IF NOT FOR THE
PERFECT STRANGER

Stories of courage, kindness, hope and healing

from

THE 2013 BOSTON MARATHON

Edited by Diane Montiel
and
Steve Alexander

BANTRY BAY PUBLISHING

Correspondence to the publisher should be by e-mail:
bantrybaypublishing@gmail.com, or by telephone:
(312) 912-8639

Printed in the United States of America
at Lake Book Manufacturing, Melrose Park, Illinois

ISBN 978-0-9850673-2-8

Organizations are encouraged to use this book as a fund-
raising tool. Contact the publisher for information
about special discounts.

Additional photo credits
Cover, front/back wrap and back center: Steve Silva, Boston.com
Cover, front left: Ken McGagh, Metro West Daily News
Cover, front center: Ken McGagh, Metro West Daily News
Cover, front right: Nicole Maneri; also background page 27, 253
Cover, back top: Corcoran Family
Cover, back bottom: Lutheran Church Charities
Background, pages 10, 74, 91, 124, 129: Steve Silva, Boston.com
Background, pages 16, 79, 153, 269: Catholic TV
Background, pages 7, 28, 36, 58, 141, 211, 258: Diane Montiel
Background, pages 4, 5, 218, 276: Hang Dinh, 123rf.com
Background, page 102, Sarah Crosby, Daily Hampshire Gazette
Background, pages 11, 49, 64, 115, 179, 199: fmua, 123rf.com
Background, page 110, Peter Pereira, The Standard-Times
Background, page 72, 239, 299: Mostapha, 123rf.com
Background, page 226: Michael Puche
Page 123, Jeremy Pavia, AP Photo
Background, page 169, 186, 220: Ruig Santos, 123rf.com
Background, page 304: Skyline Visions of America, LLC

To the Boston Marathon and all of the perfect strangers
who are the essence of its existence.

THE STORIES
. . . .

AS STRANDED RUNNER CAROL DOWNING ENCOUNTERED PERFECT STRANGERS ON THE RACE COURSE, THE LIVES OF HER DAUGHTERS, ERIKA BRANNOCK AND NICOLE GROSS, WERE BEING SAVED ON A BOYLSTON STREET SIDEWALK.

FIRST RESPONDERS — TRAINED AND UNTRAINED — RAN TOWARD THE EXPLOSIONS, NONE OF THEM KNOWING WHAT THEY WERE RUNNING TO.

IN AN INSTANT, SPECTATORS WHO HAD BEEN JOYOUSLY CHEERING THE RUNNERS FOUND THEMSELVES ON THE GROUND, BEING KEPT ALIVE BY PERFECT STRANGERS.

RUNNERS EXPERIENCED EVERYTHING FROM BEING KNOCKED OVER BY THE BLAST, TAKING SHRAPNEL IN THEIR BODIES, AND BECOMING

HYPOTHERMIC, DISORIENTED AND LOST ON THE MARATHON ROUTE. EACH
EXPERIENCED THE COMPASSION OF ONE OR MULTIPLE PERFECT STRANGERS.

OTHERS, PERFECT STRANGERS IN THEIR OWN WAYS

ACKNOWLEDGMENTS

When we started this project, the first person we contacted was Steve Silva, whose Boston.com video of the finish line explosion has been viewed over 60 million times. As a deep-rooted Bostonian, Steve provided important guidance and advice, not to mention screenshots of his stunning video and his account of that day.

As we contacted people who we thought might have inspiring stories, some declined saying that reliving those horrible moments was too much. We understood and were prepared for that. What we weren't prepared for was how wonderfully open other people were willing to be, and the intimate levels of our discussions with them. As we transcribed dozens of hours of interviews and edited the essays, tissues always handy, we felt a bond with our contributors and a responsibility to them; each was allowed to have final approval of their stories printed in this book. Our deepest thanks to all of them and to others whose stories we couldn't fit in.

Thank you to our early readers: most notably Beau Rezendes, Ph.D., of Boulder, Colorado, who tapped into the heart and soul of each story and observed how frequently the phrase, "I won't leave you," was used. Her insight was invaluable; Dr. Priscilla Zynda Otsuki, who observed that the book is about the innate goodness of people and that no person in need that day was alone. Also, Monika Miles, Kay Huemoeller, Kelley Huemoeller, Ron Main, Maggie Montiel, Lou and Katie Vidaillet, Jessica Lebsack, Erica Lebsack, and Bob Karson added noteworthy observations.

Helping us connect with people in Boston were Rhonda and Andre Tippett, Andrea Kremer, Jack Fultz, Brad Blank, Tedy Bruschi and Rob Cannon. Special thanks to Carmen Acabbo, and to Natalie Morales and her NBC colleagues Monica Alba and Mario Garcia.

On a more personal level, longtime friend and Bostonian Julia Geisman has always been our Boston Marathon "go-to person." She attended every marathon with us, organized our Sunday night pasta dinners, schlepped us around Boston, and on that day became our Command Central, helping everybody find each other.

The fine people at the B.A.A. have been generous with their time and information as have Chicagoans Dr. Leon Hoffman, proofreader Aimee Anderson, and the crew at Lake Book Manufacturing.

And last, but not least, Diane's daughter, Katie Montiel Vidaillet, who introduced us to the Boston Marathon — 2013 was her and our fourth. She has vowed to run Boston until she can't run anymore. As always, we will be there to celebrate with her at the finish line.

Editors' Note

There are many examples of heroic acts in this book, but not one of the actors will cop to being a hero. Each shrugs off the suggestion that their performance was anything more than what anyone else would do. But not anyone else did. While the vast majority of people who saw, felt and heard the bombs explode on Boylston Street ran for their lives — a very natural response, and perhaps on orders from Boston police — dozens of others ran toward the explosions. And not just the trained first responders (who were no less heroic and found themselves facing a mass casualty incident of unprecedented proportion and difficulty). There were ordinary civilians who put themselves in what might have been harm's way. No one knew if and where there would be another attack, but these people pitched in and did things they had never done before to try to save lives. They became perfect strangers.

But many of the stories in this book focus on random acts of kindness that weren't as much life saving as they were life sustaining. Hypothermic and bewildered runners who were halted just as they were grinding it out toward their triumphant finish found themselves draped in strangers' sweaters and jackets and sitting in strangers' homes. Spectators became substitute parents for runners who instantly felt like lost children.

At the worst of times, the best of people emerged. Whether it was warmth, a drink of water, a snack, a cellphone to try to reach family, a hot shower in a stranger's hotel room, or just a shoulder to lean and cry on, the common thread for the recipients of these gifts is gratitude. Lifelong bonds were formed that day, but many of the people who shared their stories with us did so in large part because of the enormous gratitude that has gone unrequited because they didn't get the names of their perfect strangers.

Perhaps you'll see yourself in one of these stories. If so, thank you. Your actions — moments of grace amid chaos — spoke louder than those deafening booms that day, and will long continue to echo as inspiration for all of us.

As for us, while we were at the finish line and were

impacted in a variety of ways by the explosions, our stories are not remarkable and are similar to those of countless thousands of others who were far too close to, but not in, harm's way. While we didn't suffer physical injury, we experienced the excruciating moments of panic and the dreadful questions you never want to ask: Is your child hurt? Is your spouse okay? Are your friends safe? Frantic phone calls that didn't go through, or went to voice mail, only heightened the concern.

After our daughter, Katie Montiel Vidaillet, had completed her fourth Boston, finishing about 45 minutes before the explosions, Diane waited in the front row of the bleachers to see her longtime friend Kay Huemoeller finish the race. Steve left, hoping to find his way to the Forum Restaurant to visit with a client. Luckily, he didn't get far because of the crush of people and headed back to the finish line. He was on the southwest corner of the library when the first bomb went off. Steve immediately texted Diane:

Apr 15, 2013, 1:50 PM

What were those booms?

Diane didn't respond, but within a few minutes Steve was able to reach her by phone. We spoke for about 45 seconds — none of which Diane remembers — ascertained that she was uninjured and police were directing them out of the bleachers. Steve waited by the entrance to the bleachers area for Diane, but she and others who had been evacuated were taken through the library and out a back door. Diane's immediate and overriding concern was for her daughter. Did she return to the finish line after running to work with her Gatorade co-workers?

Simultaneously, Katie, who was in her room at the Westin getting cleaned up, heard the explosions and turned on the TV. She recalls, "I had family at the finish line, friends running the race and Gatorade colleagues passing out drinks at the finish line. But the only person I could think of was my mom. I last saw her sitting in the grandstands. The grandstands! She's my biggest supporter and I rarely go a day without talking to her. I didn't know where she was and whether she was alive. I tried calling her and my step-dad Steve. No answer. It was terrifying and when we finally found each other, nearly an hour later, we all just hugged and cried."

At the same time, family and friends across the country were trying to get through to make sure we were okay. As you'll read many times in this book, cellphone service was inconsistent, and social media, especially Facebook and Twitter, provided alternate ways to give family, friends and work colleagues status updates.

After he knew that Diane and Katie were safe, Steve, who works occasionally as a news and business anchor at WGN Radio in Chicago, called in the first reports of the bombings, and throughout the afternoon and the next day, did a series of reports for radio, WGN-TV and the Chicago Tribune. Diane also provided eyewitness accounts for the Tribune. We met up with Katie and friends Julia Geisman and Rob Cannon at the Westin bar, from where we could see the ambulances picking up the injured from Medical Tent A.

In the following days and weeks, we began hearing and reading touching stories of how perfect strangers stepped up that day. Because of our affection for the city and our love for the Boston Marathon, we began asking people to tell their stories, hoping some good would result. We believe it has. After dozens of often teary interviews with perfect strangers or their recipients, it became clear that talking about what happened April 15th helped with their healing. And as we shared many of those stories during the editing process, we were told that being able to read about others' struggles and triumphs was also therapeutic.

We hope you'll embrace this collection of essays and that you'll consider supporting the wide array of charities our contributors have cited at the ends of their stories.

As publishers, one of our goals is to make books that matter. We hope you'll agree that this one does.

Diane Montiel   Steve Alexander

I do not at all understand the mystery of grace
— only that it meets us where we are but does
not leave us where it found us.

— *Anne Lamott*

FOREWORD

BY

TEDY BRUSCHI

Nothing in this wonderful book surprises me. Not the heart-warming accounts of how the city wrapped its arms around the runners and spectators who were victims of the miscreants who hijacked our beautiful day of civic pride and remarkable personal achievement. Nor the stirring stories of how strangers helped strangers with everything from lifesaving tourniquets to life-sustaining hugs. Nor how, along the marathon route, residents poured out of their homes with water, food, blankets, clothing and cellphones, giving desperately needed comfort to the cold and scared.

No, that the people of Boston responded as they did is of absolutely no surprise to me because I know from personal experience what this city's people are made of. When a tiny, undetected hole in my heart caused a stroke in 2005, it was uncertain whether I would recover. I couldn't walk well and had lost much of the vision in my left eye. In the days and weeks following my stroke, it felt as if all of Boston, all of New England, was lifting me. I am not exaggerating when I say that remarkable outpouring of love and support filled my heart and healed me.

April 15th left us with a hole in our heart. There remains unspeakable sorrow for families who lost loved ones. For those people who suffered life-altering wounds, we are buoyed by your refusal to be defined by the changes in your bodies and we watch your recovery with great admiration and hope. Sure, there are days when all you want to do is cry. I know. Go ahead, but never give up and never forget all of us who are pulling for you.

The stories in this book of extraordinary kindness from perfect strangers are uplifting, reaffirming and healing. But I hope you'll take them a step further: be inspired to be a perfect stranger in someone else's life. Keep that feeling of Boston Strong in your heart every day.

Please consider joining Tedy in supporting
Tedy's Team at heart.org/tedysteam

"When I was a boy and I would see scary things in the news, my mother would say to me, 'Look for the helpers. You will always find people who are helping.'"

— *Fred Rogers (PBS's Mr. Rogers)*

INTRODUCTION

BY

JACK FULTZ

BOSTON MARATHON CHAMPION

RENOWNED RUNNING COACH

"There are no strangers here, only friends you've not yet met."

T his pithy statement, handwritten on the hallway wall of a Boston University dormitory, welcomed all who entered. It was April 1972, and I was in Boston to run my second Boston Marathon. Though I knew only my friend-host when I first walked into the dorm, by the end of the long weekend I'd acquired a group of new acquaintances and felt like a resident. I had no way of knowing just how prophetic that reassuring declaration would prove to be.

Now, more than 40 years later, that maxim still resonates loud and clear. Every year, I share it with several hundred first-time marathoners on the Dana-Farber Marathon Challenge (DFMC) team as they begin their preparation for the Boston Marathon. They too feel an initial sense of aloneness despite being surrounded by so many like-minded, excited, yet nervous more experienced marathoners. The DFMC newcomers tell me those words, and the meaning behind them, are comforting and reassuring.

At the start of the 2013 Boston Marathon, on a beautiful, picture-perfect spring morning, nobody could have predicted that "there are no strangers here" would play itself out in such a profound way just a few hours later. Some of the spontaneous acts of heroism that occurred in response to the two bomb explosions on Boylston Street have been well chronicled. So have some of the thousands of acts of unadulterated kindness that occurred between "friends who had not yet met" until immediately after the detonations, and they continued for days, weeks, and months. Other stories may never be told; they'll exist solely within the new friendships forged between the givers and receivers of countless acts of compassion and caring.

When the bombs went off, I was standing less than a hundred meters beyond the finish line with Jan Ross, my partner and Dana-Farber Cancer Institute colleague. We were congratulating and welcoming our DFMC team members and other friends who had run, plus anyone within earshot and hugging distance. Activity in the nearby medical tent had been minimal because the day was so ideal for distance running: sunny and cool with low humidity. Everyone in sight — runners exuberant and exhausted, their jubilant fans, friends, and relatives, and the small army of Boston Athletic Association (B.A.A.) volunteers and race officials — was in a celebratory mood. All felt right in our world. We were cheering for the accomplishments of the runners and for the larger sense of global harmony of this renowned international event, illustrated so vividly by the flags of more than 70 countries represented in the field of 26,000 athletes.

> *These stories reveal the resilience of mankind. We are, and shall always be, Ever Strong.*

The startling sight and brutal sound and concussion of the first explosion shattered the serenity of that glorious afternoon. "What the hell was that?" we both exclaimed as a bright flash and immense cloud of billowing white smoke erupted adjacent to the finish line. There was an immediate, intense sense of fear and concern of serious injury. From our vantage point it appeared that the announcer's tent at the finish line, filled with good friends and numerous acquaintances, had blown up. Moments later, the second explosion occurred. Instincts shifted instantaneously: BOMBS.

We hurried to the nearby DFMC headquarters hotel in anticipation of our returning team members. It was there that we began receiving reports of the aid and assistance provided by perfect strangers to DFMC teammates and thousands of others who were stopped in their tracks and diverted from the marathon route.

Runners, sweaty and spent, chilled quickly. Many athletes were not from Boston and thus were unfamiliar with the area. Even many local runners became disoriented and desperate in their search for family members and friends, given the likelihood that their loved ones were in the cheering crowd lining the Boylston Street homestretch.

The Boston Marathon has been a mainstay of my life for the better part of five decades. My varied experiences here run the gamut from finishing first to absolute farthest from first, running both my fastest and slowest marathons over the Hopkinton-to-Copley Square course, disappointedly dropping out on two occasions, and excitedly exceeding my expectations on others. I'm fortunate to have been a member of the B.A.A. for more than 25 years, served as the B.A.A.'s Elite Athlete Liaison, and trained thousands of amateur athlete/fund-raisers dedicated to helping Dana-Farber Cancer Institute conquer cancer.

I am, however, only one of many thousands whose lives have been deeply enriched over the years by the magnificence of the Boston Marathon. Stories abound, from runners who worked very hard for many years to earn their "BQ" (Boston Qualifier) to those who, not considering themselves marathoners, were nonetheless empowered through their Boston Marathon experience as a fund-raising vehicle to take a stand and make a difference on behalf of a worthy organization or cause. Our hearts were broken by the horrifying attacks on April 15, 2013, and their aftermath. And yet, as the accounts in this book illustrate, our love for our fellow humans remains stronger than that senseless hate.

Many events are still unfolding. The healing process will continue for a long time. In "If Not for the Perfect Stranger," more than 40 poignant narratives are shared beautifully by those who lived them. This anthology, created and edited by Diane Montiel and Steve Alexander, themselves witnesses to the explosions, is a powerful and moving tribute to the victims and caregivers who found each other on a day that now lives in infamy. Each piece shares the circumstances and experiences of perfect strangers who quickly became perfect friends. These stories reveal the resilience of mankind.

We are, and shall always be, Ever Strong.

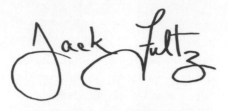

Jack Fultz won the Boston Marathon in 1976 and had two other top-ten Boston finishes among his competitive running accomplishments. He teaches sport psychology at Tufts University, and is a fitness consultant, personal coach, and motivational speaker and writer. He is the training advisor for world-renowned Dana-Farber Cancer Institute's teams in the Boston Marathon, B.A.A. Half Marathon, and Falmouth Road Race (RunDanaFarber.org).

Through his Pan-Massachusetts Challenge bike-a-thon ride every August since 2003, Jack has raised more than $100,000 to further support Dana-Farber's mission of lifesaving cancer research and patient care. Please visit his PMC fund-raising page at pmc.org/jf0068 *to read Jack's PMC profile and contribute to his upcoming ride.*

We love the fathers and brothers who took the shirts off their backs to stop the bleeding; the mothers and the sisters who cared for the injured; the neighbors and the business owners, the homeowners all across the city who opened their doors and their hearts to the weary and the scared. They said, "What's mine is yours. We'll get through this together." This was the compassion of our city at work.

Boston Mayor Thomas Menino, at an interfaith memorial service at the Cathedral of the Holy Cross in South Boston, April 18, 2013

"IF NOT FOR A PERFECT STRANGER,

my daughter would have died." Those words from Celeste Corcoran about the men who saved her daughter Sydney's life not only inspired the title of this collection of stories, it provided a memorable way of referring to the thousands of people who made others' lives less traumatic on April 15, 2013: perfect strangers.

So let's begin our stories with two men who were among Sydney Corcoran's perfect strangers, Matt Smith and Zachary Mione.

Celeste Corcoran urges you to consider supporting these organizations which have been vital to her recovery:
50 Legs (www.50legs.org);
Challenged Athletes Fund (www.challengedathletes.org).

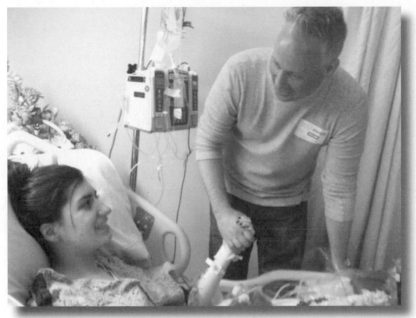

Sydney Corcoran with Matt Smith, one of her "perfect strangers"

Matt Smith

Spectator – Perfect Stranger

Age 38

Dorchester, Massachusetts

"Hey, how you doin', buddy?" I asked. Sydney Corcoran looked up at me from her hospital bed, smiled, and hugged me. She was going to be okay. Three days earlier, I was pretty sure she wouldn't be.

I grew up in Philadelphia and came to Boston in 1997 to go to college at Wentworth Institute of Technology. In 2000, I met my wife and never left.

When people ask what the best time to visit Boston is, I always tell them to come down for the marathon. Patriots Day is the best holiday in Boston. I know a lot of people say it's St. Patrick's Day, but I say it's Marathon Monday. You're outside, you've got the marathon going on, all the schools are out, everybody's in a good mood, it's a great day. If you can get tickets, you start your day off by going to the Sox game in the late morning, and when it's announced that the first runners come across, the crowd cheers for them. After the game you make your way to the Boylston Street area to watch the non-elite runners come in.

Patriots Day 2013, my wife was on the island visiting a friend who had just had a baby, so her sister, Kate, Kate's boyfriend Manny, and my buddy Bobby and I met up in the morning and took the train in from Dorchester. We went to the Fenway area, hung out for a bit and went to the game. It was a great day, sunny and nice. In fact, it was so nice we left in the eighth inning to go to a bar that had a roof deck. Other people must have had the same idea because the bars across the street were packed, so we took a cab to the Back Bay hoping to at least get a patio seat or something. The cabbie dropped us off about ten minutes before the bombs went off, about two blocks north of Boylston Street. We walked toward the finish line to try to find a place to settle in and watch the runners.

When the first bomb went off, we were just approaching Boylston and saw smoke blow out of the back of the building, and we saw the smoke in the front. I remember it as like a quiet echo; things got real quiet, and time seemed to stand still. At first, we thought it might have been a transformer. Then the second one went off. We knew they were bombs. People were running toward us to get away. I told Kate and them to run and get out of there. Why I didn't run away with them, I still can't answer. Some people go crazy, some people go stupid, both very natural responses.

I ran to try to help. I don't know why — I hadn't been in the military or in a first-responder type of job — and I didn't know what I would do, but I knew there was something wrong.

> *Sydney was asking me, "Am I okay?" "You're okay. Hold onto my shirt," I told her. "Squeeze my hand."*

When I got to the sidewalk the gates were being pulled back. People were already starting to help the injured. There was a man kneeling beside a young woman trying to stop her bleeding. Blood was pouring out and she was as white as could be.

"Hey, buddy, what's going on?" I asked the young woman as I knelt beside her.

Zach Mione, whose name I didn't know until a few days later, was ripping up shirts that the Marathon Sports people were handing out to help tie people off. He knelt down to help apply a tourniquet and put pressure on her femoral artery. Before that, another stranger, Joe, was helping and then went off to help others.

She had lost so much blood, I really thought she was done. We tried whatever we could to keep her going, but I didn't think she'd make it.

I don't remember any of the commotion going on around

me, except a loud alarm from Marathon Sports that kept blaring, and glass, heavy glass, that had fallen around us.

Someone had found her wallet so I knew her name was Sydney Corcoran. She asked me, "Am I okay?"

"You're okay. Hold onto my shirt," I told her. "Squeeze my hand."

A piece of metal from a pressure cooker had blown through the bottom of Sydney's calf and came up through her leg and tore her femoral artery. Zach and I were just squeezing as hard as we could to keep her from bleeding to death.

Sydney was so brave, talking to me the whole time. She didn't panic, maybe because of the loss of blood and shock, but if she was in pain, I couldn't tell.

"Am I bleeding?" she asked.

"You're okay. You're okay. Just squeeze my hand. Keep talking."

But even with the tourniquets, blood was still coming out and we couldn't figure out from where. I'd had my hand behind her head, and when Joe came back and took off his shirt to put under her head and I pulled my hand away, it was bloody. But we couldn't find a wound on her head; her hair was just wet from so much of her blood on the sidewalk.

There was a puddle of blood coming from her left foot. We took off her shoe and there was a hole in her foot about the size of a half dollar.

A Boston police officer, who I learned later was Sergeant Sean Burns, knelt down about that time and helped us. Within a couple of minutes, some of the people from the medical tent started showing up with supplies and Sean, Zach and I got Sydney on a flat board. The three of us carried her into the street and got her onto a gurney. That's where the medical people took her away. The other guys had wandered off, I guess, and I was just standing there in the middle of Boylston, wondering what had just happened. I was in shock. I remember seeing and hearing the bomb go off, but my brain couldn't process it. This can't be happening.

The cops were trying to clear the street. One cop was behind me, just screaming as loud as he could at me. "Get the hell out of here!" When I didn't move, or even acknowledge him, he yanked me and turned me around. When he saw my front, covered with blood from head to toe, his expression went soft and he stopped yelling.

"Kid, you want to sit down for a second?"

I just stood there; I couldn't put a thought together, much less words. He grabbed me and walked me toward Newbury Street, got me a bottle of water and sat with me for a few seconds.

> *One cop was behind me ... screaming ... "Get the hell out of here!" When I didn't move ... he yanked me and turned me around. When he saw my front, covered with blood from head to toe, his expression went soft.*

I was spitting on my hands, scratching at my skin, trying to get the blood off. I sat there for what seemed a long time, trying to piece things together in my head.

At some point, I looked at my cellphone. Kate, Manny and Bobby were trying to reach me. "Where r u?" they texted. They said they were on Mass Ave. "Come meet us." Eventually I made my way there, but I was in such a daze, I didn't really know where I was walking. I don't remember if I said anything to them, I was just happy to see them. They wondered about the blood, of course. I told them I'd helped out a girl, but didn't get into any of the details. We stopped in the Parish Café, which was chaotic, and I went into the bathroom to try to clean myself up, to wash the blood off my hands. I had no concept of time. How long it took from when that bomb went off and I was standing at the bar in the Parish Café? I had no idea. It could have been 20 seconds, or it could have been six hours.

My wife was stuck on the island because the ferries were shut down. I don't remember talking to her until later on, but Kate had spoken with her. Everybody was trying to get out of the city, but the cops were blocking off the roads. At one point, we shared a cab with a bunch of people. We finally made it home — it's usually a ten minute drive, but it took hours. We all went to a bar about a block from our home. One of my friends handed me a beer, and we spent some time trying to fill in the blanks in my memory, but nothing made sense. Even weeks later it didn't make sense until I finally had a chance to meet Sean, and later Zach. That helped.

That night, about 11 o'clock, a hockey buddy who works at the *Lowell Sun*, sent me a message.

"Hey, by chance, are you the kid with the red face, gray hair and sandals at the bombing?" He was kind of making fun of me because of my prematurely gray hair and the fact that I'm almost always wearing sandals.

I had no idea how he knew because I hadn't had the TV on and I had no clue what was going on in the media. I went to bed about two and got up at six. I walked down the street a few blocks to get a paper. When I picked it up, I was on the front cover of the *Globe* and the *New York Times*. My brother was in Belgium for work, and he said I was in the papers there, too. That's when everything got kind of weird and I got a little rattled, a little nervous. But I went to work anyway, and I thought I was doing okay until about two o'clock, when I couldn't take it anymore. I had like, I don't want to say a panic attack, but what is going on? My phone just wouldn't stop. How did these people find out who I was so fast? The media were calling, all sorts of people were calling. Some were saying, "She's looking for you, the girl you saved is looking for you."

I left work early and went home and the TV news trucks were already there and reporters were knocking on my neighbors' doors asking about me. That's when I started getting really nervous. The ferries were still locked down, so my wife couldn't get home, and I avoided everybody. All I cared about was that this girl was okay. That was the only reason I'd watch any part of the news.

Wednesday, more pieces started fitting together and I learned that Sydney's mother Celeste had been badly hurt, too, losing parts of both legs.

Thursday, a friend of mine who worked in the area of Boston Medical helped get me in unnoticed. He timed it for the memorial mass that was going on just down the street, and because everyone was there it was easier to slip into the hospital. I went to the front desk.

"Who are you here to see?" the nurse asked.

"Sydney Corcoran."

"How do you know her?"

"I don't."

She took a moment and said, "We can't let you in."

"The family's looking for me."

"How do you know her again?"

"I don't know her. I was there with her Monday and I was told the family is looking for me."

It was awkward for a little bit, but she called upstairs and gave me a guest pass. As I headed for the fourth floor, I became more and more nervous about seeing Sydney. That was the most nervous I'd been in my life. I was scared to meet this girl!

I'm sitting in the waiting room for about an hour when Kevin, Sydney's dad, comes in. Of course, I didn't know who he was, but he stood there and kind of checked me out. I guess there had been a lot of people trying to get in and see Sydney and Celeste for whatever reason, and he was being protective. He sat down and we just looked at each other for a few seconds. I told him, "I'm one of the guys who was there with your daughter."

Kevin got a little choked up, shed a few tears and gave me a big hug. "I can't thank you enough for saving my daughter's life," he said.

Talking with Kevin is when I found out that the doctors had said that had it not been for the care Sydney got immediately at the scene, she would have had only a 10% chance of making it.

Kevin went and cleared the room for me and told Sydney and Celeste that I was there; they were in the same room. I had brought them both flowers. I looked across the room and saw Syd, and I got choked up. I walked over and gave her a big hug.

I managed to say, "Hey, how you doin', buddy?"

She smiled and said, as best she could because her voice was real weak, that she was good. She gave me a big hug and said thank you. Seeing her in that bed, knowing she was okay, it gave me a breath of fresh air; it felt like I lost 20 pounds at that moment.

We just sat there for a while, not really saying anything, just looking at each other.

I went over to meet Celeste and gave her a big hug.

"Thank you," she said.

"My pleasure," I said. I was no more prepared to reply to her gratitude than I had been to tie a tourniquet around her daughter's leg.

It was great to meet the family. Celeste was always so positive, she was awesome, always making jokes and trying to keep everybody positive, which considering the loss of her legs was amazing to me. I went in there scared as could be, not knowing what to expect. It was good, it was good to meet Sydney, her parents, her brother Tyler, her grandparents, aunts, uncles and others. Just great people. But seeing that Sydney would be okay, I felt I could finally move on. It could be okay. It could start to be okay.

About a week and a half later, I got a phone call from Sean. He'd gotten my number from Celeste's sister, Carmen Acabbo. It was a funny exchange because he told me that I was so calm while we were with Sydney, he thought I was medically trained. Hearing that I was calm and appeared to know what I was doing was interesting. Shock really does play tricks with your mind and body. I had the pleasure of meeting Sean in June at the Corcoran's golf tournament. We were standing near each other, but we didn't recognize each other. At one point later in the day, we looked at each other for a while and thought, holy crap, and hugged.

In September, I met Zach at a dinner with the Corcorans.

Sydney went off to college at Merrimack in the fall. She and I speak or text weekly. She's like a little sister to me. She calls me "big brother."

We'll be friends for life, her and I. All of us.

Matt Smith encourages you to support the One Fund at onefundboston.org.

Sydney Corcoran with two of her perfect strangers:
Matt Smith, left, and Zach Mione in September, 2013

Zachary Mione

Spectator/Perfect Stranger

Age 29

General Manager, Portland Running Company

Portland, Oregon

The last thing I wanted was anyone calling me a hero. Nothing good had come from that day. That was before I met Sydney Corcoran five months later.

Marathon Sports is my connection to the 2013 Boston Marathon. I worked at Marathon Sports for about a year and a half and in that time I fell in love with the running industry. Boston is such a great running city, especially in the months leading up to the Boston Marathon. I met my girlfriend working at Marathon Sports and we both decided to pursue career opportunities in Portland, Oregon. I received a job offer with another running specialty company, Portland Running Company and headed west. Upon moving to Portland, I maintained a close relationship with Marathon Sports and made arrangements to return to Boston and help work the Marathon Expo at the Hynes Convention Center.

On Marathon Monday my friends and I awoke to a beautiful spring morning. The weather was absolutely perfect. We made our way to Washington Square in Brookline to watch the elite runners come through. We were on Beacon Street at approximately Mile 21 when the elite women started racing past. A short time later, the owner of Portland Running Company, Dave Harkin, ran past as did another co-worker Mike Orr. We saw a few other runners we knew and cheered them on.

After Mike finished the race, he sent me a text that he was at the Lenox Hotel on Boylston Street with some friends and that I should meet him for a drink. A friend and I hailed a cab and asked the cab driver if he could get us to the Lenox (which was on the opposite side of Boylston Street). He assured me that he could and we took off. But as we were approaching Copley, the closest he

Portland Running Company
April 14

Will these guys still be smiling at the finish tomorrow? Watch the 117th Boston Marathon online, live and free of charge. Coverage begins at 6:30 our time tomorrow morning.

http://www.baa.org/races/boston-marathon/event-information/tv-coverage.aspx

Portland Running Company Facebook page

My Portland colleagues, Mike Orr and Dave Harkin
at the finish line on April 14th.

could get was Marlborough Street, a few blocks from Boylston Street, and still on the wrong side of the race course for us to get to the Lenox.

So my friend and I made our way to the Boylston Street Marathon Sports store that is located at the finish line. He had never been there, so I gave him a tour and introduced him to some of my former co-workers. We were there for about three minutes when the bomb went off. The building shook as we were walking up the steps from the basement. We looked at each other and I said to him, "Did something hit the building?" My friend said, "That was a bomb."

We immediately ran outside. The air was filled with smoke and the smell of fireworks. Fire alarms were sounding, people were screaming, it was chaos.

Police officers and emergency responders on Boylston Street were trying to get to the sidewalk to help those in need, but the race barricade was still up and obstructing them from getting to the sidewalk. I helped a few other people rip down the fencing and scaffolding to make an entrance. When I turned back toward the store I noticed how many people were injured. I went back into Marathon Sports and grabbed shirts off of the racks, started ripping them up, and handing them to people to bandage wounds. That's when I first saw Sydney.

A man, who I later found out to be Matt Smith, was cradling her head while my friend was applying pressure to a wound on her leg. I knelt down to hand my friend a bandage and he instructed me to take over so he could assist others. I could see that

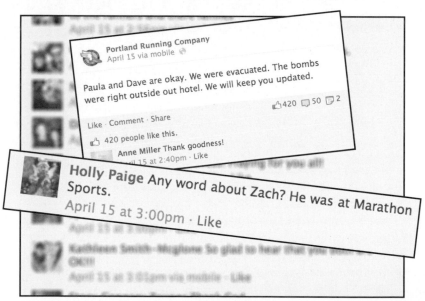

Portland Running Company
April 15 via mobile

Paula and Dave are okay. We were evacuated. The bombs were right outside out hotel. We will keep you updated.

👍420 💬50 ↪2

Like · Comment · Share

👍 420 people like this.

Anne Miller Thank goodness!

Holly Paige Any word about Zach? He was at Marathon Sports.
April 15 at 3:00pm · Like

Sydney's wound was deep and assumed it was very serious. I tied a tourniquet on her thigh and applied pressure to her femoral artery. Until that moment, I had never thought about tying a tourniquet, let alone imagined I would be in a position where I would have to. I kept pressure on her wound until a paramedic came and relieved me of my position.

I have a hard time remembering the specifics of the moments after that. For instance, I didn't remember, as Matt did, that I helped lift Sydney onto the stretcher. At some point, I remember a police officer telling my friend and I we needed to leave the area. The next thing I recall was standing in front of Stephanie's restaurant on Newbury Street.

We made our way to Beacon Street and started walking back to the apartment where I was staying in Brighton. I tried to reach my parents and my girlfriend, but calls weren't going through. I tried to text, but service was down. At some point, I was able to post on Facebook that I was okay. The long walk back was painful. I was in shock and wasn't able to process what had just happened. The day when Boston is usually at its best was now the darkest day of my life.

> *Until that moment, I had never thought about tying a tourniquet, let alone imagined I would be in a position where I would have to.*

About an hour later my phone came back to life and I was flooded with voicemails and text messages. I was able to call my mother and tell her I was okay, but did not go into any detail about what had happened. Naturally she had questions, but I just couldn't talk about it. I had a lot of messages from people telling me they saw me on the news and hoped I was okay. It was all so overwhelming. My friend and I sat down on somebody's steps and I started to cry.

When I got back to the Brighton apartment, I briefly talked to my friends about what happened. That was when I learned of the second bomb. I had no idea a second explosion occurred. I

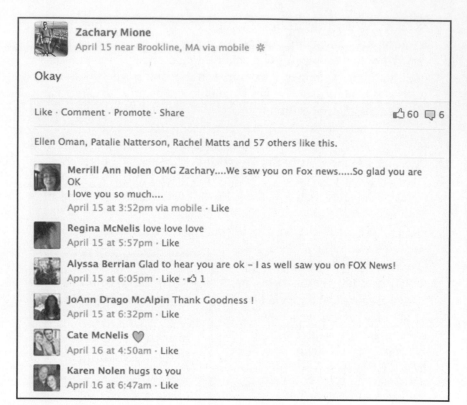

Zachary Mione
April 15 near Brookline, MA via mobile ☀

Okay

Like · Comment · Promote · Share   👍 60 💬 6

Ellen Oman, Patalie Natterson, Rachel Matts and 57 others like this.

> **Merrill Ann Nolen** OMG Zachary....We saw you on Fox news.....So glad you are OK
> I love you so much....
> April 15 at 3:52pm via mobile · Like

> **Regina McNelis** love love love
> April 15 at 5:57pm · Like

> **Alyssa Berrian** Glad to hear you are ok – I as well saw you on FOX News!
> April 15 at 6:05pm · Like · 👍 1

> **JoAnn Drago McAlpin** Thank Goodness !
> April 15 at 6:32pm · Like

> **Cate McNelis** 💜
> April 16 at 4:50am · Like

> **Karen Nolen** hugs to you
> April 16 at 6:47am · Like

reached out to my co-workers at Marathon Sports to make sure they were all okay. Miraculously, everyone was safe.

At this point I still didn't know anything about Sydney: her name, if she survived, if she lost her leg, her age …

The next day I was supposed to work at the Boylston Street Marathon Sports, but it wouldn't be opening. It was an active crime scene. That morning I avoided watching the news and went to work at the Brookline Marathon Sports to keep busy and be around familiar faces. At some point, I walked across the street to grab a cup of coffee. While in line, I picked up the *New York Times* and saw a very graphic picture of myself, Sydney, and Matt. There were no names in the caption, but that picture was in most major newspapers across the country and was spreading online. I was very uncomfort-

able seeing the picture and wanted to remain anonymous. I didn't want any notoriety or publicity.

I received a text message from a friend who recognized me from the picture and also knew a friend of Sydney's family. He told me her name and age, but didn't know what her condition was. I found out what hospital she had been admitted to and called to find out if she was going to survive.

To my surprise, they connected me to her room. I spoke with her father, Kevin. He told me the extent of her injuries and that she was facing a number of surgeries. Kevin also told me that her mother Celeste had sustained serious injuries and lost both of her legs. My heart went out to the Corcorans for what they were going to have to deal with. I expressed to Kevin that I did not want to be a part of the media and that privacy in this manner was very important to me. I wanted the victims to be the focal point. I was able to walk away from Boylston Street that day and would soon be leaving Boston altogether. I didn't have any contact with Kevin or the family for the next three months.

The next day I left Boston and went to my mother's house in New York. I needed to get out of the city and try and make sense of what had happened. A few days later I returned to Portland.

My mother diligently followed the Corcoran's story and was constantly giving me updates on their progress. She told me of Sydney and Matt's reunion and encouraged me to get in contact with her. I wasn't ready. My heart was still broken. I carry the events of the marathon with me every day. It had a profound impact on my daily life. Being in crowded public places made me uneasy, flying terrified me, any loud noise would make my heart race. In the back of my mind I thought something tragic was going to happen. I struggled to act normal.

In June, Marathon Sports had a dinner for the employees that were in the store when the bomb went off. They offered to fly me in for the weekend so we could all be together and talk with one another about how we were doing. That was the first time I was able to talk about my experience at length. I had a conversation with Shane O'Hara, the manager of the Boylston Marathon Sports about how meeting the people he assisted had a positive impact on him.

> *My heart was still broken. I carry the events of the marathon with me every day. It had a profound impact on my daily life ...*

Taking Shane's experience to heart, I decided to try to reach Sydney. I wrote her cousin an e-mail stating that I didn't know when I would be in Boston next, but would like to meet Sydney and the rest of the Corcoran family. I received word from Kevin and we made plans to get together in September. I would meet them for dinner — the whole Corcoran family, Matt Smith, and John Tlumacki, the *Boston Globe* photographer who took the photo of Sydney, Matt, and me.

On my way to dinner I was very nervous. I didn't know what I would say to any of them. I was envisioning a very awkward introduction. When we all arrived, Sydney and I embraced. It was a surreal moment. I instantly felt so much love for her. It turned out to be a very special night. The Corcorans are a remarkable family. Sydney is absolutely amazing. She's beautiful, she's brilliant, and her spirit cannot be broken. Celeste is one of the funniest and strongest people I have ever met. Kevin is a loving husband and father. Sydney's older brother Tyler is a great kid. Matt is hilarious and has a giant heart. I still talk to the Corcorans and Matt regularly.

Sydney and I had an immediate connection, though. We talk almost daily and help each other through our bad days.

Before meeting the Corcorans I didn't think I would go back for the 2014 Boston Marathon. Celeste's sister, Carmen Acabbo, is going to run the marathon again this year. She wasn't able to finish last year, stopped short just after she and a friend ran down Hereford and turned left onto Boylston. Sydney and Celeste have decided to run across the finish line with Carmen to show that nothing is going to hold them back. If they won't let fear stop them from going back, I can't let it stop me, either.

I'll be running the marathon this April to hopefully create a new, great memory of the race and the city I love. I have teamed up with my friends Steve Edwards and his wife, Olympic medalist and hopeful 2014 Boston Marathon winner, Shalane Flanagan, to raise money for the One Fund through our charity page on Crowdrise.com.

The title of this book, "If Not for the Perfect Stranger," is a great summary of my relationship with Sydney. She has had such a positive impact on my life and has helped me through so much, that she has become my perfect stranger.

Zachary Mione encourages you to join him, Steve Edwards and
Shalane Flanagan in raising money for One Fund via
this special link: www.crowdrise.com/theheroandthepro.

> I don't think that we're heroes. I think that we're people that were in the wrong place at the wrong time and just did the right thing.
>
> — *Jamis Mederios, one of the Forum Restaurant employees who aided bombing victims, on NBC News, 4/19/13*

When word of what happened at the finish line made its way back along the race course to the thousands of runners who had been stopped cold, panic set in. Many of them feared the worst. Their loved ones had planned on being along Boylston Street and at the finish line to cheer their remarkable achievement. Were they okay? Were they still alive?

Runner Carol Downing's fears were realized. Both of her daughters, Erika Brannock and Nicole Gross, along with Nicole's husband, Michael, were standing just feet from the first bomb. On the following pages are the stories of Carol and her perfect strangers, as well as the perfect strangers who saved her daughters' lives.

Carol Downing with her daughters, Erika Brannock (left)
and Nicole Gross at the 5K/10K Sticks and Bones Dog Trail
race in Charlotte, North Carolina on April 7, 2012

Carol Downing

Runner

Baltimore, Maryland

First Boston Marathon – Third marathon

Retired Licensed Massage Therapist

Mother of spectators Erika Brannock and Nicole Gross

"**M**om, why are you taking money with you?" asked my daughter, Erika, as I was getting ready to run my first Boston Marathon.

"You never know," I said. "Maybe I'll have to take a cab."

I also decided to carry my cellphone, as well as four packs of gel. Several miles into the race, just that little bit of weight was making my back ache. One of my shoes was tied too tight, and my music got stuck on one song playing over and over again. I wasn't having a great race. But I was in THE race; Boston is the race of all races. As a massage therapist, I worked on many runners, including elites, who inspired me to try it. They kept saying, "You have to do Boston. It's awesome! The crowds are amazing and it's a big party all day long." And one day I decided I was going to run the Boston Marathon.

My daughter Nicole, a triathlon coach and personal trainer at the Charlotte Athletic Club, had trained me and I originally qualified for the 2012 race. It would be my third and last marathon. But I had an injury leading up to that one and, because of the extreme heat that year which forced the B.A.A. to encourage runners not to run, I was able to defer to the 2013 Boston Marathon.

At the time, I felt very fortunate to have been given another chance to add Boston to my achievements. You probably know, because our story has been repeated innumerable times, that my opportunity ended with both of my daughters severely wounded.

It's much easier to talk about it now. In the beginning, I could not get through an interview because I was so raw. But I see the progress the girls have made and how positive they are, and that's made it easier. But it's time to stop talking about what happened to us and focus on the compassion shown us. There are so many people out there who get injured, hurt and have traumatic things happen to them and they don't have the generous financial and community support we've gotten. They don't get the things we get, and I feel so bad for those people. My girls are fortunate because they really needed the financial support for their injuries and ongoing care. It was meant for it to happen to us and we have to figure out why and how we're going to move forward and help other people.

The trip to Boston was a Christmas present for my daughters and son-in-law. Erika, Nicole, her husband Michael Gross and I stayed at a hotel in Framingham. On Saturday, we went out for lunch, picked up my packet at the Expo and I bought a marathon shirt. It was fun and Michael and Nicole took pictures of me. On Sunday, Erika — a teacher in Towson, Maryland — worked on a paper for school, Michael was under the weather and Nicole and I went shopping. Monday morning around 8:30, I was able to take a hotel shuttle to the start in Hopkinton.

We had plans to meet after the race around the Convention Center area, but I didn't know where they would be watching me run. The crowd was just as I had been told: awesome. All along the route there were people partying, having barbecues, bands were playing; it was so great. I'd never experienced crowds like that. Their cheers and enthusiasm were giving me a huge boost. Despite my aches and pains and music issues, I was doing better than I thought I was. And there was a good chance I would finish around my goal time of 4:15.

Then I hit this wall of people. I was getting close to the finish line and when I'm close, I start to dig deep. What is going on? There was a runner on the ground and there were people helping him. But why are we all stopped because of him? And then word started trickling back that a transformer had exploded at one of the hotels. Then we got word that a bomb had exploded at the finish line. I pulled out my phone and started texting my girls, but was not getting a response.

At this point, I'm not too worried. Then I got a text from Michael. But I didn't have my reading glasses with me, and couldn't read my phone's screen. Another runner, Stephen Pater from Mississippi, the first of my perfect strangers, was standing next to me and offered to help. He read the first text from Michael: "Are you okay?"

I, and my "eyes," wrote back: "Yes, I'm okay. Are you?"

"We were caught in the bomb and are in the medical tent. We can't find Erika."

A little later he wrote: "Nicole has two broken bones and we're heading to a hospital."

... I didn't have my reading glasses with me, and couldn't read the phone's screen ... the first of my perfect strangers, was standing next to me and offered to help ...

I'm stunned by the news, but I'm still thinking that it's not too bad. I figured Erika was disoriented and was walking around, lost.

I texted my husband, Skip, who was traveling and was on a layover in Kansas, telling him Nicole had been hurt.

Stephen asked me what I wanted to do.

"I don't know where I am, but I need to get to the hospital."

He said, "Come on, let's go."

We left the crowd but couldn't get to the buses to pick up our bags where I had some warm clothes. He took me to the T stop at the Prudential Building. There were a couple of runners standing there and Stephen asked them if the train went to the hospital and explained why I needed to get there.

They said, "The T is stopped, but we live here and we'll take her back to our place, give her some food, let her have a shower and we'll take her to the hospital."

This was all more than a little weird; Nicole is in a hospital, Erika is probably wandering around lost, and here I am going to the home of these strangers. I have no idea what I'm walking into. I don't know who these people are. But I was like a little puppy and said, "okay."

The couple were my next perfect strangers, Tim and Patty Island. We got to their place and I was just numb. I remember sitting on their couch and Patty giving me a bagel and a banana. I knew I needed to eat, but I was not hungry.

I said, "I need to cancel my flight." She helped me do that and asked, "Do you want to take a shower?"

I just couldn't move. The TV was on; the news coverage of what happened. Oh my God, this is awful! I really kept thinking Erika was just out there somewhere, disoriented and lost. I was feeling so bad for her, that maybe she was panicking, not knowing what to do. But I also thought someone was going to find her and take care of her.

... here I am going to the home of these strangers. I have no idea what I'm walking into. I don't know who these people are. But I was like a little puppy ...

Eventually, I did take a shower and Patty and Tim gave me a fleece jacket, a pair of reading glasses and a cellphone charger.

We went to Brigham and Women's Hospital where Patty and Tim sat with me from 5:30 p.m. until 8:00 p.m. They were so wonderful. Patty went to get us soup and coffee and they just sat with me as we waited for Nicole to get out of surgery and kept checking to see if there was any news on Erika's whereabouts. When Michael's brother, Brian, arrived at the hospital, Patty and Tim left after we exchanged phone numbers and e-mail addresses.

FBI agents came to get me and told me they had found Erika. They took me to Beth Israel Hospital, just around the corner, to the Intensive Care Unit. Erika was already out of surgery and a doctor and nurse met with me. But they needed me to identify her before they would discuss any of her injuries with me. I went into the room, looked at her and honestly didn't know if it was her or not. Her hair was singed and her face was swollen. When I realized it was her, I didn't want it to be. I just wanted her to be wandering around lost.

I didn't know the extent of her injuries. All I saw were breathing tubes and IVs; never the way you want to see your child. They then told me about her injuries, that she had lost one leg and had extensive injuries to her other one. A lot of that is still a blur to me, but I remember staying with her, still in my running clothes.

When I went back to see Nicole, she was already out of surgery, too. They'd put a rod in her broken leg and her other leg had severe soft tissue injuries. Both her legs were bandaged up. She was awake and talking and she wanted to know right away about Erika. I felt like I had to be honest with her and I told her. She said, "Mom, it's all my fault. I made Erika move." And we've been dealing with that. Michael had some lacerations and some burns to his head and arms. He probably could have been released the next day, but he stayed with Nicole and they let him stay in the room.

Erika started to come to on Tuesday night as they reduced the sedation. She still couldn't really talk because of the tubes. But she asked about Nicole and Michael, and wanted to know what her students at her pre-school had been told. She asked me about her leg. She kept putting her hand down there and I looked at the nurse and I asked her what I should tell Erika. She said, "We can do this together." And she stayed there with me. But Erika already knew; she just needed confirmation. She got teary-eyed, not hysterical, just teary-eyed.

Nicole had been doing really well. But because she had so many surgeries for wound care and to clean out shrapnel, the doctors decided to put a filter in her abdominal area to prevent blood clots. Soon after, she began having severe abdominal pain. Ultrasounds showed the filter had dislodged and perforated her small intestines. That required major surgery, which set her back. She couldn't eat for ten days.

Nicole is such a private person and struggled with all of the news coverage of her and the other victims. And the picture of her, sitting on the sidewalk in a daze that was plastered all over the world? That bothered her. I told her, "When I saw the picture, I thought of how beautiful you still were." It was a big issue, but we've all come to terms with it.

Erika and Carol cuddle at Beth Israel Deaconess Hospital in Boston.

My husband, Skip, arrived and we stayed at a hotel for a few days. Michael continued staying in the hospital with Nicole. Family members arrived and Brian got hotel rooms for everyone. Tim and Patty stayed in touch, as promised. Patty offered a fully furnished apartment through her company. They came to the hotel, Tim drove my husband to the airport to return our rental car and met us back at the apartment. The apartment was full of food; the refrigerator and cabinets were stocked.

We had family come up and Erika's good friend, Jillian Ball, came. Because she wanted to stay with Erika every night, it allowed Skip and me to go back to the apartment. Skip is a doer and handled a lot of the paperwork. I'm more of a, "I need to sit with my child because she's injured," kind of person. Despite being numb and in shock, I went into "mother mode," just taking care of my daughters, going back and forth between hospitals. It was so fortunate that Michael was able to be with Nicole all the time. Erika's aunt and uncle, Debbie and Ronnie Atkinson, came up and stayed for a month. They were a huge help, as were many others. We had great support.

And I had Patty and Tim. They continued to be amazing,

Photo courtesy Tim and Patty Island

Tim, Patty and Carol taking a break on the banks of the Charles

keeping in touch with me and letting me know they were there for me. "What do you need?" "How can we help?" "Call if you need anything." On one nice day, they picked up wine and food and took me for a picnic along the Charles River. They took me out to dinner another time. They made sure I knew where I was going and how to get there, offering me rides, telling me where to run when I started running again. They kept checking in. They were so sweet, telling me they didn't know how much to interfere, that they didn't want to be a burden.

Nicole left the hospital after three and a half weeks for Spaulding Rehab for five days before returning home to Charlotte. When Nicole and Michael came back to Boston to visit Erika and me, they, Patty, Tim and I went out to dinner. The four of them just hit it off and Nicole ended up training Tim to run the New York Marathon.

Other perfect strangers? I can't say enough about the compassion we felt from the two hospital staffs and the doctors and nurses. They treated us like family. Erika was one of their favorite patients and the nurses were always in her room, painting her fingernails and toenails. The Beth Israel people treated our family so well over the 50 days we were there and we really got to know each other. They gave Erika a surprise going away party and presented her with a scrapbook of pictures, including ones of nurses just lying in bed with Erika and some other special times they shared with her. They were so compassionate and are still in touch, so interested about her recovery progress.

All over Boston, people were so caring and supportive. I was in a gift shop and found a glass heart that I wanted to get for Tim and Patty to thank them for all they did for us. The store owner asked me what brought me to Boston. I told him our story and why I was buying the glass heart. He said, "There's no charge for this." That kind of thing happened all over the city. Everyone just wanted to help. People from Baltimore would say, "I've got relatives or friends in Boston. What do you need? Do you need clothes? Do you need food? Do you need a place to stay?" Everyone was ready to open up their homes to us.

There were other significant and amazing perfect strangers, including:

CHRIS SPIELHAGEN: Chris, one of Nicole's perfect strangers, had just completed his second Boston Marathon and was getting water about 50 yards beyond the finish line when the first bomb went off. Chris is an Army Sergeant who is stationed at Fort Carson, Colorado, but was born and raised in Boston. His three tours of duty in Iraq helped prepare him for saving Nicole's life. He sprinted for the bomb site and saw that Nicole needed help. As he worked on her injuries and got her stabilized, he told Nicole that all she had to do was trust him, and that she was going to get through this.

AMANDA NORTH: If not for Amanda, Erika would probably not be here today. Amanda, from California, was watching her daughter run and was near Erika when the bomb exploded. Amanda had some cuts and lacerations and her ear drums were blown out, but she crawled over to help Erika right away. She kept Erika calm and focused. She called for help for Erika and gave her belt to a responder to use as a tourniquet on Erika's leg. Amanda stayed with Erika until she was taken away. Amanda is such a kind, generous, compassionate woman. She came to stay at our house in October and it was like sitting around talking to an old friend, she's so easy to be around. And Amanda just loves Erika, caring about her so much.

I've thanked these people over and over again. We've hugged, we've cried, and more recently we've laughed together. They are part of our family now, our extended family. We will always be in each others' lives. We keep in touch, texting back and forth. Perhaps my biggest "thank you" to them is paying it forward. Seeing how they reacted in such a traumatic situation inspires me. If I'm ever called upon, I hope to respond with great compassion.

Erika went back to teaching at her pre-school on a part-time basis to begin with. Being with her students brightens her life. Her boss has been terrific at working around the doctor visits. Some days are challenging with many hours of appointments. She's also in the process of finishing her master's degree in Early Childhood Education.

> *We will always be in each other's lives ... Perhaps my biggest "thank you" to them is paying it forward.*

As you would imagine, all of our lives have changed. I retired from my massage business in November of 2011, but kept my license, thinking I would volunteer at hospices and do some other things I never had time to do before. But those things will have to wait. Right now, I am being a mom, tending to Erika and helping Nicole as much as I can from a distance. It has been a learning experience, to say the least. In the beginning, I was in denial: I thought I could care for Erika and still have my life and that my life was not going to change. I have surrendered to the change and learned to be patient with the process. And it's been fine. As I told my husband one day, "I am feeling irritable today and it has nothing to do with you." He asked, "Do you want to talk about it?" I said, "No, and tomorrow will be better." And it will be.

Erika is amazing and never complains, even when she has setbacks in her recovery. Because of her visibility, Erika has gotten to do things she never would have, but she would still rather have her leg.

Through it all, I continue to run. I did a half-marathon in Charlotte in November, 2013. Nicole was the race starter and many family members and friends were there. Tim and Patty flew in from Boston, Amanda came from California, and her daughter, Lili, came down from Boston. Nicole's perfect stranger, Sgt. Chris Spielhagen came, too, the first time we had met him. In the 5K,

SportPhoto.com

Erika's friend Bre pushed her wheelchair to 100 yards from the finish line, gave her a walker and then Erika, Nicole and Michael walked across the finish line together (shown on the previous page).

The Boston Marathon is a goal I was so close to attaining. I plan to run this year, but I'm excited and apprehensive about it. I have a feeling I will be recreating in my mind what happened last year. Is somebody going to try to replicate the attacks? I just have to trust that nothing will happen and my family will be safe. And I don't want Boston to be a negative feeling for me. I want to think of it as a place of healing and celebration. It has been one year, we did it and we're okay.

The plan is for Erika, Nicole and Michael to meet me at the spot on Commonwealth Avenue where I was stopped last year. And we'll finish the race together.

Carol Downing encourages you to considering supporting
www.bestrongstaystrong.net.

Stephen Pater

Runner/Perfect Stranger

Over 30 marathons, two Bostons

Age 42

Teacher, George County High School

Lucedale, Mississippi

My first encounter as a runner with perfect strangers happened when I was six years old. My dad was in seminary in New Orleans and I went with him one Saturday morning to the public library where he was studying. I was goofing off and decided to run outside to our car. I had a towel safety-pinned to my shirt and I was pretending to be Superman, which probably had a little bit to do with me being hit by a car as I ran across a street. As I lay there with my leg severely injured, two women came to my rescue, comforted me, and went inside to find my dad.

On April 15th in Boston, there were a lot of perfect strangers and Carol Downing was one of mine. I know that she has credited me with being one of hers, but as you'll read, I believe it was the other way around.

The reasons I run can be traced back to that accident when I was six. The damage to my leg wasn't catastrophic; it could have been much worse save for the shoes I was wearing. My mom was washing my tennis shoes that Saturday morning, so I was in my Sunday dress shoes, which were sturdy enough to keep my foot from being crushed by the weight of a 1970s solid metal automobile. My mom still has that shoe and sock.

The doctor told my dad and me that I would probably be able to walk reasonably well but he wasn't sure I'd be able to run again. Since then, I've used that as motivation to not only prove him wrong, but prove him way wrong. I ran track in high school and was a casual runner throughout college, but it wasn't until I took the teaching and coaching job at George County High School in Lucedale, Mississippi that I began distance running and marathons. Thirty-some marathons later, I've enjoyed the opportunity to go to different places and run different races, but no place and no race is like Boston.

It is the Super Bowl of marathons. It's the Holy Grail. However you want to put it, it's held in such high prestige. The way I explain it to my students is, "You may be a good driver, but if you aren't in the business already you're probably not going to be able to race at Daytona or Talladega. But when I run in Boston, I'm running the same race against, technically, the world's best marathoners." There is something special about that. Not to diminish smaller races and the competition in those races, but in Boston, you know that most everyone has qualified to run there, that you are among the best runners in the world and that the person next to you has gone through the same sacrifices that you've gone through to get to that point.

I was hoping to finish in 3:30 to 4:00. My training had gone well, but when I arrived in Boston, I had a change of plans. I said, "You know what? This will probably be my last time to run Boston as a qualifier, so I'm just going to soak it in. I'm going to take pictures along the route. I'm going to stop at Wellesley and kiss the coeds. (Many of them hold up signs saying they want to be kissed. When I ran in 2011, I found a girl from Tupelo, Mississippi, to kiss. This time, I didn't find a Mississippi girl, but I did find a young lady from Louisiana, where I grew up. I gave her a little peck on the cheek and a fare-thee-well.) I'm going to high-five the frat boys at the end of Heartbreak Hill as well as all the little kids along the route. I'll enjoy the screaming and yelling as I go through Boston College and on down to the finish line. I was just going to immerse myself in it all instead of killing myself trying to have my best time.

What's different about the crowds in Boston is that this is their race. For example, at the New York Marathon, no families showed up with trays of oranges, or had their own little water stop in their front yard. In Boston, you've got the little kids handing out popsicles and water all along the route. Bostonians turn it into their own private sporting event.

As I ran along, enjoying every bit of the experience, I was thinking that if this is my last time to celebrate the Boston Marathon, I really picked a great day. It was a perfect weather day for running and the crowds were big and into it. When I ran past Fenway, the Red Sox had just had a walk-off win, so I stopped and sang "Sweet Caroline" with some of that crew. I might have gotten a sip of somebody's beer, too.

I was nearing the iconic "right on Hereford and left on Boylston" where spectators are piled up eight and ten deep and was looking forward to catching that rush again and taking it, or it taking me, through the finish line. I liken the experience of making that turn to driving, at night, out of the mountains into Los Angeles and as you come out of a dark mountain canyon, there are all of a sudden the lights of the city sprawling before you. In Boston, when you make those turns, you are swallowed up and carried by screaming fans. At that point you are exhausted, you're spent, you've given it all you've got, and the spectators pick you up.

The first indication that something was wrong was near the underpass before you come up to take the right onto Hereford. There was a bottleneck and police officers were running in the direction of the finish. After the fact, I thought I may have remembered hearing a boom, but I wasn't thinking that at the time.

Immediately, I texted my wife, Kristy. "I'm all right, please don't worry."

She responded, "Yeah, I know you're all right. Have you finished yet?" She and several other teachers — Kristy is a kindergarten teacher — were tracking my progress on the B.A.A. website. My little runner on the site had stopped.

I texted, "Something blew up at the finish line."

"What do you mean, something blew up?"

"Something exploded, we don't know what."

There was a woman standing next to me. Her name was Carol and I had seen her off and on during the race. We had been sort of running side-by-side for a while, and probably nodded and smiled at each other the way runners do. I'm not a social runner; I had my iPod on and I don't talk to people a whole lot while I run,

cheaters. But she was able to hold her phone further away than my
arm could reach and I was able to read her messages for her.

Carol had been very calm, but she began getting upset
about not being able to reach her people. I told her, "You know
what? The finish line is this direction; come with me and we'll try
to find our way there."

Although we still didn't know what had exploded,
it became more and more apparent that something bad had
happened because the police had sealed off the finish line area as
a crime scene. We could not find access. We tried back alleys and
a couple of different streets that I thought would get us there, but
we couldn't get through.

Carol tried to explain to a policeman that her daughters
were in there, and he just said, "You can't come in here."

The police were trying to get us off the streets, so Carol
and I went into a shopping mall type of area. That's when a text
came in on her phone that I read for her. It said her daughter was
injured and had been taken to Brigham and Women's Hospital. We
immediately found a security guard and asked him how far it was
to the hospital.

"It's about five miles right down this road," he said.

Our hearts sank. I said, "We've just run a marathon and
can't go another five miles. Where's the nearest subway station?"

"The subways are closed."

A man and a woman were standing nearby and overheard

52

our conversation. The man said, "What's your problem?"

I told him, "Her daughter was one of the people injured at the finish line."

He said, "We're from Boston. Our car is four or five blocks from here. You come with us. We'll get you to the hospital."

I asked Carol if she was okay going with them and she said she was, that all she cared about was getting to the hospital. I gave her a hug and told the guy, "Please take care of her, because she has taken care of me."

In the process of getting from the underpass to where we now stood in the mall, and as concerned as Carol was about the plight of her family, she also worried about me. She stopped somebody along the way and asked for their Mylar blanket because the guy she's walking with is from southern Mississippi, me, and is cold. A bit later, we stopped and talked to somebody else and she got this guy to volunteer to give me his warm-up clothes that he had on before the race and were in his bag. So, all of a sudden, I'm wearing a pair of adidas sweat pants and a 2006 Boston Marathon t-shirt that this guy just gives to me, thanks to Carol. Her kids have been hurt, and she's worried about me! Who cares whether I'm cold when her children are in the hospital?

After Carol left, I bought a phone charger so I could get in touch with Kristy. I always carry some cash in my shoe and, for the bigger races, a credit card and ID. When my phone had enough of a charge, I called my wife. This was about 4:30 or so, and she was, naturally, upset, but okay that I was safe.

I was starving and went and got a bite to eat. I asked the waiter where was the nearest subway terminal that was open, because I had to get back to my hotel in Quincy. He said he didn't know, but suggested the Back Bay. I said, "Where's that?" He said, "Six blocks that way." So I headed there, but it was closed. I spotted a cab on a street corner about a block away. I took off in a dead sprint for this taxicab and the driver says, "No, no, I've got a fare." I said, "Can you get a cab sent to this street corner? I'll just wait here for the next one." He said, "No, we're not taking calls."

The passenger in the cab said, "Where are you going?" I said, "You know what? Anywhere but here!" He said, "I'm going to the airport." I said, "If you can get me to the airport, I can get to where I need to go."

It turns out he had run the marathon, been to his hotel, changed his clothes, gotten his bag, and was heading back to London. He not only shared his cab with me and made sure the cabbie dropped me off at the subway station by the airport, he refused to take any money from me. He said, "I was going to the airport anyway, certainly not. I only wish I could take you the rest of the way to your hotel." And this is the thing about runners: they're always there for each other. It's an amazing tight-knit group of people.

I took the subway to Quincy. When I got to the hotel, I told the lady at the desk that I wanted to pick up my bag. I had checked it that morning, knowing that after the race I would pick it up and go to another hotel by the airport for an early flight Tuesday morning.

She said, "Do you have your claim ticket?"

I said, "Ma'am, it's somewhere on Boylston Street."

Something clicked and she said, "Oh, you're the runner!"

I said, "Well, yes, I am a runner, but there were probably 40 or 50 of us staying here that were running the marathon."

She said, "No, no. You're the only one who hasn't picked up his bags yet. We were worried about you!"

She got my bags and I headed back to the airport hotel. My phone was dead again because every student and teacher and everyone in my contact list were calling, texting and posting on Facebook, trying to find out if I was okay. It's amazing, you can't keep your number from students. They're resourceful.

It was 9:30 p.m. before I got into my room and plugged my phone in again. I called my wife and she was upset, but very thankful that I was fine.

Before the race, and all while I was running it, I was looking forward to repeating my 2011 post-race dinner: lobster and a cold Sam Adams. All afternoon, I kept thinking that all I wanted was a warm meal and a cold beer. Finally, nearly 10 p.m., I headed down to the hotel restaurant and had a burger and a beer. A TV was on and I watched the news with a heavy heart. It had been a long day.

Tuesday morning, I flew back to Mississippi. One of the

most troubling images I'd seen in the coverage of the bombings was that of Martin Richard, the eight-year-old boy who died. When I got back home Tuesday and my eight-year-old son, Jayce, came running up the stairs to me and jumped into my arms, that was the best hug I've ever had. Kristy joined in and we all just held on to each other, nobody wanted to let go.

I didn't know whether Carol found her children, nor what had happened to them. I didn't know Carol's last name. All I knew was that she was from Baltimore. So when I pulled up the Internet, I Googled "Carol, Baltimore, injured," something like that. The Baltimore ABC affiliate had done an article on Carol, Erika and Nicole.

Reading what happened just took the air out of me, it sucked some of the life out of me. I knew her daughters had been hurt, but you don't ever think it's "that person." Her daughter was one of the ones that was very badly hurt. I almost felt guilty that I didn't stay with her and left her in the hands of the couple that took her to the hospital. I was thinking, Stephen, you should have stayed with her. You were the only person she knew at that moment. Not that she really knew me, but I felt bad about that. As it turned out, she was in great hands with Tim and Patty Island.

> *Reading what happened just took the air out of me, it sucked some of the life out of me.*

We hadn't been in contact, and I didn't know if she would remember me and, you don't know, given the trauma of the day, if someone wants to talk to you. I went to Baltimore to run in October because I heard that her daughter was the starter of the marathon and I was hoping I might get to see Carol.

As her daughter gave a very inspirational speech before the start, I saw Carol near the podium. I was able to walk to the edge of the stage and I shouted her name a couple of times. She looked over and there was that moment before the recognition set in and the look on her face was, "Oh, there's that runner!" We hugged and chatted for a bit about how we each had wanted to find the other but didn't know how, or in my case, wasn't sure she wanted to. We exchanged phone numbers and off I went to run the marathon. As I finished the race, I thought that I would send her a message later, but there she was in the finishing chute. She had waited three and a half hours to talk to me. We talked for 30 or 40 minutes and took a picture together. It was cathartic to reconnect. It warmed my heart to see her and to see that her family was on the road to recovery. She means the world to me and I'll never forget that in her moment of need, a situation that no parent should be in, she was helping me.

Everything else aside, not finishing the race is heart breaking. I know I have a time, a projected finish time that B.A.A. assigned me, but I haven't finished that race. I'm very jealous of all of the people who got to finish, or mirrored where they were and got to finish later that week. When I go back in April, I'll be going to the course on Saturday or Sunday and start where we were stopped and trot to the finish.

On Wednesday, April 17th, when I went back to class, I told my students in first period what had happened. Between classes, I went to the restroom. When I came out, the students had lined the halls to cheer me on and had taken a piece of police tape and held it across the hall. They said, "Okay, come finish." So I ran about 30 yards down the hall and broke through the tape. I keep some of my running medals on display in my classroom and one of my students had pulled out my 2011 Boston Marathon medal. When I "finished," they draped the medal around my neck.

That was my finish.

Stephen Pater urges you to consider supporting the recovery of Carol Downing's children at www.bestrongstaystrong.net.

*Carol Downing, right, with two of her perfect strangers,
Boston residents Tim and Patty Island*

Patty Island   Tim Island

Spectator/Perfect Stranger   *Runner/Perfect Stranger*

Ran Boston in 2012   *Fourth marathon, first Boston*

Merchandising Executive   *Inventory Planning and*

Boston   *Management Consultant*

                                  Boston

Tim decided to run Boston, his first marathon in 17 years after having witnessed what a wonderful experience Patty had in 2012 as part of the Dana-Farber Marathon Challenge team. Patty was diagnosed with breast cancer in 2010 and was treated at the Dana-Farber Cancer Institute. The quality of care and the people she met through the Dana-Farber organization inspired her to run Boston in 2012. So 2013 was Tim's year to run and raise money for Dana-Farber cancer research honoring his mother who died in 2000 from pancreatic cancer, in support of his step-father recently battling multiple myeloma, and in support of Patty.

Tim's experience and journey with fellow team members leading up to the marathon was extraordinary. The running community in Boston is tightly knit and provides important physical, mental and social outlets during what can be tough winters of snow and cold weather. Since moving to Boston five years ago, the marathon has become a large part of Tim's and Patty's lives as both runners and spectators. The energy in the city on Patriots Day weekend is infectious and April 15th 2013 began as a beautiful day in Boston — a perfect day to run 26.2 miles. Tim and Patty walked a few blocks from their South End home, through the Public Garden to Boston Common where Tim met a teammate and boarded one of the hundreds of school buses that took the runners out to Hopkinton. Seeing Copley Plaza and the Common filled with eager and anxious runners on Marathon Monday is inspiring to witness.

Patty took in the sights and sounds along the finish line area on Boylston before taking the subway out to the Woodlands T stop. That's at Mile 17 just before the start of the Newton/ Heartbreak Hills, and a common training ground for 10-mile evening winter runs. Tim was aiming for a sub-4:00 marathon and his training and conditioning all pointed to this being achievable. Through Mile 17, he was on pace but realized he needed to slow up a bit as his legs just didn't feel as they had throughout all the training runs. Tim was able to text Patty updates on his progress because he opted to run with his iPhone. With the knowledge that Tim was slightly slower, Patty changed her meeting point plan from the finish line area to the corner of Commonwealth Ave and Hereford. She would hop in and run with him over the last 700 meters. All was as planned and Tim was soon to finish the historic Boston Marathon.

The Boston Marathon spectators are intoxicating, from the children along the course in Natick with their hands out for high-fives, to the screaming Wellesley girls begging for kisses, to the students of Boston College on the Heartbreak Hill descent, to the children handing out orange slices along Beacon Street through the mentally tough Miles 23-25. These fans make the runners feel special, cheering them on as if they are winning the race.

In an instant, the beauty of the day vanished and running the race was suddenly unimportant.

Patty was at Commonwealth and Hereford when the bombs went off and spectators turned toward the sound, but couldn't tell what happened. Suddenly the race was halted and what seemed like hundreds of police officers emerged on foot and bicycles, all heading toward the finish line.

Tim was close to Mile 26 under Mass Ave when a friend next to him said "What was that?" As they ran out of the underpass toward Hereford, people started yelling: "Stop running! Stop running! Stop running!" He thought, what the hell? That's impossible; how can the marathon be halted as there are some 5,000 runners behind him flowing like an untamed river. His friend pulled up on Twitter that there were multiple explosions at the finish line and he said, "This is a terrorist attack." Patty and Tim texted and quickly found each other, remarkably only 50 yards apart and so relieved she had moved from the finish line. Having his phone that day proved to be very important, as so many runners were without communication of family and loved ones.

The weather also had rapidly changed from sunny and beautiful to cloudy and cold. This made it more difficult for the runners to stay warm and make rational decisions. Everyone wanted to know what was happening, and tried to piece it together as they learned news from phones or text messages. It was chaotic.

Patty and Tim made their way toward the Dana-Farber post-race headquarters in the Copley Plaza Marriott Hotel, but were unable to proceed beyond the back of the Prudential Center at Huntington. Many strangers and runners came up to them and asked to send text messages on their phones to their families. Just inside the south entrance of the Prudential shopping complex, a runner from out of town walked up to them with Carol Downing. He said, "This woman needs to get to Brigham and Women's Hospital to find her children. Do you know how to get there?"

Tim said, "We're from Boston, we have a car and live just a few blocks away. Come with us to our home, put on some warm clothes, have some food, and we'll quickly get you to the hospital to find your daughter." They didn't know at that moment that Carol would become one of their closest friends and someone they would communicate with over the next year on a nearly daily basis. As they sat on the Island's couch refueling, taking in news coverage, trying to get warm and charging their phones, Carol calmly read some of her text messages from Michael Gross, her son-in-law. He wrote that Carol's daughter Nicole had two broken legs and was going into surgery. Carol was calm and stoic, but informed them she still had no idea where her youngest daughter, Erika Brannock, was and whether she was injured.

SWAT security was protecting the hospital entrance and when asked if Patty and Tim were family, Carol responded, "Yes," so they sat with Carol into the evening until another family member arrived.

Patty and Tim communicated via text and e-mail with Carol over the next week and on Wednesday morning, Tim picked up Carol's bag and her marathon medal from the B.A.A. offices. Going there was an incredibly cathartic event of closure for Tim.

Photo courtesy Tim Island

As he left, gently weeping, he thanked a woman of the B.A.A. and said that someday he'll cross the Boston Marathon finish line. The woman said, "Well, you have now. You just did." Tim hadn't noticed the small finish line B.A.A. staffers had created so that runners entering the room would be able to "finish" the marathon. It was a simple but poignant gesture.

Carol and her family are a gift that came out of a horrific event. Their attitudes throughout this ordeal have been incredibly positive, uplifting and inspiring. Patty and Tim feel so grateful to have them in their lives, and felt fortunate to be able to surprise Carol on her birthday in November at the Thunder Road Marathon in Charlotte. Erika and Nicole started the race and gave inspirational speeches. Nicole and Michael welcomed Tim and Patty into their home and treated them as part of the family, including them in some private celebrations. It's a friendship that will endure.

Patty and Tim are both running Boston this year with the Dana-Farber team, and they'll be running in memory of those who lost their lives and were impacted by the bombings. Carol will come to Boston to run the marathon again and her kids will be here to cheer her on. It will be an amazing reunion and celebration of the human spirit, and of Carol and her family's resiliency. It will be an important and emotional weekend for the entire Boston area and those from all over who were affected.

Boston and its citizens showed a great deal of humanity in

the days and weeks after the bombings and, contrary to what Tim and Patty were told when moving from the West Coast, Boston is a town of warm and friendly people. Get to know a New Englander and you may have a friend for life.

Patty and Tim encourage you to support the recovery of Carol Downing's children at www.bestrongstaystrong.net.

Courtesy: Carol Downing

LEFT TO RIGHT: *Tim Island, Erika Brannock, Carol Downing and Patty Island*

*Erika Brannock, right, is reunited with her "perfect stranger,"
Amanda North, a month and a half after the bombings.*

Amanda North

Spectator/Perfect Stranger

Founder, Artisan Connect

California

Marathon Monday capped off what had been a wonderful weekend visit to New England. I arrived in Boston on Friday and my daughter, Lili, and I spent time with some friends over the weekend and also had a lovely time visiting my mother in New Hampshire. Lili and a college friend were running the Boston Marathon for a charity. Her friend's family had us over for dinner Sunday evening and, Monday morning, helped me navigate the spectator areas of the marathon.

I had no idea how big the Boston Marathon was. I was overwhelmed. At every step along the marathon route there were throngs of people. It seemed that everybody was out. We watched for Lili and her friend at Mile 10, on Heartbreak Hill and then headed to the finish line to see them cross. I remember feeling so elated, so proud of my daughter. She worked so hard for this, training through an especially brutal New England winter. As I waited at the finish, some of Lili's friends called to say our runners were close. It was a beautiful day; crisp and cool. The music was playing and it was so emotionally charged. I was surrounded by people cheering on their loved ones. It was family oriented; simple and pure joy. I remember that moment, tears welling up in my eyes and thinking, this is one of the happiest moments of my life.

And then the first explosion happened. My first thought was that it was an accident. When the second one went off, my thoughts shifted immediately to an attack: we were under attack. I remember looking at the sky for airplanes. Was this like 9/11? I have a clear memory of what happened. The first bomb was right behind me and it knocked me over. I was on my side, and there was so much smoke.

A feeling of calm came over me as I looked around. To my right, about two feet away, was a young woman. I saw that she had a huge, gaping wound on her lower left leg. She was conscious and I thought maybe I could do something for her. I can help! It was as if another force took over, like I was watching someone else in a movie crawling over to help her. I realized I had burning embers on my jacket and took it off. I brushed the embers away and put it around her. I held on to her hand. I really didn't know what else to do, but my grandfather was a surgeon and somewhere along the line I must have heard the basics of trauma care: keep people calm and keep them from going into shock. Maybe, at an unconscious level, I was thinking that I needed to hold her attention and keep her calm.

I asked her name.

"Irene," I thought she said. There was a lot of confusion and my hearing had been diminished by the explosion. It seemed unearthly quiet.

I said, "I'm Amanda, and I'm not going to let you go. Look into my eyes. I won't let you go. Hang on, help is coming."

It was so smoky and chaotic and every minute was critical in whether people survived or not. I yelled for help, and one of the responders took a quick look at Irene (whose name I later discovered was Erika Brannock) and yelled, "Does anyone have a belt?"

I did, and I gave it to him to use as a tourniquet on Erika's leg. It bought us a few minutes until the official responders came and took her away.

I really thought it was the end; we didn't know if there were other explosions coming. There is a wonderful line from *Lord of the Rings* where Frodo says, "I am glad you are here with me. Here at the end of all things, Sam." That is the emotion that went through my mind. It was as much about me having Erika's hand to hold and drawing comfort from her, as it was her holding my hand. I've since told Erika that she helped me as much as I helped her. That human touch at such a critical moment helped calm me.

It may have also distracted me from my own injury. When

Erika was taken away, one of the rescue workers said, "Hey, you're injured!" I looked down and there was a nine-inch long, two-inch deep incision on my upper thigh. It was probably from a slice of glass. On my other leg, there were third-degree burns. It looked like a ball bearing landed on my leg and burned through my coat and jeans. I hadn't felt any pain and it was interesting that my wound was not bleeding. And, when I arrived at the medical tent, my vital signs were near normal. I told the surprised medical staff, "I know, I feel fine!" And I really believe it was because I had focused on Erika. It calmed me down. It gave me something to do. And I believe it not only contributed to my immediate well-being, but my injuries healed very quickly, too. My perforated eardrum healed itself. I was incredibly lucky.

As I try to describe what it was like when Erika and I were on the ground, it was as if everything else in my life stopped. There was a strange melding, almost like a life force going from me into her. I felt as if we were hardwired together and there was nothing else in the world but her. That's how strong our connection felt and how focused I was. After they transported Erika and took me to the medical tent, my focus shifted to my daughter, and I lost some of that calm, wildly asking questions about what had happened and if the runners who hadn't finished were okay. I knew Lili was about a half mile from the finish line.

There were several anxious hours before I knew what happened to Lili. I couldn't call her because my phone was still in the pocket of the coat I had put around Erika. Lili and her running partner were between the two bombs and were thrown off their feet. They ran off the course, and a perfect stranger loaned her a phone and she called her dad to let him know she was okay. But she couldn't reach me and didn't know where I was. And it wasn't until later on, when I was at the hospital, that a social worker got through to my son, Logan, at college in Colorado.

She told him, "Your mom is going to be okay." Logan had no idea what she was talking about and what was going on. He had just come out of a mid-term, feeling good about putting that behind him, then was blindsided with the news of the bombings.

Detectives came and took my clothes for evidence, and

they also asked for a hair sample. My hair had been singed on the right side and they reasoned with me by saying, "You're going to have to cut it anyway!"

Lili and I reunited at the hospital later that night and I was released around midnight. Because my clothes were gone, I left the hospital dressed in scrubs.

The next day, Lili said, "Mom, we were spared by a miracle. Our lives will never be the same and we need to think about our passion and our purpose." It was a powerful moment. I agreed. We had seen all too clearly that life can change very quickly and I wanted to act on my sense of purpose and my passions now, not at some later time. I decided on the spot to leave my career and do something completely different.

What am I passionate about? Where is there a problem that I could use my experience and expertise to help solve? I spent 30 years in the technology business as a marketing executive in a variety of companies. My thoughts went to the developing world. My daughter, son and I have traveled extensively there, and along the way I met with a lot of artisans who told me that their way of life is becoming extinct because they're not getting paid enough to sustain themselves in their traditional livelihood. What is it they need? I had been volunteering at Santa Clara University with some social entrepreneurs in developing countries. And although they have been providing the artisans many things, I realized what was lacking was market access. Well, I'm a marketing professional, I understand technology and I can create an online marketplace that connects the artisans to buyers who will pay them appropriately for what they do.

I've founded a new company: Artisan Connect (www. artisanconnect.com). It is an online marketplace offering high-quality home décor products from artisans in developing countries. As a social venture, we are dedicated to sharing the profits from our business to help sustain these artisans in their traditional livelihood. We celebrate the artisans by telling their stories and providing additional means of connecting with them, through direct donation, visits and volunteer opportunities. It is for-profit but distributes the wealth. It's been exciting, exhilarating and terrifying. And it has changed my life. The Boston Marathon was a catalyst for me.

Several times in the weeks after the marathon, I thought of trying to get in touch with Erika to find out how she was doing. I would think about her every night and would feel myself beaming energy into her, not knowing who she was, where she was or how she was doing. I describe it as an umbilical cord. We had such a shortlived but powerful connection and I continued to feel that way. I am a person of faith and I did pray for her. But I didn't know how to contact her without going to the media. And I did not want to be part of that.

On June 3rd, just before leaving Beth Israel Hospital in Boston to go home, Erika told a CNN reporter, "I really want to

Anderson Cooper 360
June 3, 2013

Do you recognize the woman in this photo? We believe her name is Joan and she's from California. She's a hero to a Boston bombing victim, Erika, who lost part of her leg in the attack. Help Erika with her search for the woman who saved her life. If you know Joan, email findjoan@cnn.com and tune in now and at 10 p.m. ET to hear Erika's story of survival.
More info: http://on.cnn.com/11SDrjZ

Courtesy CNN

find the woman who saved my life. I think her name was Joan and she's from California. I don't know if you're even watching, but Joan, I would love to find you and tell you thank you and give you a big hug."

CNN showed a picture of me bending over Erika at the explosion site. My brother had been watching, texted me: "You're on CNN!" I thought he was pulling my leg, as he has been known to do, but some of my friends soon started texting that they had seen me as well. CNN also posted a plea to find "Joan."

That night, I e-mailed "findjoan@cnn.com" and wrote, "That's me!"

The producer wanted to make sure I wasn't part of a hoax and I was vetted very thoroughly. I told them I was overwhelmed that she had remembered me and wanted to meet me. I told them I wanted to find out what happened to her and would like to support her if she needed to raise money for her medical care. I was not after any publicity. The people at CNN were very sensitive in protecting Erika.

They asked if I wanted to meet her.

"Of course! When?"

They said, "Tomorrow."

So I jumped on a plane and flew to Baltimore where it was an amazing moment when I reconnected with Erika on June 5th. That is when I first met her mom, Carol. I had never thought of myself as having saved Erika's life, but Carol and Erika have said that if it wasn't for me, Erika wouldn't be here. I think they give me too much credit. But it shows how doing one small thing can make such a big difference.

After CNN showed our reunion, I received so many kind messages from all over the world. Many people thanked me for reminding them that kindness to strangers can happen and that there is goodness in the world. As my pastor at Menlo Park Presbyterian Church, Reverend John Ortberg, noted: even in moments of chaos and terror, God speaks clearly to us; that there is goodness in the world, and it's worth fighting for.

Once we connected, we've stayed connected. I look for Erika's Facebook postings and I celebrate with her along the way.

Visiting her, going to the school where she teaches and meeting her kids and co-workers was incredible. I've gotten to know her as a person. Her spirit and courage is so inspiring to me. It's so powerful.

In November, Erika told me she was just getting ready to use her prosthesis and asked if I would meet her in Charlotte for the Thunder Road 5K and Half-Marathon. Her goal was to walk across the 5K finish line and she wanted me to watch her. Carol invited Lili to run the half-marathon with her, so we got to watch them run and finish, too.

Also in Charlotte were Patty and Tim Island, two of Carol's perfect strangers from Boston, and Chris Spielhagen, Nicole's perfect stranger. It was wonderful meeting them and putting more of the pieces of the Boston Marathon puzzle together. There is something so healing in doing so.

I need to mention that I, too, was the recipient of the kindness of strangers. From the people who knelt beside me at the bombing site, to those who took me to the medical tent, to the medical personnel there and at the hospital, and to many others along the way, I am forever grateful.

Like so many whose lives were affected by the bombings, I will be back this April for the Boston Marathon. Lili is running it again for a charity, and I will be there again to watch her finish. Tears will well up in my eyes and it will be one of the happiest moments of my life.

Amanda North urges you to consider supporting the One Fund at onefundboston.org, and the recovery of Erika Brannock at www.bestrongstaystrong.net.

Anderson Cooper 360
June 5

This moving photo captures the moment Erika Brannock had been hoping for. The Boston bombing survivor finally got to meet the hero who saved her life. Thanks to our amazing viewers, Randi Kaye was able to reunite the two women who profoundly touched each other's lives. Amanda North says she never stopped thinking about Erika; they share a deep bond. Don't miss their remarkable story on AC360 at 8 and 10 p.m. ET tonight. Read more: http://bit.ly/13ltVnG

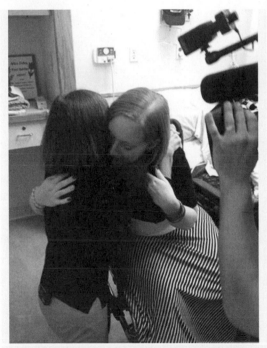

Like · Comment · Share   2,007   117   152

Courtesy CNN

*Army Master Sergeant Chris Spielhagen after running
the 2013 Boston Marathon. Minutes later, his
combat experience saved a woman's life.*

MSG Chris Spielhagen

Runner/Perfect Stranger for Nicole Gross

Age 34

U.S. Army Team Sergeant • 10th Special Forces (Airborne)

Fort Carson, Colorado

The vibe you get when running the Boston Marathon is unbelievable. Being born and raised in Boston, it's a very emotional experience for me as I run through each town with so many people cheering from start to finish. The B.A.A. donates slots to the military and police officers and I ran it for the first time in 2012. It was very hot, but I finished in just under four hours.

My wife, Kristie, who is an Army 1st Lieutenant, and five-year-old daughter, Brianna, came to watch me run the marathon on April 15, 2013. I told my wife that morning, "You'll either see me in an ambulance or at the finish line." I was surprised I actually finished. I had not trained as I should have and although I was exhausted, I only added seven minutes to my 2012 time.

After finishing, I had my picture taken by a volunteer and as I grabbed a bottle of water and cracked the cap, the first explosion went off. It sounded like a celebratory cannon, which I thought was weird. I turned toward the sound, saw smoke rising about 50 meters away and said, "Oh crap!" My military experience told me something bad was going on. Then the second one went off farther down the street. I knew that people were hurt or killed. I needed to get in there; they needed my help. I've been in similar situations in combat and knew I had more experience than most of the people out there. I started to run, but my legs seized up. Moments later, adrenaline kicked in and my legs started working properly. As I sprinted toward the first bomb site, a volunteer tried to stop me. I told her I was in the military, people needed my help and I moved her out of my way. I ran to where the police and others were pulling down the barricades and jumped over the fences to get to the injured.

Medical staff had not arrived yet, and as I moved through the site assessing the injured, I saw a man leaning against a wall and, although he was bleeding from his lips and chin, he was not in need of critical care. I saw a woman who had lost her legs and had people helping her. And then I looked down at my feet and there was Nicole. She was sitting up and appeared to be in shock. I told her, "You need to trust me. I need you to be calm and listen to what I tell you," and told her to lie back and that I would take care of her. She was in bad shape and losing blood from a deep laceration on her right leg, almost down to the bone. On the same leg, the Achilles tendon was severed and her other leg was shattered. Because of my military experience, this was a familiar scene and I was able to stay focused on helping this woman. I told her I needed to straighten out her legs so I could work on them. A volunteer came over and I took his windbreaker, which I used as a bandage. Another medical volunteer came up and I asked her to keep talking to Nicole, to keep telling her everything was going to be okay. Two National Guard soldiers asked me what I needed and I directed them to a bench that could be used to make a litter. A firefighter came up and asked what I needed and I ripped open his First Aid pouch and pulled out supplies.

I told Nicole I would have to check her hips and back. I lifted her up, which had to have been painful, but she didn't make a sound. I tightened up the bandages and tied her legs together. We did more triage on her leg as a medical volunteer struggled to get an IV in. Nicole was still bleeding and, with the help of a firefighter, we put a tourniquet on her left leg and I started an IV. I kept telling Nicole, "You're going to be okay."

This was about 10 to 15 minutes after the first explosion. A hand tapped my shoulder. An EMT said, "Sir, we've got it from here." And I handed over my patient to them. A physician volunteer asked the status of the patient. I started explaining in detail and she interrupted me; "No! One, two or three?" I said, "I don't know what 'one, two or three' is!" She said, "Is she urgent, litter or ambulatory?" I stated, "No she is urgent surgical," which means she had priority over anyone that is urgent. They moved her onto an ambulance litter and as they prepared to carry her away, I held her hand and told her, "Don't worry. Everything will be okay." She later told me she remembered my voice, but paired it to the female medical volunteer's face.

As I walked down Boylston, I started texting my wife and finally reached her. She said they were in the Prudential Center, but when I got there, a cop told me that everyone had been evacuated from the building. Texting wasn't working again, and for close to an hour I walked around the area trying to find them. I entered the Shops at the Prudential Center and heard, "Chris!" It was my wife and she and my daughter came running up to me. It was such a relief to find them. I kissed them and put my daughter on my shoulders. My wife had bought me a zip-up sweater thinking I might be cold. She was right. We hugged again and I said, "Whatever happens you need to stay with me." We eventually met up with others from the B.A.A. and State Troopers and flew out early the next morning for Fort Carson.

As I replayed what happened over the next several days, I felt blessed that my wife and daughter were okay. They were so close to the second bomb, standing just across the street. They saw the explosion and my daughter has some PTSD she's working through. After we got back to Colorado, I had to get ready to leave for training 48 hours later. It was pretty emotional leaving. I wanted to help my daughter through this experience.

And I wondered about the woman I helped. Who was she? How was she? I remembered what she looked like and what she was wearing. The next day, on the front page of the *Wall Street Journal*, there was a photo of her, unidentified, just after the bombing, sitting up and looking bewildered, pretty much just as I found her. Within two days, my sister, Jessica Keegan, found out her name was Nicole Gross, but we didn't know how to reach her. About three months later, my sister found an interview Nicole did with a local news person in Charlotte, North Carolina. I e-mailed him and from that connection, I was able to contact one of Nicole's assistants. She shared my story with Nicole and about a month later, Nicole contacted me and invited me to Charlotte for a race and a thank you dinner for all the people who supported her.

So in November, almost seven months to the day since the bombings, I flew to Charlotte to meet her.

I attended the gathering wearing a Boston Strong ribbon pinned on my jacket. I recognized Nicole and walked up to her asking, "Nicole?"

She responded, "Hi, I'm Nicole."

"Hi, I'm Chris."

Her eyes got big and her mouth dropped open and she said, "Hold on a second."

She went to get her mom, Carol Downing. Carol came over and Nicole said, "Mom, this is Chris. This is the man who saved me."

Carol started crying and I said, "Please don't cry, because I will start crying too!" We just stood there and hugged.

At dinner, I sat next to two of Carol's perfect strangers, Patty and Tim Island, and the next morning, Sunday, we all par-

Nicole Gross and her perfect stranger,
MSG Chris Spielhagen

ticipated in the race. Nicole invited me to a family dinner that night and I flew back home the next day.

I didn't go there looking for a parade for what I did; a simple thank you was plenty. And there was plenty of that. They all told me how grateful they were. Nicole and I texted on Thanksgiving and we exchanged Christmas cards with the family. I hope the bond will continue; a long-lasting connection.

I'm running again this year. My wife will be on deployment but I will bring my daughter to the marathon. Boston is my home town and this town can't be held back. So I want to run for Boston and to support Nicole, Carol and the rest of their family.

I believe God put me there that day for a reason. I was needed there. I find peace and calm with that.

Chris Spielhagen encourages you to support Carol Downing's children at bestrongstaystrong.net, as well as the Wounded Warriors at woundedwarriorproject.org/Donate.

The Downing/Gross/Brannock group in November, 2013
LEFT TO RIGHT: *MSG Chris Spielhagen, Nicole Gross, Michael Gross, Erika Brannock, Amanda North, Carol Downing, Tim Island, Patty Island*

On Monday morning, the sun rose over Boston. The sunlight glistened off the Statehouse dome. In the Common and the Public Garden, spring was in bloom. On this Patriots Day, like so many before, fans jumped onto the T to see the Sox at Fenway. In Hopkinton, runners laced up their shoes and set out on a 26.2-mile test of dedication and grit and the human spirit. And across this city, hundreds of thousands of Bostonians lined the streets — to hand the runners cups of water and to cheer them on.

It was a beautiful day to be in Boston — a day that explains why a poet once wrote that this town is not just a capital, not just a place. Boston, he said, "is the perfect state of grace."

President Barack Obama, at an interfaith memorial service at the Cathedral of the Holy Cross in South Boston, April 18, 2013

THE FIRST RESPONDERS

Volumes of analysis have been written about why some of us run toward danger. The majority of us who don't are grateful to the men and women of fire, police and EMS departments who signed up to face danger each day. But on Marathon Monday, those brave souls were joined by another group of first responders: the people who had no training and no business being there, but still ran in and saved lives.

As President Obama said at the Boston interfaith service:

You displayed grit. You displayed compassion. You displayed civic duty. You displayed courage. And when we see that kind of spirit, there's something about that that's infectious.

It is infectious, isn't it? The people who ran in and, as described in the previous section by Matt, Zachary and Chris, held people's lives in their hands, make all of us want to be better.

Whether they were trained and doing their jobs, or were simply civilians who still can't explain why they ran toward the explosions, none of them expected the horrific scene awaiting them. Three people died instantly. That so many more did not die in the following hours was miraculous and a testament to the quick actions of the first responders. Rick Kates, an off-duty EMT and high school track coach in Hingham who was recording official finishing times, was kneeling next to the wounded within seconds. He tweeted that night, "I tried my best." His best, and the best of all of the dozens of first responders, was more than good enough.

Not one of them likes hearing it, but they are heroes.

NDATF
@RickKates
Head Track & Field Coach, Physics Teachery, Asst Executive
Director Mass State Track Coaches Assn, EMT #BostonStrong
Massachusetts • ndahingham.com

1,660   211   368

Follow   👤▾

Tweets

NDATF @RickKates   Apr 15
I am safe everybody...thoughts and prayers to all those affected........I
tried my best
Expand   ← Reply   ↻ Retweet   ★ Favorite   ••• More

NDATF @RickKates   Apr 15
Good luck to all running the BAA Marathon today...see you at the
finish line
Expand   ← Reply   ↻ Retweet   ★ Favorite   ••• More

Rick Kates

Track and Field Coach and Physics Teacher
Notre Dame Academy, Hingham, Massachusetts
Part-time EMT, Carver, Massachusetts

My first thought after hearing the explosion near the finish line was that it was some sort of salute to Dick Hoyt, who pushes his son Rick's wheelchair each year in the marathon. I had heard rumors it would be their last Boston, their 31st, and they have been such an inspiration to so many people, so a tribute like that would have been fitting. The boom sounded like when the Patriots score a touchdown, when the muskets are fired, except a lot louder. Then there was a second explosion and people started bolting and I knew it was something else, something bad.

This year's marathon started out as one of the best ever. Perfect weather, just a great day. There's no other marathon like ours. It's the oldest continuously running marathon in the world and is one of the few marathons you have to qualify for. As a kid growing up in Dorchester, I got to go in to see the marathon. It was such a special event that we looked forward to each year. It brings international and local flavor together and it showcases our city. When you go to other marathons, you realize how special Boston's is. It's held on Patriots Day and you've got the Red Sox game going on, too. The marathon is right before the college kids are getting ready for exams, and they are out in force along the route. It's just fantastic!

I was working at the finish line as an official for the Massachusetts Track and Field Officials Association. It is responsible for recording the top 100 official times for male, female and wheelchair runners. My job was recording the wheelchair finishes. Our official uniform is a blue jacket and green hat, the same uniform worn by officials at all the high school and college meets. I wear that same uniform for my other officiating duties. I'm heavily involved in high school athletics and I am the cross country and track coach at Notre Dame Academy in Hingham. Last year I did about 160 events in an officiating, meet director or hosting capacity. I'm also the state high school director for track and field. My wife Livvy is a runner and coach, too. She has run Boston a couple of times and won the Cape Cod Half-Marathon. We're a track and field family, although she's the only runner for now. Our eight-year-old daughter Emma is too young, and I don't run anymore after falling 40 feet from a ladder eight years ago. The amazing surgeons and nurses at Boston Medical saved my life and put me back together with 13 screws in my hip.

That day in Boston, 18 to 20 of my former high school runners and coaches were participating in the marathon. Some had qualified to run, and a lot of them were running for charities, such as ALS and Dana-Farber. The neat thing is that even though their competitive high school years are over, they keep their passion for fitness for life. They love the atmosphere of road races and the physical challenges of competing. So it's always awesome for me to be at the finish line to congratulate and take pictures of them finishing. And I always put notes about them in the alumni newsletter.

At the time of the explosion, we still had about 10 runners that hadn't come in. One of my first thoughts after the blast was about the students. Some of the current high school kids had been sitting in the grandstands and were standing on the sidewalk. Oh, my God. Could someone I know have been hurt? It was mindboggling, and there were a lot of emotions going on simultaneously.

There were people around me saying, "Oh my God! What the hell just happened?" Then the second explosion went off, panic set in, and many people just started running, started bolting. The police, National Guard and volunteers started ripping down the fences. I hopped over pieces of the fence to get to the injured. As EMTs, we're trained to assess the scene: What do you have and what do you need? Burns and wounds? I'm already thinking about infections. How do you stop the bleeding? What type of resources do you need? How are you going to communicate with people? How are you going to get the people in that you need? All of this was going through my mind.

I've also been an EMT for over 25 years. For the past nine years, I've been a part-time EMT for the town of Carver, Massachusetts. I work 60-80 hours a month responding to 9-1-1 calls. When first I saw people down on Boylston, I was probably in shock for a few seconds, but then went into "EMT mode" of, "Let's take care of business. Let's go!" I grabbed some medical gloves and ran, as best my hip would allow, to see what I could do to help. In EMT training, we're told not to become a victim, that safety comes first. My brother, a Boston firefighter, told me later that terrorists often plan a second attack, timed to injure or kill the responders. That never occurred to me and I blew the safety first rule right away. I was in the middle of it, horrified by how much blood was on the ground and how many bones I saw sticking out and limbs that were no longer attached. Here we were at a marathon where people need their legs to run, and people were losing them.

> *There were so many of those unsung heroes, the perfect strangers who had every reason to flee, but were willing to do whatever they could to help.*

So many people were down I didn't know who to help first. So, as trained, I did Rapid Assessment. I went from one person to the next as fast as I could. I would initiate treatment, doing my best to reassure them. Other people were asking me what they could do to help. I told them, "Here, put direct pressure on the wound to stop the bleeding." There were so many of those unsung heroes, the perfect strangers who had every reason to flee, but were willing to do whatever they could to help. One man asked me, "What do you need?" and I said, "I need something to wrap this up with." He ripped his shirt off and wrapped it around the victim's leg to help stop the bleeding. In those early minutes, it was all about stopping the blood and elevating the wounds. Direct pressure, elevation and tourniquet. That's all I was thinking about. As I was working on one person I was able to tell someone else what to do. Many people were using their own shirts, or ones that had been brought out from Marathon Sports, and were helping to stop the bleeding.

I keep playing it over and over again in my head but I think we treated about 10 to 15 people, either putting on tourniquets or applying pressure to wounds.

We had no medical supplies, nothing, for five to ten minutes. Another local track coach who had been handing out silver blankets at the finish line brought me a box of gauze. He said, "I don't have much, but take this." I could've kissed him, I was so glad to see someone I knew and he came with something I could really use at that moment. At some point after the gurneys showed up, one of the responders was doing CPR and working on a victim and was struggling to move him out. I jumped in to help and said, "I'll go with you." We walked with the stretcher to the medical tent.

When I left the tent to go back to the Marathon Sports area to help, there were many more uniforms there and it was really "scoop and go" at that point; get everyone to the medical tent. That's where the doctors and triage were. This was 20 minutes in and these people really needed surgeons. They were past the point of needing direct pressure, these were traumatic injuries and they needed to get to the hospital. Luckily for all of the injured, and for all of us who live in the Boston area, we have many of the greatest hospitals in the world. They were all on standby. Let's go, I thought! Get these people there!

Some weeks later, I was fortunate to be able to meet one of the victims I treated on the sidewalk. She thanked me and said, "You told me I was going to be okay. And I needed to hear that." I'm a very religious person and I always have rosary beads in my pocket. I felt that I wanted to hug each one of the injured and pray for them to be okay, because I did not know if they were going to make it. I thought about their families. Did they have kids? Were their kids here? I prayed they were okay. I wanted to ask if I could call someone for them, but the cellphones were not working at the time. I was trying to get ahold of my family, too, but didn't until later. My wife and daughter had gone to Wellesley to watch some friends run, and I worried about them and I was sure they were worried about me. When I had service and a chance to check my phone, I must have had 200 text messages and voicemails from family and friends asking if I was okay.

When the bomb squad arrived and told us to get out, I knew I could leave and go home. I tend to listen to the guy with the badge and the gun. I started walking. People stared and asked me if I was okay and I responded, "Yeah, why?" I didn't realize I was covered in blood. I told them I was just one of the helpers. The T wasn't working so I took the long walk down Boylston and hit the Common. I listened to what people were saying. Many of the runners were crying. Some people coming out of work had no idea what was going on. I stopped in one of the hotel lobbies and watched the TV. It was amazing how many of us were watching the news together to see the video and find out what was going on. People were trying to call loved ones. My phone was dying but I had my phone charger in my bag and plugged it in and let other people use my charger. I was texting my brother to make arrangements to pick me up. I still hadn't talked to Livvy. When I got to South Station I finally got through to her. We talked about 15 minutes and every minute, I had to reassure her I was okay.

> *And there was the ambush factor; on that glorious afternoon, I was not in a disaster mindset. I was in a mindset of celebration and pride in officiating at one of the greatest marathons in the world.*

My brother picked me up and I was feeling numb at this point. He did a mental check on me. As a firefighter and Navy veteran — he had served in Desert Storm — he knew what questions to ask and what signs to look for. While driving home, we saw the smoke from the JFK Library and didn't know if that was related to the bombings. On the ride home I was quiet. Turned the radio off and closed my eyes for a little while. I was replaying the day's events in my mind like it was a Hollywood movie. I had never seen anything like this in my 25 years as an EMT. When a 9-1-1 call comes in and we respond, I'm ready for anything, and I have seen some awful things over the years, but nothing that big. And there was the ambush factor; on that glorious afternoon, I was not in a disaster mindset. I was in a mindset of celebration and pride in officiating at one of the greatest marathons in the world. And getting to be with some colleagues I get to see once a year. I'll never ever forget how much blood was on the ground and how many people were down. The bones and muscles exposed. The missing limbs and the crying and screams for help. Those memories will be etched in my mind forever.

When I got home that evening, it looked like I was arriving at my own funeral. There were so many people there; my family, friends and neighbors. They had all seen the footage and were concerned and just wanted to see me, I guess. I hadn't cried that day, but welled up when I hugged Livvy and Emma for the first time. Emma had seen me on TV and said, "Proud of you, Dad," and gave me a hug. And then she went back to her activities. Emma knew her mom was upset, but our good friend, Steve, had already arrived at the house to distract Emma from what was going on.

Everything that happened on that day didn't sink in until a month later, partly because I was so busy dealing with the remnants. The press hounded me. I didn't sleep well for the first few nights, so I e-mailed and called about 100 people to let them know I was okay. So many people cared and that was overwhelming. And it was emotional to attend the first practice with my girls' track team after vacation. I didn't realize the broad impact that day had on people.

One of the most satisfying times came in September at the home opener of the Patriots' season. We were guests of Andre Tippett, as were many of the injured. Getting to sit next to them and see them walk onto the field and have fun and enjoy themselves; that was a satisfying and healing night. I was so happy to see them recovering. So many people came up to them and patted them on the back. A lot of the emotion turned a page that night. The Red Sox also honored them at a game, not only the injured but the first responders and medical personnel. That's one of the amazing things about Boston; the organizations that put those events together and really support the community.

I am aware that some of my former and current students have praised my actions on Facebook and called me a hero. I'm no hero. The heroes are the people who were injured and are going to have to deal with this for the rest of their lives. I just did what I was

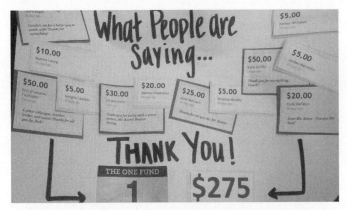

When Rick returned to his classroom at Notre Dame Academy in Hingham, Massachusetts, a week after the marathon, he found this poster that co-workers and students created to collect donations to the One Fund.

supposed to do, what I was trained to do, and I feel blessed that I was able to help. It was flattering that people were proud of me. But I'd rather the focus be on the people who were hurt. I watched video in October of how some of them were taking their first steps with their prostheses. I almost started bawling at that. Their recovery, and that they get to hug their kids, are more important to me than anything. Maybe I played a little part in their being able to hug their kids another day.

Will I be back at the finish line next year? Of course! I may be a little nervous and apprehensive, but I wouldn't miss it.

Sometimes we can find humor amid tragedy. My mom is yelling at me to this day because she saw me on television running down Boylston to get to the wounded. I'm not supposed to run because of my hip, and she was mad!

I'd like to end with a heartfelt "thank you." To all who have reached out in support during such a tragic event, especially my family, colleagues, friends and students, I am forever grateful. Collectively, we have changed this to a story of overcoming adversity and making our community truly what it is today: Boston Strong.

*Rick Kates encourages you to support his fundraising efforts
at Notre Dame Academy which provide financial
aid and scholarships for girls' educations.
www.ndahingham.com/donate*

*Coach Rick Kates and four members of
his Notre Dame Academy track team*

*Editors' note: As word of our interest in Rick's story spread, we
received notes from his co-workers at Notre Dame Academy:*

I'm lucky enough to call Rick Kates a colleague. We are so proud of
Rick. His actions on this horrific day come out of a lifetime of making
choices for the good of others. He has always used his gifts and his training to make others better.

Sister Barbara A. Barry, SNDdeN '69
President

We've always been grateful and proud to have Rick here at NDA, but
the events of 4/15/13 amplified that. My office manages, among other
things, alumnae relations and the school's FB presence. We spent so
much time that day responding to alumnae and parents who were worried about Rick. He's touched so many people in his time on campus. We
are thrilled that he is being recognized.

Lynn Page Flaherty
Director of Institutional Advancement

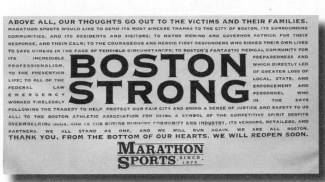

*This poster covered the boarded-up Marathon Sports
front window during its 10-day restoration.*

Shane O'Hara

Manager, Marathon Sports on Boylston Street

Should I dial 9-1-1? After the first explosion blew out the front of our store my brain was overloaded with options: What to do first? What to do next? Which of the injured to help? I struggled to make the right choice. Wondering whether I should dial 9-1-1 wouldn't be the last nonsensical thought that passed between my ears in the next hectic minutes.

The third Monday in April is usually a gorgeous time of the year in Boston. Spring is in the air, we're done with the winter and it's a beautiful feeling. We're full of hope that the Red Sox will do well and all these wonderful, nice people arrive in our city to be part of one of the world's greatest marathons. It's a fun atmosphere with lots of families and great excitement. Family members and friends are cheering on their runners, and spectators are cheering for anyone and everyone. If a military person is finishing you can hear the giant roar of the crowd. It's a fun and controlled environment.

The Boston Marathon is a bucket list run. It's one of the world's oldest and toughest marathons. I ran it in 1999 and I've been at every marathon since 1995.

Until 1995 the only one of our stores open on Patriots Day was the Wellesley store and, along with handing out energy gels to runners, we turned it into a barbecue and party for the staff. I lived for that day! In 2001, I became manager of the Boylston store. After we started staying open on Marathon Monday, I sometimes apologized to employees about having to be away from parties with family and friends. But we work hard and have our own little celebration. It's usually not a huge sales day — mostly apparel, not many shoes — it's more a day of celebration. We usually have a good number of staff running the marathon and their family and friends gather at the store. In front of the store on the sidewalk, we set up a temporary corral, probably 20 feet square, to save space for our people to watch the race. I've been fortunate to watch it for so many years, so I send employees out to enjoy the race. Come 6:00 p.m., I close the door and go home. That's the way it was supposed to work.

On the afternoon of April 15th, all the staff was in the store. A few old colleagues had also come to help out. The front door was wide open, the sun had shifted and it was getting chilly. I pulled on a sweatshirt. Around four hours into the race, the store was busy and some of our staff had finished the race and were stopping by to receive our congratulations.

At 2:50 p.m., I was selling a pair of shoes to Katherine Lavelle, a former colleague, and we were having a great conversation. She was testing out some shoes; one on, one off. And the bomb went off. That was my first thought: it was a bomb. It never occurred to me that it was anything but a bomb. The building seemed to shake and it felt like my whole body fell. I looked toward the front of the store where the sound came from and there was an instant cloud of smoke covering the sidewalk. Something really, really bad just happened. Our fire alarms went off. There was shattered glass everywhere outside and yet when I watched the video later, it looked like the glass and our signs on our window were intact. It was very confusing to me until I realized that only the outside pane of the two-pane glass broke. Windows up to the fourth floor were cracked. Analyzing it later, it looked like the force of the pressure cooker blew up at a ten o'clock angle instead of coming straight into the store. We were very lucky. There were about 30 people inside the store and everyone seemed to be okay. But, outside …

As I stepped onto the sidewalk, a woman came up to me and said, "I need to find my sister. Have you seen her?" She had smoke coming out of her hair and was injured. I said, "Let me get you inside so you can sit down." As I was bringing her in the second bomb went off. Katherine was outside yelling, "We need help! We need help!" I looked down at the woman and saw blood coming out of her leg. My adidas rep, Andrew Dailey was nearby and I asked him to bring some shorts so we could apply pressure to her leg. As I felt her leg to find the source of the bleeding, I was expecting to find a broken bone sticking out of her leg. We used the shorts to apply pressure but the ooze of blood seeped through my fingers. Somehow — I still have blank spots in my memory — I must have turned the woman over to Andrew because I heard shouting from the police outside that they needed help getting the scaffolding pulled down. As I ran out, I remember thinking we were under attack and people were going to come out of the Boston Library windows and start shooting at everybody. Just like the movies. Two bombs go off as a diversion and now we were all going to get shot.

> *... if I was going to die, it would be OK ... I would go to a happy place. I thought I would see my dad again and one of my favorite uncles. It was peaceful, just peaceful.*

It's crazy how the mind works. I wasn't scared. Leaving didn't occur to me. I guess I could have run out the back door and down the alley. But as I was standing on the sidewalk, critically injured all around, everything slowed down. I had the thought that if I was going to die, it would be okay. My guardian angel was with me, my family would be taken care of, and I would go to a happy place. I thought I would see my dad again and one of my favorite uncles. It was peaceful, just peaceful. It was so powerful that it was like a light shining on me from my guardian angel. I really went to a different place. And then, just like that, the moment disappeared.

Chaos and confusion returned. I was hearing all kinds of sounds: the relentless BEEP-BEEP-BEEP of the fire alarm, screams, yelling. I didn't know what to do first. Who do I help? Who do I not help? It was such a difficult decision. People started bringing wheelchairs and I heard Katherine yelling, "We don't need wheelchairs, we need gurneys!" There was not a single victim standing, everyone was on the ground. The only ones standing were people trying to help. Everyone else was down. One man yelled, "We need stuff for tourniquets." So we — employees and strangers — pulled armloads of apparel off the racks and were rushing them outside to give to the medical crews. In the middle of all this, I'm having these really dumb thoughts, as only a manager would, such as: My entire inventory was going out the front door! How am I going to correct the inventory? There is blood on the floor! How are we going to clean this up? Like I said, dumb thoughts of a mind in shock.

I had been in and out of the store several times carrying supplies before things started to quiet down. As I headed back in to check on my employees, I ran into a Boston police detective who didn't want to let me in. I told him who I was and why I had to get back in the store. He said, "I know who you are, you've sold me shoes. But you can't go in." The police were clearing regular people out of the area and securing the crime scene. I was able to talk my way back into the store where a couple of injured people were being tended to by EMTs. I looked over at Katherine and said, "There isn't anything more we can do and they want us to leave." We walked to Copley Square, down Boylston Street and around a back alley where the rest of my staff had gathered.

At this point, I hadn't talked to my wife, Joanne. She's an Executive Producer for Channel 5 and even though she had the day off, I knew she was going to hear about this. I needed to call her to let her know I was okay. Most of our cellphones were not working, but one of our former employees had a working phone and everyone was taking turns making calls from her phone. I waited until last to make my call. As I went to dial, I couldn't remember Joanne's number, so I was trying to open up the speed dial on my phone to get it. But I was shaking like a leaf and could not type her name into my phone. One of the others had to do it for me.

Meanwhile, Joanne was at Foxborough with our children. They were in line to get into the Jump House.

Our daughter said, "Mommy, your phone is ringing."

Joanne pulled out her phone and saw it was work calling.

One of her colleagues said, "Joanne, have you heard what happened?"

"No, I'm out with my children."

"There was an explosion down at the finish line."

Joanne thought they wanted her to come into work and she said, "I can take my children to a friend's house and I can be there in about 45 minutes."

Her co-worker said, "No, Joanne, you didn't hear me correctly. The explosion was at Marathon Sports."

The initial report said it was inside Marathon Sports. Joanne lost it right there. In her mind, I was dead. She couldn't get in touch with me. It was such a scary time for her. Our seven-year-old daughter started to cry when her mom did. Our five-year-old son asked, "Is Daddy okay?" Joanne told him I was, and then he was okay.

Some of the staff headed for a friend's house, but I was still in manager mode, I guess. Katherine, Melissa Cunningham, Sole Mendez and I just stood there looking at each other, trying to process what had just happened. Melissa had just run the marathon and didn't even have her shoes on, Katherine had been trying on a pair of shoes and her things were still in the store, as were Sole's. I had a spare key, so we headed back to the store. It made sense to me at the time that, as manager, I should make sure my employees got their belongings, that everything in the store was secure and check to see if there was anybody still left who needed help. As we walked down the alley, two firemen told us we needed to get out of the area. I told him I was the store manager and had a key to the building. They let me unlock the door, and one of them went in, but the other wouldn't let us follow. He escorted us to Exeter and Newbury. As we were going around the corner, we ran into Colin Peddie, the Marathon Sports owner. He got tears in his eyes and gave all of us a big hug. He was in his car when he heard about the bombings. Then we saw Zach Mione, a former employee, who was carrying a stack of shirts. Zach was featured the next day on the front page of the paper for his extraordinary actions helping the injured Sydney Corcoran. But when we saw him, his face looked like he had seen a ghost. He just handed me the shirts and walked away.

Colin asked, "Is the door still open?"

"As far as I know," I said. "The front door and the alley doors are open. The lights are on and the computer is still on."

A few hours after the explosion, about 4:30 or 5 p.m., I walked across the Mass Ave Bridge to meet Joanne. She was going to pick me up on Memorial Drive by MIT. As I waited, I was watching people on the north side of the Charles River. They were jogging and families were strolling. It was as if that side of the river didn't even know what had happened. People were out and about doing regular things while our city had just been attacked. It seemed bizarre.

When Joanne pulled in to pick me up, it was almost comical. She nearly sideswiped another car, and then she couldn't undo her seat belt. Tears bounced off her cheek as she was saying, "I love you. Are you okay?" We were trying to hug through the seatbelt. I told her, "We're okay, I'm okay."

Our children were staying with our good friends and we went there. I had my first beer, and saw my first footage of the explosions. When we made it home that evening and got the kids to bed, Joanne and I sat on the couch. She didn't ask me what I had seen or done. It took about four days before she asked for details. Even then I said, "Do you really want to know what I saw?" I think she realized how traumatizing the experience had been for me.

The shock left me with such a time warp, there's so much I don't remember and over the last several months, I've been trying to fill in the blanks. Looking back at my text messages helped me figure out some things. I took Tuesday and Wednesday off. Tuesday morning, I watched the TV footage to see if I could see myself. I was curious about the light that I felt was on me, my guardian angel. That's how real it seemed at the time. On Thursday, I was ready to get out of the house, but our store was still closed. I didn't want to go to another store with a lot of people, I wasn't ready, and so I went to our warehouse. The only people I felt comfortable talking to at this point were the ones I was with the day of the explosion. Other people would say things, not meaning to be insensitive, I'm sure, and I wanted to say, "You weren't there. You don't understand."

Dan Soleau was there. He had been blown off the bench he was standing on in front of our store by the force of the explosion. He was knocked unconcious briefly. I only remember seeing him one time. He was taking a case of water outside and I remember thinking he must have been in the basement, where the water is kept, when the bomb went off. And then I was wondering why he was carrying a case of water. (Again, the human mind!) A few people from New Balance came by the warehouse and we started hearing their stories. It was so emotional. We all were crying. It was really tough.

On Saturday, the 20th, Colin told us we were invited to attend the Red Sox game the next day to be honored. I told him how awkward I felt, and that I didn't really want to go. Colin told me, "This isn't about you and it's not about Marathon Sports. It's about our city and our country. This is something we have to do." It was the first public event for us and it was a bizarre experience because we stood on top of the Red Sox dugout, facing a stadium full of fans giving us a loud, standing ovation. The normal response is to smile and wave to the crowd, but we couldn't. We were so sad. Colin, Dan, Dave Moynahan and I just stood there. As we headed back to our seats, Colin asked if anyone wanted a beer, and I said, "I'll take two!" People were shaking my hand, patting my back and touching my hand. It was overwhelming. I started getting text messages from everyone. A friend of my brother wanted his son to meet me because, "This is what a real hero is like." I still feel that hero isn't appropriate or accurate.

I grew up on a dairy farm in upstate New York. It was a good life, but a hard one and we were raised to never think that we were better than anybody else, and to never brag. So when I saw, because of the video and photos from the media, that I had become one of the faces of the bombing and was being called a hero, I was really uncomfortable. I didn't save anybody's life. I didn't run someone to an ambulance. I felt like I didn't really help anybody. The second guessing and guilt I mentioned earlier was getting to me. I felt guilty that I was always being asked to tell the story of what I saw.

On the following Tuesday, the 23rd, Colin asked Dan and

me to go to the Boylston store because someone tipped him off that there were cleanup crews inside the store. He assumed that he would be responsible for the cleanup. We raced over there, but we didn't have security clearance to get into the secure zone. Managers from the cleaning company, A.R.S., met us at the Westin and escorted us over and let us in the back door. Workers had already taken up the rug and the tile. Furniture and display racks had been moved to lift up the rug. One of the managers said they'd been hired by Mayor Menino's office and were told that Marathon Sports was "Priority One." "You guys were first on the list," he said. "You'll be the first one to reopen. We need to get you guys up and running." I guess it was because we were the closest to the first bomb, plus we are a running store, and we'd become a symbol of Boston's resilience.

It was tough to be there because of so many fresh memories. As we walked toward the front, we saw hazmat workers in their moon suits scrubbing the walk. The corral looked like it had been shot at with pellets, shards of glass were everywhere and I wondered how Dan didn't get hurt. Boylston wasn't open to traffic, but they allowed pedestrians and residents to come back. My car was still parked behind the store and I wasn't able to remove it yet.

> *... people left flowers outside the store. There were people at our door all the time ... A couple of Boston firefighters came by each day to make sure we were okay.*

When the streets opened up, people left flowers outside the store. There were people at our door all the time. We re-opened 10 days after the explosion. We had our first running club that Wednesday. A couple of Boston firefighters came by each day to make sure we were okay. Strangers came in to give me a hug and thank me. It was so humbling, and a struggle to deal with. I didn't lose a leg, I didn't get hurt. I'm sure I have mental scars, but those things I can hide. All I did was hand out apparel that the first responders used as tourniquets and compresses.

Courtesy Shane O'Hara

*One of the bittersweet but awkward moments of the past year:
We celebrated the Red Sox World Series win while honoring the
bombing victims, first responders and perfect strangers.*
LEFT TO RIGHT: *Red Sox players Jonny Gomes and Jarrod
Saltalamacchia, Marathon Sports owner Colin Peddie, me, and
Dan Soleau, with the World Series trophy on the finish line.
Thousands of people sang "God Bless America."*

It wasn't until I talked to a professional counselor that I began to put things into perspective. A therapist was made available through Joanne's employer. At first, I thought the counseling would be a waste of time, but I'm glad we did it. She helped me make some sense of my actions after the bomb blew out the front of our store. She said, "You helped people." It was such a relief to hear that, like a cement block taken off my back, because I had accumulated plenty of self-doubt and guilt about my role in those crazy, horrific minutes. She said, "You've been a manager for a long time. You managed so many things that day. You gave people the apparel to do what needed to be done. You brought a person inside. And you stayed." I need to live with that, that it was the right thing to do.

One of the few light moments in the weeks after the bombings came during one of our phone therapy sessions.

"Are you staying away from alcohol?" the therapist asked.

Joanne and I – sharing a beer — looked at each other and couldn't help but smile.

This year, I'm running the marathon. I've got to run this. I'll never forget what happened that day but this will be a great way to move forward. One reason I want to run is because I don't want to be in the store that morning. I want to finish around the same time as the explosion. I will run my race, cross that finish line, go back in the store to work, and lock the door at 6:00 p.m.

Like I should have done last year.

Shane O'Hara will be running the 2014 Boston Marathon in honor of the victims of the bombings and to raise money for One Fund: onefundboston.org.

Photo by Sarah Crosby, Daily Hampshire Gazette

Dr. Pierre Rouzier, a finish line medical volunteer

Pierre Rouzier, M.D.

Finish Line Medical Tent Volunteer
Family Physician and Sports Medicine
Team Physician, University of Massachusetts
Age 56
Amherst, Massachusetts

I volunteer each year for the medical team of the Boston Marathon and my role has been as a triage doctor in front of the major medical tent, Tent A. When a runner finishes the race and might be staggering or appears ready to collapse, a volunteer with a wheelchair swoops them up at the finish and brings them to the front of the tent. Personality wise, I'm a good fit for triage. Jokingly, I tell people I'm kind of like a Wal-Mart greeter for runners who finish the marathon. Some feel it's a hard job, but not me. When the runner comes staggering up or is wheeled up, the first thing I do is tell them my name and I ask, "What's your name?" "How'd you do in the race?" If they say they have a little cramp in their leg, it's one thing. If they have a difficult time communicating and appear confused, they're either overheated, sodium is really low or they are dehydrated and we go into the tent to figure it out. Part of my job is to decide whether they need to be in the tent, whether they are really ill and need to be in the intensive care part of the tent, or if they just have a leg cramp and need to drink a little bit of Gatorade and walk it off.

Charity runners are typically a little slower and maybe a little less equipped to withstand the difficulty of a marathon, so most of the action in our tent happens between 3 ½ and 5 hours after the start. And it's very busy; we see cramps, dehydration, low sodium, heat illness, chest pain, breathing difficulties — all levels of distress. When it gets busy, there could be 10 to 30 wheelchairs lined up to be triaged in. So I make the decision on what level of help they need by meeting and talking to each runner and assessing what's going on with them in about 20 seconds or so.

Our group is part of a sports medicine fellowship and we

train younger doctors. One aspect of their training is to work the Boston Marathon. I go with them as their faculty member. In the tents, we have doctors and nurses with a variety of specialties. There are cardiologists, family physicians, internal medicine specialists, emergency physicians, lab techs and clerical and computer people to manage records. It's a well-oiled machine. The spirit of volunteerism is part of what makes the Boston Marathon special. Doctors, nurses, support staff, college students — everyone just volunteering to help. That's what I like the most, being part of the spirit of volunteerism.

On April 15, 2013, it had been a piece of cake, an uneventful day. There were four of us triaging outside the tent; two doctors and two nurses. It was a beautiful, cool day. As we stood there, someone said, "Wow, we're past the three and a half hour mark and we haven't been that busy." And then the boom went off.

At first I thought it was a celebration and said, "Oh, someone just shot off a cannon." A tech guy next to me said, "I think one of our transformers just blew." But as we're guessing, we're thinking, what was that? Just puzzling. And then the second explosion went off about 10 seconds later. I said, "Something happened." One of my former fellows, Chad Beattie, was standing next to me. This is a kid I love like a son. We agreed they were bombs, and debated where we would be more valuable; staying at the tent, or running to the site? The instruction inside the tent was for personnel to stay and not go down to the explosions. But for those of us outside the tent, the people normally making the decision of where we should go weren't available at that moment. We needed to make our own decision. There were two nurses next to us. The first injured person arrived in a wheelchair, with a head laceration, and we thought, well, that is not a big deal, maybe we stay at the tent. The second person came with an open fracture of the tibia and fibula, the broken bones had broken through the skin. Chad and I looked at each other and said, "We've got to go." I gave a nurse my phone number and told her we were going to the scene and to call me if they needed us back here.

As we headed out to the unknown, I texted my wife and kids: "I'm going to where the bomb went off. Say a prayer." I was really texting them a goodbye message. Just in case. My wife, Arlene, had her phone in her purse and didn't know what was happening, and my kids live in Florida and they didn't know what was going on. But I was thinking about them as I was heading to the bomb. I was not scared for myself at this point. Chad and I just felt we needed to help. We had nothing with us, just medical gloves in our pockets and the clothes on our backs.

I wasn't expecting to see what we did. It was the most surreal scene I've ever experienced. I've done a lot of emergency care and I've seen a lot of trauma, but this is the Boston Marathon; there shouldn't be 50 people lying in pools of blood. I've just never seen that many injured people in one spot where they didn't belong. This would be a new experience for anyone who was not a combat physician.

My first thoughts were: What is this? What is going on? Where am I needed most? It was about three minutes after the explosion and the barricades had already been pulled down. We had to hop over a man's severed legs to get to the injured. The worst injuries were easy to see but it was challenging figuring out the degrees of the other injuries; who was critically hurt and whose injuries could wait. The first responders — trained and not — were already helping people. Initially, it was challenging figuring out who was injured and who was helping. I did a lap around the scene trying to figure out who were the victims, helpers and consolers. For every one person injured, it seemed like there were at least two people with them; somebody helping and somebody consoling. People, the perfect strangers, just jumped in to help. Controlling bleeding was the primary job. Who is most seriously injured?

I saw the director of EMS and asked her, "What do you need me to do?" She said, "Make sure everyone has tourniquets." That made sense. I took off my belt and went over to a leg wound and realized they already had a tourniquet. I went to the next person to put on a tourniquet and they also had one on. I took my belt off and put it back on three times because people already had them on. Most of the tourniquets were belts; some were t-shirts. At that point, I wrapped up my bloody belt and put it in my pocket.

I spotted an injured girl who appeared to be with her

parents. Her mom was curled up on the ground next to her and her dad was next to her, holding her mangled right leg. He was asking, "Somebody please help my daughter's leg." I can help this family, I thought. I found a piece of stick from a barricade and a discarded poster. I rolled up the poster and added the stick to make a splint for her leg. But I had no way to attach it. I had the dad hold it to his daughter's leg until we could get something to secure it.

Just then, I feel somebody reach over and grab my arm and pull me down. It was a woman, probably in her 30s. She said, "I'm going to die right here and right now and no one is going to know where I am." She was by herself. The bones in her left leg had broken and were protruding through the skin. I took her hand and said, "You're not going to die." It bothers me to this day that I didn't say to her, "I'm Pierre Rouzier," and ask, "What is your name?" But it was chaos and I still didn't know what was going on around me. Were we in danger? What else was going to happen?

Everywhere I look, there are people in need of the kind of medical attention and supervision I can provide. As I'm working on the young girl and talking to the other woman, I see someone next to me getting CPR and they're dying. But that person has people helping and these people need my help. I've committed to helping the family and the other woman versus leaving to instruct others what to do and how to do it. I felt I needed to be a hands-on guy.

What I needed at that moment, among the many things I could have used, was something to secure the splint on the girl's leg. The injured needed stretchers, IVs, antibiotics and surgery. There were a ton of ambulances behind the tent, but they weren't on Boylston yet. All of a sudden, someone with roller gauze was attaching the splint. People were coming with supplies, but we need to get these people to a wheelchair or a stretcher and get them in ambulances. Little by little, you can see motion happening; this injured person and that injured person are being moved. And then the young girl with the injury to her right leg and her parents were taken away. My other woman, with splintered bones breaking through the skin on her left leg, was still there. She had a tourniquet on, but someone came with a better tourniquet and as they put it on she screamed in pain. Somebody brought a wheelchair, but she really needed a gurney. We didn't see one, so I got her up in a wheelchair, supporting her injured leg. And then a gurney showed up. I apologized for the imminent pain, "I'm so sorry but we need to move you to a gurney." Funny, she had the wherewithal to ask, "Where's my bag?" I saw a bag and held it up: "Is this your bag?" So now we have her strapped to the gurney along with her bag. In the pool of blood where she'd been lying, I saw a phone. "Is this yours?" It was. I handed it to her. And then she was gone, to an ambulance and to a hospital. I never got a chance to introduce myself and that still kills me. I could've done better. I wish I had gotten her name and I wish I had told her mine.

As she was being wheeled away, I turned around to see whom else I should help and there was nobody left. There was glass, shrapnel and blood everywhere. Time was a blur. I didn't know if I had been there for 10 minutes or an hour. Then someone on the loudspeaker says, "There's another device. We need to evacuate the area." I'm okay being in danger helping others, but I'm not okay getting blown up by myself on an empty street. It was very unnerving. My thoughts turned to Chad, because I didn't know where he was and I prayed that he'd be safe. His wife had just delivered their second child one month earlier. As much as I didn't want to die, I REALLY didn't want Chad to die.

I went back to the tent to help and found that it was very controlled. It was chaos in the street but complete order in the tent. People were being treated and were in the process of being transported. And there was plenty of help, volunteers everywhere. And there were a lot of people in tears. The tent had at least 100 cots, but these injured didn't need the tent — they needed the hospital. The goal was to get the injured into the long line of ambulances and on their way.

There were also several runners in the tent needing attention for running-related problems, and as I tried to help them, I also had to tell them, "There's been a bomb and we want to give you as much care as you need. But they've warned us that our medical tent may not be safe and they may tell us to evacuate. Until then, I'm not going let you go too soon, but you should leave the tent if you are able to." Moments later, a bomb squad person came through and said, "You can't stay here. You need to leave the tent."

So now what? We are at the peak time for helping runners. We knew there were thousands of runners in Boston who needed help, but where were they? So groups of doctors and nurses went out on the Boston Common thinking there would be runners needing help, but it was fruitless. We couldn't find runners. We were approached by family members of runners who said they couldn't find their relatives and needed to know if they got hurt. At least we were able to say, "No runners got hurt." They asked, "Where can we meet them?" We didn't know what to tell them. People wanted information we didn't have.

Finally it was time to leave. Our volunteer group usually has dinner after the marathon at Legal Seafood in Copley Plaza. Jay, the organizer of the dinner, thought we still needed to go. So we're walking around in bloody clothes and shoes and went to Legal Seafood but we couldn't get in because of the lockdown. We kept walking and found a restaurant where I ordered comfort food: mac and cheese. Except there was no comfort. It was a weird dinner. We were wondering about how the victims were doing. We didn't feel the trauma yet, we were mostly shell shocked. We felt the city was still in danger and wondered whether bombs would be going off in other cities. We should be safe in western Massachusetts, but what about New York or Chicago, and the London Marathon coming up? We talked about 9/11.

I wasn't going anywhere for a while. My car was parked in the Westin, which was on lockdown, so I had no way home. Nobody could get their car from the center of the city, so we walked out of town to the Northeastern University area to get to where someone could pick us up. Another doc had parked his car at a T stop along the Pike and we finally got there. I didn't make it back to Amherst until after 11 p.m.

When I undressed that night, I left my pants on the floor of my closet. I looked at them twice a day and thought about whether I could touch them. I just couldn't bring myself to wash them. I finally threw them away two months later. I threw my shoes away in October. I made the decision to throw my bloody belt away before I left Boston and later wished I hadn't. The belt that never got used. I spent months shopping for "just the right belt" — the one that will make a good tourniquet. I'm never going to cover a mass event again without a good tourniquet belt around my waist.

Facebook saved my soul. When I posted, "I was at the site of the Boston Marathon bombing. I'm OK. Pray for the victims," the response was overwhelming. I got hundreds of supportive and caring messages, and so many students showed an outpouring of support and care for me. People told me I was a hero, but I didn't feel like I was. Our priest at the UMass Newman Center asked me to say a few words after mass one day, and he simplified things for me by saying, "A hero is someone who runs toward danger." And that finally made sense.

Some of the medical responders didn't want to talk about what we went through, but I did. Talking about it is therapy. At UMass, I gave a talk to about 300 students. For many of them, growing up, attending the marathon as spectators was a family event. It was as if somebody just bombed their family picnic. It was a sacrilege against their family and they needed to understand what happened and wanted to hear about the bombing from someone who was there. I am in a mentor role for many of the students and there was a role-modeling aspect to this. My decision to run toward the bomb served as a lesson for them: you don't want people to run into harm, but you want to do the right thing.

In 2010, I went to my father's native Haiti after the earthquake to help. The devastation and loss of life was shocking and I was tortured because I wanted to help more than I was able to. That was a real tough one for me and I had a bad case of PTSD after that. The marathon bombing happened at the time I was making a decision about whether to go back to Haiti to help teach a sports medicine course. I was hesitant because I was a such a wreck after my last trip there. At a sports medicine conference in San Diego shortly after the marathon, one of my colleagues who was planning to go to Haiti advised me, "You should go. It will make everything better." I went and he was right. We did good things, and it was a step forward for me.

Trying to deal with the emotions of the marathon has been challenging. My wife and two sons have been incredibly supportive. I had several sessions of EMDR (Eye Movement Desensitization and Reprocessing) therapy for post traumatic stress and it's been tremendously helpful. In May, my wife and I went to a Celtics playoff game. I NEEDED to be around Boston sports fans and to buy a Boston Strong t-shirt. As the game started the PA system blared Dropkick Murphy's song, "I'm Shipping Up to Boston," with the haunting line "… I lost my leg," and I sank into my seat uncontrollably shaking and crying. After the game, Arlene and I walked to the finish line of the marathon. I stood where the front of the tent had been, reliving the sights and sounds of April 15th, then walked with my wife to the bomb site. I could feel the scene again. I knelt in the area where I had been with the young girl and woman. Then I stood up, hugged my wife, thanked her and told her that I loved her.

We've all been grappling with our feelings about what happened at the marathon; what we could have or should have done differently. Some volunteers were told by authorities to run to safety. They did, and they felt guilty. They felt maybe they could have helped more. Had I a do over, I would have done the same thing. Only better. I would have told those patients my name, and asked for theirs. I'm envious of the responders who have met the people they helped.

I will be back at the tent for Boston 2014 and I will have my new belt on. And I will be ready.

The Challenged Athlete Foundation has a special fund for marathon victims who will be learning to be active again with their disabilities. Last summer I was able to do a fund-raiser for the CAF while on a week-long bike ride across Iowa (the RAGBRAI). Special thanks to those who made my "fun-raiser" a success. You can support CAF at challengedathletes.org.

Chad Beattie, M.D.

Primary Care Sports Medicine Physician

Hawthorn Medical Association, Dartmouth, Massachusetts

Age 34

Dartmouth, Massachusetts

"This is a slow year compared to last year," I said to Dr. Pierre Rouzier as we stood outside Medical Tent A waiting for finishing runners who needed help. "Last year" was the 2012 marathon, the hot year, when we did not stop treating patients until 6:30 p.m. 2013 was my fifth year as a volunteer in the medical tent. The Boston Marathon is such an important part of the community and it's important for me to help out any way I can.

My specific job was working triage in front of the tent. We would assess the runners' conditions as they arrived and determine what level of treatment they needed. But, as I said, business was slow.

Within minutes, I would be sprinting down Boylston with Pierre, the hysteria and chaos of two explosions all around us, and for me, at least, the fear of more. Would there be a third? I immediately assumed it would go off right across the street or by our medical tent. So I sort of braced myself for another explosion. But then there was a pause of about a minute, and then another, and then I thought we would be okay.

That's when I transitioned from figuring out how to protect myself to figuring out how to help others. What should I do next? I turned to Pierre and asked, "Are we more useful here or in the field?" We decided there was sufficient medical staff in the tent and we grabbed latex gloves and ran to the first explosion site. I have a wife and two small children and I sent a text message to my wife and also my family back home in Canada: "Bombs at marathon. I'm OK."

I wasn't running into the site fearing for my life. I was nervous from a professional standpoint. I'm not trained in trauma; I'm trained in family medicine. So I was trying to wrap my head around what I was going to have to do, what bare essentials were available and what skills I was going to use.

As I was running through the smoke, I saw people with some lacerations on their faces and the soot and ashen look of burnt hair. When I got through the smoke and could better see the site, I was shocked. There was a pile of bodies, it looked like a battle scene in a movie. And all I had were gloves and what I wore that day.

As I circled the wounded, what struck me first was, even though I got there no more than a minute or two after the explosions, the sidewalk was already packed with people helping the victims. Everyone who was injured had someone. There were men and women kneeling and lying on the ground beside the wounded, consoling and getting help for them. There was so much consoling, so much compassion. A first responder approached me and said, "We have two damaged limbs. Do you have a tourniquet?" I took off my belt and applied the tourniquet.

> *Everyone who was injured had someone ... There was so much consoling, so much compassion.*

But it was apparent that there were enough people helping there. I needed to get to the next explosion site. So I ran down the street, having no idea what the second site would be like, nor how difficult it would be to get there. Boston police had begun sealing the area as a crime scene, and even though I had my bright fluorescent jacket on, clearly showing I was a physician, they were yelling at me, "Don't go over there!" "Don't touch that!" I was getting screamed at repeatedly and had to zigzag my way there. When I arrived it seemed to be a calmer scene than the first. That could have been because more time had gone by. People were being loaded into ambulances and there was some semblance of a triage center. Injured people were being evaluated for degree of injury. I grabbed gauze and used it to make tourniquets and made several splints for broken bones out of wooden fence slats and cardboard congratulatory signs. That's all I can remember. I know I was there for 40 to 45 minutes, but I can only remember a few minutes of it. Only a few minutes of memory.

At some point, I realized I was one of the only people left on the street. There were no more victims, everyone but a few police officers was gone and there was nothing else to do. I headed back to the medical tent and started treating victims, although most of the acute patients had been transported to hospitals.

Then there was a rumor of another bomb. The police told the medical director there was a potential bomb right outside the tent. They started to evacuate us and announced they were going to do a controlled explosion; another tense moment in the day. I had not feared for my life until that moment.

As soon as we walked out, just two steps out of the tent, there was media everywhere, asking for interviews. But I didn't talk to them. We are trained not to talk to the media; there is a procedure for responding to the press.

I got kind of lost at that point, separated from the rest of the medical tent group. There was this feeling of total loneliness. I called my dad in Toronto and that was the first time I broke down that day. It all kind of hit me when I talked to him. He didn't know what had happened. He had been busy all day and hadn't understood my text.

The city was packed, but I was wandering around alone and just wanted to talk to someone from my team. I really wanted to talk to Pierre, to rehash what happened. But phones weren't working. Such a weird feeling, a sense of loneliness in the midst of so many people. I did finally find out that the doctors had gone to Boston Common to help runners who needed aid. Eventually our whole team reunited and we had the chance to decompress and talk about things that night at dinner. After dinner, I was able to get my car out and head home, but I don't remember anything about that hour drive home. A complete blackout.

It was a few days before I was able to process it. The first few days were a total obsession with CNN. I couldn't get enough of the information about the event and the manhunt. Through it all, I thought about my family and what could have been.

The 2013 Boston Marathon experience will carry me for many years. I saw so much compassion and strength from victims and the perfect strangers who were helping them. Aside from all the hustle and bustle of life, compassion is what people are about. From a professional standpoint, I'm not sure I did much that day — from what I remember, anyway. I'm sure it made the wounded feel better, gave them some degree of comfort, when they were lying on the sidewalk and saw that a physician was looking over them.

In 50 years I'll likely look back on that crazy day and realize it had some huge impact on my life that I haven't even started to figure out yet. This year? I'll be back and I don't know anyone from the medical tent who's not going back, not even hesitating about it. The one-year mark will be a good reflection for all of us. I'm looking forward to it.

One more thing: humor can show up at the most unexpected times and in the most unexpected ways. Early on in my story, I mentioned that I pulled my belt off to use as a tourniquet. The pants I wore that day were way too big and without the belt, they were in constant danger of falling to my ankles. I was always hanging onto them and pulling them up. Eventually, I grabbed a piece of tape and wrapped it around my waist.

Dr. Chad Beattie urges you to consider supporting the One Fund at onefundboston.org.

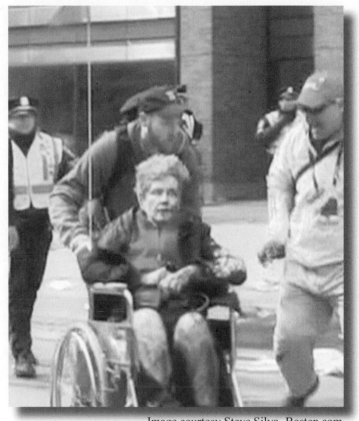

Image courtesy Steve Silva, Boston.com

*Stephen Shinney pushing a bombing
victim to the medical tent*

Stephen Shinney

Spectator/Perfect Stranger

Age 29

Union Electrician, IBEW Local 103

Dorchester, Massachusetts

Before April 15th, I never carried a pocketknife. Now, I always do, but I hope I'll never need it for the reason I carry it.

Marathon Monday began for me as it has for the past 12 years. I was at Fenway, where the Red Sox were playing their traditional 11 a.m. baseball game. I work at the ballpark for Aramark. That day I was in the left-field stands at Gate E, helping the vendors stay supplied with beer.

When my shift ended at 1:30 p.m., I jumped on my bike and rode to my friend Brendan Pires' house in Cambridge, and we both rode our bikes into the city and parked them at the house of another friend, Luigi Juarez. We walked over to Boylston with some other friends to watch the race. A friend, Scott Long, was running and we saw him go by as we stood near the finish line next to the Lenox Hotel. He didn't see us, so we walked to the other side of the finish line where the runners got their medals, Gatorade, bananas and everything to try to see him and say congrats. We couldn't find him, but our rendezvous point was to be the Rattlesnake Bar, which is just down Boylston another two and a half blocks past the finish line. We started in that direction, and as I was on the phone with my sister, who was also in the finish line area, the first bomb went off. Somehow, we both knew exactly what it was. The phone went dead. I was less than 100 yards away from the explosion, and took off running toward it.

I started yelling at everyone around me, "Run, run, run! It's a bomb!" and yelled that repeatedly as I ran. No one moved. No one ran. Nothing. They just stood there, stunned. I was having trouble moving very fast through the crowd and thought I could get to the bomb site faster if I got onto the street. So I tried to hurdle the metal crowd control barrier, but my toe caught the top of it as I went over and I smashed to the ground, coming down on my elbow. I didn't feel it right away but later that night and for days I could, and I had a nice black-and-blue patch for a week. I got up running again and was going the wrong direction down Boylston, past the medical tent and through the finish line when the second bomb went off. That's when more people started to react, you could hear more screams, and people were running away.

When I arrived at the bomb site, the first person I came upon, whose name I learned later, was Krystle Campbell. She was already gone. I had never seen a dead person outside of a funeral, and certainly not a victim of such violence. I was in shock and couldn't look away or move for a few seconds. When I was able to look around for someone I could help, there was an older woman on the ground, covered with blood. Another person was trying to help her up. I remembered that, as I was running through the finish line, there were several wheelchairs parked nearby. I ran and got one of the chairs, and ran back to where the woman was being assisted. It appeared she had a badly injured forearm and hand. We got her into the chair and the woman who was helping her told me that the lady's husband was injured badly and needed to go to the hospital. I ran her to the medical tent. The wheelchair wasn't the best. One of the front wheels was making noise and it rolled like a grocery cart with a bad wheel. But we got there and a triage nurse started asking me her name, age, where she was from, and I didn't know any of the answers. I kept saying "I don't know, I don't know. I just brought her in."

So as I ran back toward the bomb site, I grabbed a different wheelchair, but when I got to the finish line, the police had it sealed off and weren't letting any more people in unless they had official IDs. I pleaded that I was just there to help, and had already brought someone out, but they wouldn't budge.

Right next to me, the police were looking for more bombs, and thought they might be hidden under the bleachers and other structures around the finish line, so I briefly helped pull down the tarps that covered the underside of the bleachers. As I was doing so, it dawned on me that this may not be the best idea, looking for bombs. So I walked away.

I decided to run back over to the medical tent and see if I could help. About then, I got a text from my older brother, who was vacationing with his family at Disney:

Our mom works in an office by Fenway and even though it was closed for Patriots Day, she went in to catch up on some work and keep track of my sister's boyfriend's progress. As he got close, she walked over to cheer for him as he ran by, then went back to her office. My sister was concerned that there would be an attack on Fenway and that Mom was too close.

When I walked into the big medical tent, it seemed to be pure chaos, although I guess there was some order in the madness. Medical personnel were running around trying to help victims and get them organized by the severity of their injuries. I noticed a smaller woman struggling to take down the IV bags that had been hanging above the rows of cots, waiting for dehydrated runners. She could barely reach them, but I'm fairly tall, about 6'3", and went over to take down the IVs for her and pile them in one spot in case they were needed.

"Excuse me. Can you help us?" Two girls were lying on cots, IVs in their arms, waiting to be transported. They had blankets over them and I couldn't tell how badly they were wounded. They weren't among the most seriously injured.

"Yeah, sure," I said and kneeled down in between them.

"We're trying to call our families, but our phones aren't working," one of them said. "Can we use yours?"

Somehow I knew that only text messages were going through and told them that. They asked me to help them with their texts, so I typed in messages to their families that they had been injured and were being taken to a hospital and that they would let them know which one. They said they were thirsty, so I got them some water, but a doctor came by and told me they didn't need any more fluids, they were getting enough from the IVs. They were taken away in an ambulance shortly after that.

I noticed a paramedic examining a person and he was trying to roll him over to check for injuries. He was alone and I knew that it takes at least two people to roll someone up, holding their neck properly, so I helped him get a look at the patient's back.

From then on, I was just doing whatever seemed to be needed; I was bringing gauze and what not to the EMTs and helping move people from cots onto gurneys and get them loaded into ambulances. As quickly as one person was loaded and the ambulance left, another one was backing in and another person was loaded.

As most of the patients had been transported and things were slowing down, an announcement was made for group leaders to do a head count of doctors and nurses, and if you didn't need to be there, they were dismissing you. That's when I realized I didn't need to be there anymore, so I decided to walk over to the Rattlesnake where my friends were going to be. On the way, I looked at my phone and saw that I had a ton of missed calls and text messages in the 45 minutes I was in the tent. Everyone knew I was okay, but no one knew where I was. I texted my wife, Colleen, and told her to go home; just leave work and go home now. I texted my sister Suzanne.

Another sister hadn't been able to get in touch with me and asked our brother to try to reach me because they both thought I was in danger in the tent. I didn't see his texts until later:

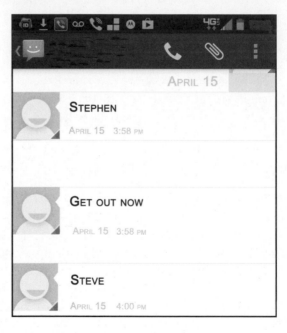

I went into the Rattlesnake. There was blood all over my clothes, but if my friends noticed, they didn't say anything, and I didn't really tell them anything about what I had been doing for the past couple of hours. When I saw what was going on on the TVs, I couldn't turn away. I just kept watching, and as I did, everything kind of sunk in; the emotional part of what had happened and what I'd seen. I just wanted to go home, see my wife and be in my own place. My friends weren't ready to leave, so I asked Luigi for his keys so I could go to his apartment and get my bike. My plan was to bring his keys back, but as I left, a cop told me that they weren't letting anyone back into the area, so I went back and told Luigi I'd just leave his keys under the mat.

After I got my bike and headed home, I rode by the line of ambulances that had been lined up to take victims from the tent to hospitals. There were so many; they seemed to go on and on.

As I pedaled the two miles to my house in Dorchester, I was replaying what had happened and found myself choking back the tears. When I got home, the first person I saw was my landlady. She knew I had planned to go to the finish line that day, and she opened up the door and started crying. She said she was so happy to see me and that I was okay. I started breaking down, told her I'd talk to her later, and went upstairs to our apartment. I broke down for about 15 minutes. My sister and my cousin called and said they were on their way over. Then my wife came in the door, crying.

As for the older lady I pushed in a wheelchair, I was able to find out her name was Mary Jo White of Bolton, Massachusetts, and she was watching the marathon with her husband, Bill, and their 35-year-old son, Kevin. They didn't know anyone in the marathon, they just decided to have lunch in Boston and watch the race. I found an e-mail address through Jeff Bauman's aunt. I wrote to them and told them I hoped they were doing okay — I had heard that her husband had lost part of a leg, and her son had been wounded, too — and let them know that I felt bad for splitting up her and her husband when I wheeled her away. I had heard later what a difficult time people were having finding their loved ones because of all of the different hospitals they were taken to. Mrs. White went to Boston Medical Center and her husband to Mass General. I felt bad that I didn't get her name and make sure she knew which hospital her husband was going to.

They wrote back and said they were doing better, and asked if I wanted to talk with them sometime. I decided not to. I just wanted to apologize for splitting them up.

When people started leaving shoes and flags and flowers and candles and everything at the memorial on Boylston, Colleen wanted to go. I didn't. I didn't want to be in the area at all. My mom convinced me to go. She said, "If you run from it now, you're never going to be able to deal with it. The problem will never go away." So I went with Colleen. It actually helped, and talking about it has helped. I didn't talk to a psychologist, I talked to friends and family who could understand what I saw that day.

As far as how my life has been different since the bombings, in the first few months, I was a little jumpy. Working construction is noisy and every time someone would drop a piece of steel, the noise would take me back to where I was that day. I could see it all perfectly, just as if I was watching it on the news; where I was standing, everything around me; I could see it all.

About the only thing I do differently now is carry a knife. I didn't have a knife with me that day and it would have been real handy cutting cloth for tourniquets.

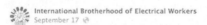

International Brotherhood of Electrical Workers
September 17

Boston Local 103 member Stephen Shinney (third from the left) was standing less than 100 yards away when two bombs went off at the Boston Marathon last April. His first response wasn't to run however, but to help, transporting the injured to safety. Read more about Shinney's heroics: http://bit.ly/16hnIIN

Like · Comment · Share   👍 178 💬 4 ↪ 27

Another difference in my life is that I've been honored by Aramark, the City of Weymouth, the Red Sox, and the IBEW for my "heroic" actions. I'm not a fan of that word, hero, and I don't think it's appropriate for me. I was always the kid at the back of the class. Out of sight, out of mind. It was nice to be recognized, but I'm glad that my sister was also honored. She did the talking so I didn't have to.

I've had several months to think about that day, over and over, and I still don't know why I ran toward the explosion and grabbed the wheelchair. I do know that if Colleen had been with me, I would have done the opposite. I would have grabbed her and run the other way.

Stephen Shinney encourages you to donate to the One Fund at onefundboston.org.

Boston EMS Lt. Brian Pomodoro (center with helmet) helping transport one of the wounded

Lt. Brian Pomodoro

First Responder

Boston EMS

EMT Instructor — Specialist in Emergency Preparedness Certified by U.S. Homeland Security as WMD Instructor

My first perfect strangers weren't really strangers, but they sure were perfect. Boston EMS has a very well-developed peer support program, and Lt. Ginny Famolare is the head of the team. She works with a group of civilian practitioners as well. I don't know where they came from, I don't know how, but right in the shank of the incident, after we evacuated all of the victims to the medical tent and as we're stabilizing them and beginning to do our transports, she grabbed one of the mental health people — Hayden Duggan, I think, who is the chief psychologist for the peer support team — and came to the scene lights and sirens screaming. As I'm working on a patient, out of the corner of my eye I saw Ginny and the doctor, and I let out an "All right!" Talk about the right instinct; this is exactly where we needed them and when. To have them come right to the scene, everyone who saw that was bolstered a little bit because we knew that they were there to help us, to look out for us. To check on us and ask, "Hey, do you need us to call anyone at home to tell them you're okay?" Stuff like that. That was such a shot in the arm to see them come to the scene, and not wait until days after the event.

Keep in mind, we had been taking care of people all day, from 8 a.m. when the marathon started, to when the runners started coming in and needed help. What a lot of people don't realize is the medical tent was already nearly at capacity when the bombs went off. We were already working a mass-casualty incident when this thing happened. We had been taking care of runners most of the day, and then the explosions; all of a sudden critically wounded people needed our help. But when the stress team showed up, it was, as selfish as it may sound, "Hey, someone's showing up to take care of me." These people weren't there to help with the mass casualties; we had that well in hand. They were here for me, for us. That was a real shot in the arm. What people really needed at that point was a break, but that wasn't possible. There was no time and no place to go; it wasn't like we had a break room. But that didn't matter; 99% of it was that the peer support team was there, somebody had our back.

My wife, Barb, had the day off and was at home. A neighbor called and asked, "Have you been watching what's going on at the marathon?" She hadn't, and snapped on the TV to watch. I tried calling her, but cell service was down. Texting got through, but you should see me text; it's like Brother Dominic transcribing with a quill pen. There's no way I had time for that. Later, one of our public information people had a satellite phone and asked, "Does anyone need to call home?" I said I did and proceeded to dial. What I didn't think about was the Caller ID read "City of Boston," and when Barb picked up the phone and saw that, she had a flicker of dread; like this is how they notify the widow, right?

Later on, it was starting to get dark, we had not eaten, we had nothing. This was after we had transported all of the patients, but we were still on duty, station keeping, standing by, not doing anything. That's the worst part, standing by, and we didn't know for what. We kept hearing reports from all over the city about suspicious packages; there was a backpack in the lobby at Children's Hospital, a report of an explosion at JFK Library. These things were trickling in all afternoon, so as far as we were concerned it was still an active incident and we had no idea if something else was going to go off somewhere. So we were still as tense as kittens, but we had no patients left at that point. About then, employees of the Fairmont Copley Hotel came across the street with a perfect stranger type of invitation. Their kitchen —when this thing started — someone knew that food was going to be important and they shifted into top gear and started cooking stuff. They told us, "If you want, come over and you can go downstairs in our employee kitchen, have a seat and eat. There's plenty of food for everyone." That was so neat, to be able to get away — maybe for only 15 minutes — to get away from the scene, and even though it was just across the street, it seemed like we were in a different world because we were downstairs in the kitchen area. They opened up this incredible spread for us with all sorts of chicken dishes and comfort food and beverages. They did that spontaneously, and here's another nice thing: there were no TVs, there were no radios. In other words, we really did feel like we were away from the scene.

After we had eaten and were walking back upstairs — keep in mind we were in uniform, carrying our helmets and ballistic gear and appeared quite bedraggled from hours of working on victims — to get out we had to pass through the Fairmont lobby. As a few of us were walking by, people stood and applauded. That was a surprise, something that's reserved for military people, not us. I kind of got a little tear in my eye with that.

When I drove home, it was great to see my wife, of course, but she said our youngest son, a Marine who is based in Hawaii, had been calling. "Sam's been calling all night. He wants you to call him right now." Sam had served in Afghanistan and he's seen what IEDs can do. Talking with him was kind of my own stress debriefing because he was someone who knew what happens when a bomb goes off. Now, my wife is an emergency physician and is no stranger to trauma and it was nice to be able to talk with her about it, but talking with Sam, who surprised me by how he knew when to just listen and let me talk, really helped, too.

At the Boston EMS Academy, it's my duty to train people in mass-casualty care. I'm constantly teaching how to respond to explosions, chemical spills, and biological and radiation leaks. I'm always teaching and we do mock disaster drills, but we rarely do these things for real. On April 15th, we had a conglomeration of everything: mass-casualty incident, multiple trauma, and a security scene all wrapped up into one. You can do exercises all you want, and we've had some serious accidents with buses, and multiple shooting victims, but we never had this scale of people injured before. What we learned was that our training works. Keep in mind that other than the three unfortunate fatalities, the people killed instantly, we didn't lose any patients and there were some very critically wounded people.

What training does not do is insulate EMS responders against the shock of the trauma. Training prepares you for what to do, but cannot prepare you for how you will feel. And it doesn't mean you won't do what's needed, and do it well. On April 15th we worried about some of our younger people who hadn't been on the job that long and how they would respond to such mass trauma, and the threat that there might be another attack, possibly on the tent. An example was one of our younger EMTs working in the medical tent; she was crying her eyes out, literally bawling, but she never stopped working. She would wipe her eyes with her elbow while applying a tourniquet. She was crying while carrying a stretcher to an ambulance. It was amazing. She did not panic. If anything, she was the most well-adjusted person among us because she was letting her emotions show and never missed a beat. I'll never forget that sight.

Until you put the training into real world application, you don't know if the training will work, and by gum, it worked!

In Washington, DC, there are memorials to fallen Firefighters and Police Officers, however there is no similar site for EMS people who have died in the line of duty. The national average is about 80 fatalities a year. An organization was started in Boston in 2007 to raise money for a site and a permanent memorial to be erected. Please consider donating to the National EMS Memorial Foundation at: emsmemorialfoundation.org.

Photo by Ken McGagh, MetroWest Daily News

Boston firefighter and paramedic Jimmy Plourde carrying one of the injured.

Jimmy Plourde

Firefighter/Paramedic

Engine 28   Jamaica Plain Firehouse

Boston Fire Department

Age 36

I saw two engagements at the finish line, two runners proposing to their girlfriends. One guy knelt down and pulled a ring out of his shoe. I'll never forget that. I was thinking, one, that's amazing that he carried it and, two, that it didn't give him a giant blister. I know myself, the moment I took that ring out of the box to give to my wife, it was like a winning lottery ticket. I couldn't help checking that it was still there, still there, still there. So to run 26 miles with it in his shoe was pretty amazing. The other guy, when he crossed the line, someone ran up to him and handed him the ring, and he went over to the railing and proposed. So, two of the happiest times in people's lives just before one of the worst.

A regular duty day is at the firehouse, waiting for alarms. But on Marathon Mondays and other special events, we're sent out along the race course on fire watch detail. If an alarm goes off along the course, we don't want to unnecessarily stop the race with big fire trucks going down Boylston Street. Instead, they have us go over on foot and check it out and if it's something big, then we'll call in the cavalry. But besides that, we're also there for the runners; we have medical kits and if someone goes down, we're there to render first aid.

When the first bomb went off, I was at the corner of the library at Boylston and Dartmouth, next to the main medical tent. This was my fourth or fifth marathon and I was commenting to the fire lieutenant that, "Jeez, it feels like it's been a slow day." He agreed, and said he'd been listening to the radios for EMS and other agencies and everybody had kind of been saying the same thing. It was kind of interesting how slow it went, and then how fast it got so quickly.

When we saw the explosion, my lieutenant said, "That's not right. That's not right." And we both took off running straight down Boylston Street, which was kind of crazy since the race was technically still going on. Some runners that had already passed the bomb site looked at us funny, like, "What are you doing? I'm finishing up the race here!" But within seconds victims were running onto the street with clothing ripped and covered in blood.

It didn't seem to me like it was anything but a bomb; not a gas leak or a transformer. As some other people were pulling the barriers away in front of Marathon Sports, I ducked under and about that time, the second bomb exploded. At that point, I was sure it was a terrorist attack. About a week before, I was teaching a Mass Casualty Incident class at fire headquarters, and part of what is taught is that the first blast is for the average Joe on the street and the second one is made to kill first responders.

Over the years I've seen my share of trauma, from people shot, to people jumping off buildings and I thought I was pretty well versed in what I would see while working for the city, but all of a sudden to come up on that, well, it was just a horrific sight.

As I looked at the blast site, I saw glass all over the sidewalk, and I thought, all right, the blast must have been inside and it blew everybody out. That's when I ran into the first building I saw, which was the candy shop, Sugar Heaven. Once I stepped in the doorway, I knew the blast had been outside, the glass just shattered outward. I turned around to go back out, and yelled to everybody inside that they had to get out of there. A guy named Bruce Mendelson, who had been upstairs at a party and came down to see what was going on, was kneeling with a girl right in front of the counter. I said to him, "You gotta get out of here."

Bruce had started to tie a shirt around her leg as a tourniquet. I said, "I got this," and I tied it tight. There was another woman there with her. She said, "I have to go, my husband is outside." I told her, "I'll take care of her. I promise I'll get her to an ambulance."

At the time, I thought she was probably 12 to 14 years old. She had black leggings on and was lying in a pool of blood.

But after what I'd seen outside, I assessed her injuries to not be the most critical of the wounded and others needed my help, but I decided I couldn't leave this girl. I told her, "We gotta go." She screamed and said, "No!" She was afraid to go back outside. I just scooped her up and ran. As I hit the sidewalk, I turned left on Boylston Street and saw two people I knew from Boston EMS, Danielle Hickey and Janelle Jimenez, running up with a stretcher. I laid her down and knew they'd take good care of her.

I went back to the sidewalk and began trying to help people. It was a tough scene. The hardest part about that many patients and limited resources at the time was, really, who do you help first? One guy was unresponsive, but wasn't bleeding and had two people doing CPR on him. Next to him were two people who were bleeding out, so I told them, "Leave him. We've got to help these people." I took my knife out — which was weird because I never carry a knife, I just happened to grab one that morning — and started cutting people's clothing to make homemade tourniquets. I used strips from a pair of pants to tie a tourniquet around one man's leg. I tied it as tight as I could, to the point where I actually had to put my foot on it to get it tight enough.

These things I'm telling you? For a long time I couldn't talk about without having a tough time, but my family has been great; my wife's a great listener and I did talk to a professional, which some people didn't, but should. I recommend it to put a lot of these feelings out there and deal with them.

The way people jumped in to help the wounded was amazing. The people who stayed and came over to help just dove into it. They got down on the sidewalk, they put their hands in the blood, they put out fires on people. There was no hesitation that day; it was, "Hey, that person's bleeding and I've got to stop it." They decided to take a stand and said, "You know what? I'm going to help save a life today." In that regard, they became true patriots on Patriots Day, helping their fellow Americans.

I saw people pulling off their belts, taking off their shirts, running out of Marathon Sports with handfuls of apparel that they used as bandages and tourniquets. They were handing me things as I needed them. I said, "I need a tourniquet," and a guy gave his belt to me. It was interesting to see that so many people, knowing it was an attack, ignored the danger and stayed around. That's what I'm trained to do and am paid to do; that's why the police are there, that's why EMS and Fire are there, but so many other people risked their lives. It was the average Joe, you know? People who work in an office building who've never taken a medical class, they've never trained for it, but they just knew the right thing to do because it had to be done. And it saved lives.

Boston is a major city, but it has a smaller community feel. People are always looking out for each other. I think the marathon really proved that. Some people think the "Boston Strong" phrase is a little cheesy, but it has been something that we could all get behind. It wasn't corporate, it was spur of the moment, just a couple of college kids who came up with it and it didn't matter what part of the city you were from, what your profession was or anything; it brought everyone together.

> *... it was amazing to me to see so many people risk their lives. It was the average Joe, you know?*

My wife, Michelle, who at the time was five months pregnant, and our daughter Ceileigh, were in front of Marathon Sports before the bombing. Like I said, it was a slow day, so I had time to check my texts. She was letting me know what they were doing and where they were. At 2:30, she texted me, "We're tired, we're heading home." If I didn't get that text, knowing where they had been, I probably wouldn't have been able to help anybody until I knew they were safe because, you know, my entire life would have changed that day as 19 minutes later, the first explosion occurred.

I was able to send Michelle an e-mail to let her know I was okay, which was a good thing because the picture of me carrying the young woman went viral and everyone was calling her. News crews were outside my house within a couple of hours. That was stressful for my family.

Come to find out, the girl I carried out of Sugar Heaven,

Victoria McGrath, had gotten to the marathon about five minutes before the blast and she was about to go into the candy shop when the bomb went off — the two of us have tried to piece things together through pictures and talking to other people — but she either crawled on her own or her friend, Krystara, helped pull her into the candy shop because her leg was pretty well cut up. She was gravely injured, her artery was sliced and most of her calf was ripped apart. The best thing to come out of it is knowing Victoria is all right. I got to meet her a few days later under better circumstances. It was on the "Today Show," where they put us together in her hospital room at Tufts Medical Center along with Bruce and two

> *"Live your life to be greater than yourself."*

people from the medical tent who helped her.

And she's not 12 or 14 as I had guessed; Victoria is a 20-year-old student at Northeastern. She has been over to dinner at our house and met my family and she's just an all-around amazing girl. I'm so blessed because in this job we never really get to know the people we treat. We rarely know what happens to them, other than whether they make it or not. I'm grateful that everything came full circle and that Victoria survived and is doing so well. I'd like to think that the efforts of not only myself, but other people, too, saved her life and she can go on and do great things.

I graduated from Siena College in upstate New York and one of the things I took away from there is a quote from Father Kevin Mackin, the former president of the college: "Live your life to be greater than yourself."

Jimmy Plourde encourages you to support Lupus Foundation New England at www.lupusne.org.

The ER nurses from Lowell General
in Medical Tent A before the bombings.
LEFT TO RIGHT: *Kristene Pinheiro, Jessica Fiore,*
Diane Forsyth (back), Molly Coughlin (front),
Rachel Cockerline and Marie Patenaude

ER Nurses from Lowell General

The following account is taken from a group conversation involving nurses Rachel Cockerline, Molly Coughlin, Jessica Fiore, Diane Forsyth, Kristene Pinheiro, and Marie Patenaude.

We had very few runners coming into the tent that afternoon and it was a little boring. In fact, we thought about leaving at 3:00 p.m. because there was just nothing to do. We were just chatting with some of the 100 or so other medical staff and peeking outside the exit flap to watch the marathon.

We heard and felt the explosion, could feel it rattling in our chests and knew immediately something was not right. Everyone in the tent stopped what they were doing and it was silent. Just an eerie scene. Two of us went outside and we expected to see people running, but there was nothing. Then there was a police officer with an injury, a wide open leg. We ran for dressing and tried to wrap his leg. And as we did, the second one went off and the chaos began.

People came running into the tent yelling, "There was a bomb at the finish line!" As medical professionals, we knew we had to hold it together and get ready for the injured. We quickly ran to our phones and texted our families to let them know we were okay.

We remembered feeling like sitting ducks. All these people who someone had tried to kill were now being brought to us to help them. We were afraid there was another bomb in the tent and it was going to go off at any second. And we did think about leaving, but an overhead announcement confirmed that bombs had just gone off and there would be mass casualties. "Clear out your runners. Everyone stay at your stations." There was calm in his voice and calm in the tent. We looked at each other and it was like looking into each other's souls. Nobody said anything. We kept watching each other. If one of us had said, "Let's go!" the rest of

The 2013 Boston Marathon

us might have run, too. But nobody did. We said to each other, "Don't leave me." This is what we do and we will stay together as a team and do what needs to be done.

And then we went to work. As the injured arrived, we checked vitals, helped stabilize the bleeding and started IVs. The injuries were severe, especially the legs. The life saving work of the first responders, the perfect strangers as it turned out in many cases, was evident: homemade tourniquets made of belts, shirt sleeves and volunteer ID lanyards tied around people's legs; homemade splints cobbled together with cardboard and scraps of wood. Efforts that saved lives and maybe limbs.

We didn't want to believe this was really happening, that it was this bad, that bombs had done this. Their injuries were not just cuts and scrapes. We were seeing severed legs. We quickly realized we didn't have the supplies we needed to treat such severe injuries. We only had 2" x 2" gauze and we ran out of gloves. We were low on alcohol prep pads, hand sanitizer, splints, and pain medication was only available in the EMT trucks. When we think back to the scene, it's as if we were watching a movie. It was awful. We had never seen or experienced anything like this. When you're in an ER, you have all your supplies and medications and you have a heads-up as patients are brought in. An EMT tells you what the injuries are and what happened to the patient. You are ready for it. But on Marathon Monday, we had little warning, inadequate supplies and we were working in a potentially dangerous area.

... belts, shirt sleeves and volunteer ID lanyards tied around people's legs; homemade splints cobbled together ... Efforts that saved lives ...

Most of the patients were conscious and asking, "What happened?" "Why can't I feel my leg?" A woman asked her husband if her feet were still there. One of us treated a woman telling her, "I'm so sorry this happened to you and it's going to be okay." But the woman and I looked at each other and we both knew how terrible this was. We wanted the injured to know we were with them and we were there to help. We asked their names and told them ours. Many of them were in shock but seemed grateful that we were trying to help them. We remember Celeste Corcoran, who ended up losing parts of both legs. I asked her name and where she was from as I gently brushed her hair off her forehead. We talked as though it was a regular conversation, making sure she stayed conscious, keeping her calm. "We're helping you and we'll get you out of here and to the hospital," we told her and others. We had eye contact with the injured and kept telling them we were here to help them. All the while, we were thinking, holy shit! Many of the people had such severe injuries, we weren't sure they would survive. When Jeff Bauman came through, we truly thought he wasn't going to make it to the hospital. We had never seen a patient look that bad, have such severe injuries, and actually survive.

We held it together because we had to. We couldn't show our horror and emotions while treating the injured. We worked as we were trained, talking to each other while treating patients saying, "I'll go get the gauze and you handle the IV." We worked as team. And this goes for others in the tent, everyone pitched in as needed. Everybody in the tent had the same goal. Get these people stabilized and get them out and to a hospital! In the beginning, we didn't have enough ambulances, but then they kept coming in a steady stream. As one pulled away, another one arrived. Where were they all coming from?

All of a sudden we looked around, and there were no more patients. About 50 minutes had passed. We looked at each other in such shock and we didn't know what to do. So we started to gather our belongings and that's when we lost it. We looked at each other and broke down crying. We no longer had to hold back our emotions for the injured. We no longer needed to be calm and together for them, and it hit us hard. We were so proud of how the injured were treated that day. All these different groups of responders worked together, helping where needed.

We headed out of the tent, some of us covered in blood. Now what? How would we get home to Lowell? What was our plan? We started walking. It was again like a movie scene; abandoned cars were all over, and there were numbed looks on faces. And yet, as we moved farther away from Copley, some areas looked like life as normal. You could see some people hadn't even heard about the bombings. I remember walking by two girls and they were discussing what color shirts to wear, and we remember getting annoyed by that. How could they have a normal conversation about such a silly thing? But they hadn't been where we were and they didn't witness what we had.

We didn't know where we were going but decided to head for the Garden. Some of our family members wanted to come get us, but they couldn't; there was no way into the city. Because we work in the ER, we have friends who work for the ambulance company. Through texting, Facebook and a call to dispatch, we were told they were sending an ambulance for us. We all piled in the back of the ambulance and while it was a comical scene, we started to cry again. Someone was taking care of us. We were going home. The ambulance took us to our hospital, Lowell General, where our families picked us up, *... we started to cry again. Someone was taking care of us. We were going home.* which was one of the most emotional moments of an emotion-packed day. One of us remembers not wanting her daughter to see the blood on her pants.

Safely in our own homes, we watched footage of the event all night long. In some cases, our family members questioned whether we should stop watching. But we couldn't. We started wondering if it really happened. It was all we could think about.

Lowell General was fantastic and very supportive of us. Management met with us to do a crisis briefing, and later presented us with plaques honoring our contributions on the day of the bombing. And they told us, "Whatever you need."

We've followed the progress of some of the patients through their postings on Facebook and Twitter. It's so uplifting to read about their progress and we worry about some of the injured who were not high profile. Are they okay?

As the days passed and the trauma eased, we remembered an odd, if not funny moment from the tent. One of the injured had on a down jacket and we had to cut through it to get to her injuries. Feathers flew everywhere! Feathers mixed with blood stuck on the pavement floor. One was on the bottom of my shoe when I got home.

How has this experience changed us? Some of us have difficulty in crowded places and feel panicky if we don't see a quick way out. Loud noises, fireworks and sirens sometimes start our hearts racing.

One of us has an obsession with her cellphone. It must be on her and fully charged. If she can't get ahold of her husband and mother, she starts to freak out. She gets anxious and feels unsettled. Some of us get anxious when our children are not in sight. Panicky feelings. On a positive note, we realize how lucky we are, and appreciate what we have even more.

Are we going back to work the marathon this year? Three of us are. We just have to. There was a bomb and people got hurt, but we're not going to let that scare us. We will be back in the tent. Three of us don't feel ready yet, and are concerned about not being able to do our jobs because we would be looking over our shoulders and feeling so anxious that we would not be productive.

We have an incredible bond after what we experienced on Marathon Monday. We don't know that we feel proud of what we did that day, but we know we did the best we could with what we had. Whatever each one of the medical staff did, it worked that day. When we returned home that first evening, we remember thinking so many people were going to die from their extensive wounds. As the night went on, and as days passed, we were astonished that there were not more deaths.

We text each other at night and we stay very connected. We can talk to each other about the experience in a way that we can't talk to anyone else. What happened on April 15, 2013, will never go away in our minds.

And we got tattoos! They say "Boston Strong" with the

marathon leaves and a nursing cap in the middle that says "R.N." and the date of the marathon. Six leaves, each a different color, representing the six of us.

Lowell General Hospital

Complete connected care.℠

These nurses urge you to consider supporting the One Fund at onefundboston.org

THE SPECTATORS

Spectators are the heart and soul of the Boston Marathon. Runners will tell you the best part of running Boston is the crowd. Unlike most marathons where spectators gather at the start and the finish, but sparsely in between, Boston spectators line all 26.2 miles and do so with gusto. Their high-fives, their orange slices, their cups of water and most of all, their encouragement shouted at total strangers, lift the runners and carry them over the hills and to the finish. Spectators are novocaine for the runners' pain.

And to be standing elbow-to-elbow among the crush of joyous fans, straining on tiptoes to see their runners, snap their photos and scream their names is, itself, an experience that lifts and inspires. It isn't for the claustrophobic, but people make room for each other, moving an inch this way or that way so everyone can get a peek. So for this group to be targeted by the cowardly attackers, who no doubt knew that they and their backpacks would be welcomed as just another couple of celebrants, was especially insulting.

Among the injured spectators were Lee Ann Yanni and her husband Nick, and Sarah Girouard. Their stories, and how perfect strangers entered their lives, follow.

Nick and Lee Ann Yanni after Lee Ann finished the Chicago Marathon, only six months after being wounded in Boston.

Lee Ann Yanni　　　　　Nick Yanni

Spectator　　　　　　　　　　　　*Spectator*

Age 32　　　　　　　　　　　　　　*Age 33*

Physical Therapist at Joint Ventures　　*Student*

Boston　　　　　　　　　　　　　　*Boston*

L EE ANN: My husband Nick and I were watching the marathon from the VIP corral area in front of Marathon Sports. I had a couple of patients running the race and we'd come back from seeing a friend at Mile 17 and just saw her cross the finish line. There were five of us in our group and Nick and I were standing next to each other. I had just looked up my friend's race time and we were discussing who would let her know her official time. Then the first explosion happened. I felt something warm brush against my leg and I thought that was really weird.

NICK: My back was against the store window and I was in front of and to the right of Lee Ann. What just happened?

LEE ANN: Why would they have fireworks going off now? I looked down and saw the broken bone sticking out of my leg and it felt like a hose was attached to the back of my leg, just pouring blood.

NICK: I remember being jerked back a bit. I saw and smelled smoke. It sounded like a crate being dropped on the ground, but magnified. Shattered glass from the floors above Marathon Sports was falling down on top of us. The explosion felt like when you're sitting in the ocean and a wave sways you back and forth. I could feel that sway. The only thing I could hear was a consistent high-pitched ring. And I saw blood, missing limbs and people screaming and running. I think I was in shock and my brain couldn't process it yet. This was all in a span of five to ten seconds.

LEE ANN: Then the second explosion happened. I forgot about my leg and instinctively tried to get away, but when I tried to walk my left leg kind of buckled and I jumped back onto my right leg. I saw that my friend's mother was on the ground and had also been hit.

NICK: I looked over at Lee Ann and saw her hopping. Why is she hopping? It was hard to make sense of some of the things I was seeing.

LEE ANN: I stood up and hopped into Marathon Sports. My shoe was filled with blood.

NICK: I looked down at her leg and I saw bone sticking out and a lot of blood. She was sitting on the floor of the store, and blood was pouring out of her. I grabbed a shirt off the rack and she told me to wrap it around the leg.

LEE ANN: I was telling him where to tie the tourniquet. As Nick applied my tourniquet he was saying, "I can't believe this is happening." I kept telling him, "I'm okay, I'm okay." At one point I grabbed my leg and tried to push my bone in. That didn't work out so well. I just kept moving my toes and I didn't see anything else wrong. Even though there was a lot of blood, I still thought it was just my bone.

NICK: I grabbed more shirts and kept wrapping them around where the bone was sticking out. Lee Ann said, "I'm all right. I'm okay. Go check on our friend's mom." I tried to go outside, but another woman collapsed in the doorway and her leg was pouring blood.

LEE ANN: I remember someone lying on the floor by the register and seeing someone collapse in the doorway. Nick went to help the woman in the door. "It will be okay," he told her. He went into a protector role and did a pretty damn good job! I'm really proud of him because Nick is not one who does well with blood and needles. And he did an amazing job helping others.

NICK: Through the ringing in my ears, I heard people yelling, "Where are the injured?" And I heard other yells of, "In here!" I was able to help the woman in the door until the paramedics got there. Then I went to our friend's mom who was still on the ground outside in the corral. The EMTs had just started working on her and she handed me her phone and said her husband was on the other end. As I'm surveying the scene, I'm telling him, "It's not good, it's not good. You need to get over here." And the phone disconnects. Oh God, he probably thinks she's dying!

LEE ANN: I was processing my injuries and knew that I'd have to have surgery and that they'll put a plate and screws in, but I'll be okay and I'll be able to run again. It's just my fibula. Being a physical therapist, I instinctively went into figuring out how I was going to get back to running. I was completely calm and was telling the first responders coming in that they didn't have to treat me right away, that they should help the others. There were a couple of women just holding my hand and talking to me. I could see the fear in their faces. They stayed, though, just being with me.

NICK: I tried to get back into the store to check on Lee Ann, but a policeman stopped me from going in. I told him I needed to get to my wife, but he said, "No, you need to leave."

LEE ANN: I didn't know how severely my leg was injured until Boston firefighter Greg Conlon knelt down and tried to work on it. He didn't know if he was going to be able to wrap it and the only things he could find to make a splint were a hanger and a shoe fitter. When we met up again days later, he told me it was the worst injury that he'd seen in his 25 years as a firefighter. He said that he had been looking for me on the amputee list because he thought for sure I'd be on it. While he was telling me this, I was just shaking my head; all I thought I had was a broken bone.

Nick: I was still trying to get back in, but the policeman said, "There could be another bomb. Leave." I wouldn't, but within a minute or two I saw them taking Lee Ann out of the store.

LEE ANN: I wasn't in pain once the tourniquet was on, but when there was a rumor of a second device, firefighter Conlon and a Boston police officer picked me up and ran me out of the store. My leg was dangling and that did hurt! They put me on a cart to take me to the medical tent. That's when a man named John Mackie, who said he was an Army medic recently returned from Afghanistan, appeared. He thought it was an IED and hopped on the cart with me. He held my leg as we headed to the medical tent.

Once I was in the tent, I was lying down and they put a sheet in front of my face to shield me from my and others injuries. John Mackie took charge of my care and started asking for this and that. He told me later that an official asked him, "Why are you in here? You can't be in here, get out!" John said he replied, "Dude, have you ever seen anything like this before? I have." And he kept working on me. He was just amazing.

There were a lot of people screaming and crying in the tent, but it was controlled chaos. I remember telling the medical professionals, "I'm a physical therapist. Don't sugarcoat it. I want to know exactly what's going on." I told them that it was just my fibula, that's all. They said, "No, it's your fibula and tibia." I insisted they were wrong, saying, "No, it just hurts on the outside!" Seriously, I was out of my mind! All the responders did such a wonderful job. I had nurses in the medical tent trying to call my husband.

NICK: I needed to be with Lee Ann but they wouldn't let me in the tent. I walked around the back and snuck in, just acting like I was supposed to be there. When I saw her being taken out on the gurney to be put in the ambulance, I said, "That's my wife!" and they let me sit in the front of the ambulance.

LEE ANN: I feel like I remember everything except for much of the time in the ambulance. The last thing I remember saying before finding myself in the Tufts Emergency Room was, "Do they have an orthopedic surgeon?" Of course they did, but that's just another sign of how out of it I was, despite appearances that I was in good shape.

My surgeon told me later that she saw me texting and thought to herself, "Oh, this girl has to be doing okay." I came out of my first surgery with a cast and a wound vac.

NICK: The doctors told us how close Lee Ann came to possibly losing her leg. If her body had been turned just half an inch at the time of the explosion, the shrapnel would've gone right through her leg instead of skimming it and breaking the fibula.

LEE ANN: Looking back at the post-operative reports, I realize my leg was quite a mess. The injury severed the nerves in two spots and the doctors had to take pieces of my fibula. I can't feel the top of my foot. I was in the hospital for eight days and had three surgeries. I was finally able to get a skin graft on my third surgery, because in the second surgery they had to take out more tissue, muscle and bone and weren't able to do the graft at that time. I do have some permanent damage, but as a physical therapist, I know what to do to recover. I had a punctured ear drum, which is healing, but Nick has permanent hearing damage.

This experience changed my outlook on life. You never know what's around the next corner. Appreciate life and the people around you because life changed in an instant that day. I can never say thank you enough to my husband for what he did, to Greg and John, and to my family and friends. And to my co-worker who is taking time out of his schedule to work with me on my physical therapy. I have a scar I have to look at every day. It makes me angry sometimes, but I was stronger than what tried to hurt me.

A major accomplishment in my recovery, physically and emotionally, was the Chicago Marathon. My physical therapist co-worker and I decided on a plan that took into account my new gait. We decided on a "walk four minutes, run two minutes" plan. At the starting line, I was excited, nervous and scared. My friend, Stephanie, ran with me. It was difficult, but I was able to run the final quarter of a mile and as I crossed the finish line, I threw my hands in the air and tears filled my eyes as the announcer said, "Lee Ann Yanni, Boston Marathon survivor, running today!"

Am I going to run the Boston Marathon this year? Heck yeah! Both Nick and I are going to run it.

Lee Ann and Nick encourage you to support cancer survivors by donating to the Livestrong Foundation at www.livestrong.org.

Sarah Girouard

Spectator
Age 21
Falmouth, Maine
Environmental Science major at Northeastern University

This was my third Boston Marathon. Since moving to Boston
to begin college at Northeastern, Patriots Day had become
one of the highlights of the year. I immediately fell in love
with it. It was a day to visit friends and rejoice in celebrating other
people's amazing accomplishments. The marathon represents so
much more than simply a competitive race of runners. It is an
event that brings the city of Boston together as it weaves its way
through towns and culminates in the heart of the city. Everyone is
connected. All of the colleges have Marathon Monday off, spring-
time with all of its beauty is in full bloom, people are out and
about, restaurants open up their outside seating, kids are on their
parents' shoulders, barbecues are on roof decks and there are end-
less flags and posters supporting the runners. It's all so much fun
and so inspiring.

The 2013 Marathon was going to be different for me.
The previous two years, I had visited high school friends attending Boston College and participated in the "Heartbreak Hill"
festivities. This year my roommates Sarah Mackay and Brittany
Gavrilles and I were going to the finish line.

The hours before we left our apartment were very mellow,
relaxing and spontaneous. After watching the top finishers on TV,
we got dressed and headed toward Boylston Street, which is less
than a five-minute walk. We stepped around the blockades and
walked towards Newbury Street to grab a quick lunch at a sushi
place before the bigger wave of finishers would cross. After lunch
we moved farther down Boylston towards the finish line where
another group of our friends were, right in front of the Forum,
ironically. I was amazed, and motivated, by how supportive the
crowd was in that area. I vividly remember leaning toward Brittany

and saying, "Just by watching this, I want to run the marathon. I feel so inspired!" We were continuing to trade messages with our friends who were closer to the finish line, so we decided to join them there and we continued walking along Boylston.

We gave up looking for our friends and found a place to watch the runners right between Marathon Sports and Sugar Heaven. I looked up and saw that we were under the Swedish flag. A chilly breeze had picked up, so the three of us huddled up in a triangle: me, the tallest, in the back right corner. We were talking about whether we should start heading back, possibly getting a warm apple cider on the way. The crowd was as lively as ever, new people replacing those who'd already seen family or friends cross. There was a man who had his daughter on his shoulders a few feet to my left, and the fence was maybe three people in front of me. Behind me, there was a bit of an opening in the crowd.

When the first bomb went off all I remember was a loud bang followed by mass confusion. Immediately, my right ear began ringing, a high pitched ringing. That's all I heard. I grabbed my ear to try to make it stop but of course that didn't help. I smelled burnt objects and found that the right side of my hair was singed and there were articles of clothing, paper and other things on fire falling from the sky. I felt a pinch or a slight sting on my lower leg and when I looked down, there was a quarter-sized hole in my jeans and a little blood. Not thinking anything of it, I looked up and all I saw was my roommate Sarah screaming. I couldn't see Brittany. The next thing I heard was a second bang, a distance off, and instinctively I grabbed Sarah and we tried to run to our left. Only getting a few feet because of my leg, we sought cover near the next closest building in a doorway with another woman. "What was that? What's happening?" I kept asking. "Sarah, what's going on?" When first responders came up to us to tell us to move, I realized that I couldn't. There was a large, flowing puddle of blood under my right foot. My wound was more extensive than a simple scratch. That's when I started to panic, but having Sarah there was reassuring. She's a biology and pre-vet major and instinctively started putting pressure on the leg, without reference or worry about the blood pulsing through her fingers.

A man came up to me, the first of my perfect strangers,

and helped lay me on my back and elevate my leg. He took over the pressure from Sarah, who was desperately trying to calm me but also was looking for Brittany. As Sarah left to find her, I began freaking out. But the stranger holding my leg up and keeping pressure on my wound started talking to me.

"You're going to be okay, Sarah," he said. "I'm not going anywhere. You're going to be okay."

I was amazed at the level of calm that came from him. As I lay on the sidewalk, leg extended, shaking from shock, my second perfect stranger arrived.

"How are you doing?"

I was shivering from shock and the cold.

"You're going to be okay," he assured me as he took off his heavy, warm, leather jacket and draped it over me. Then he left, probably to try to help someone else who was in distress. Later, before I was taken to the hospital, a nurse gave me the jacket thinking it was mine. She was shocked when I told her how the man had left it with me, because there were a set of keys and a wallet in the pockets. To think that a complete stranger had such little concern for such valuable items is unbelievable.

Sarah returned soon after and told me that Brittany was unharmed and was heading back to the apartment to call her dad and tell him about the three of us. As police and first responders continued to try and clear the area, I was determined to get up and hobble out of the way. I couldn't, and found out later that I had a fractured heel with a big chunk of metal in it, and a piece of shrapnel had pierced a bone in my leg. Three men ran over and helped "perfect stranger number one," who was still holding my leg, pick me up. As they were carrying me toward the medical tent, a nurse came running over with a wheelchair and the men placed me in it. The nurse wheeled me away, Sarah at my side.

It crossed my mind that my parents, friends and other family knew nothing of our whereabouts and how we were doing. I handed my phone, still in my pocket, to Sarah and told her to call my mom or my sister Lauren who I knew would have their cellphones near them. As she tried, the cell service began to fail, so she tried texting everyone in my phonebook. Come to find out later, the blast burst the microphone in my phone, so although I could hear the person on the call, they couldn't hear me. We first reached my sister, and after reassuring her that I was hurt but okay, told her to contact my parents. Once in the medical tent, I was inspected and labeled with a yellow tag. The doctor reassured me that although I was in a lot of pain, I was going to be one of the last people to be transported to a hospital, and that meant I wasn't too bad.

Along with all I received from my "perfect strangers numbers one and two," countless other strangers gave me reassurance and support — just like you'd hear if you were running the marathon itself. "Just hang in there, you're doing great!" or kind acts like tossing an extra blanket on top of me, or keeping my eyes shielded from other victims being brought into the tent. Every little bit helped get me through that day.

When the details emerged afterward, we figured out that we were less than 10 feet away from the bomb and I'm still amazed — and grateful — that of all 10 of our friends gathered there in that small area, I was the only one that was physically hurt. What doesn't make sense to me is that as close as we were to the bomb, the injuries weren't worse. Luck, or something, was with us.

A few weeks later, my parents wheeled me around the Boylston Street bombing site where I tried to piece the events of that day together in my mind. We saw the memorial to the victims, and my mom and I were so touched and honored by the support we felt from so many around us.

In the months following the bombings, the random acts of amazing kindness and support have continued. I received offers of help from as far away as California. And in Boston, The Greg Hill Foundation called and said it was raising money for those injured in the marathon and asked if I would like to receive a donation. Not really thinking anything of it, I agreed. A few days later, I received a check that far exceeded anything that I imagined. To this day I'm surprised and honored.

I will be back at the 2014 Boston Marathon and, for what it's worth, at the same spot. It's important to prove to myself that my future actions won't be impacted by what happened, and by standing at the finish line, I'll prove to myself that I've overcome this event. I considered running, knowing that if I ever wanted to do it this would be the year, but I think simply standing on the sidelines, cheering on those who represent everyone affected will be enough for me.

Sarah Girouard urges you to consider supporting the great work done by the Make-a-Wish organization, at www.wish.org.

Courtesy Sarah Girouard

Sarah, in her hospital bed with college roommates and friends.
Left to right: Brittany Gavrilles, Andrea Bloom, Sarah Mackay,
Sarah Girouard and Sanah Ahmed

Our prayers are with the injured — so many wounded, some gravely. From their beds, some are surely watching us gather here today. And if you are, know this: As you begin this long journey of recovery, your city is with you. Your commonwealth is with you. Your country is with you. We will all be with you as you learn to stand and walk and, yes, run again. Of that I have no doubt. You will run again. You will run again.

President Barack Obama, at an interfaith memorial service at the Cathedral of the Holy Cross in South Boston, April 18, 2013

THE RUNNERS

What we learned from our conversations with runners who are featured on the following pages is that after running for over four hours they are physically, mentally and emotionally spent. And to be stopped cold in their tracks not only threw their muscles into spasm, it left them mentally confused and emotionally devastated.

Who could blame them? They had no idea yet of the deaths and injuries closer to the finish line. All they knew at that moment was they had been punishing their bodies every day for months, making huge sacrifices for the moment when they would dig deep and somehow find one last drop of energy that would push them across the finish line of arguably the world's greatest marathon. The Holy Grail, the crown jewel, the bucket list marathon.

But there were Boston police officers standing in their way, telling them to turn around. Leave. Go home. The race is over.

As hypothermia rapidly set in, runners from out of town were understandably lost, but even runners from the Boston area were so addled they didn't know which way to walk to find familiar landmarks if, indeed, their legs would carry them.

Many needed not only directions, but physical assistance. Luckily, there was no shortage of perfect strangers.

*Rick and Dick Hoyt, in the flesh and in
bronze, with sculptor Mike Tabor*

Dick and Rick Hoyt

Runners

31 Boston Marathons

Holland, Massachusetts

Kathy Boyer

Spectator in Grandstands

Team Hoyt Office Manager

Holland, Massachusetts

DICK: Tears were streaming down our cheeks. It was April 8th, a week before our 31st Boston Marathon, and Rick and I were at the starting line in Hopkinton for one of the most unbelievable moments in our long running career. A life-size bronze statue of us was unveiled. It's a familar pose: Rick with joy and determination on his face and his arm stretched forward with his fist clenched in triumph, and me in full stride, pushing his wheelchair as we've done over a thousand times in races around the world. What an incredible honor, and we're eternally grateful to John Hancock Financial for commissioning the work.

It has been an amazing journey since 1977 when Rick, then 15, told me he wanted us to enter a charity race. I had never run a race before and the thought of pushing his wheelchair while running a long distance was daunting. Nearly 1,100 races later — including 240 triathlons, six Ironmans and 69 marathons — we're still going, although, at ages 73 and 51, we're slowing down a bit. We are humbled that our efforts have affected so many people in positive ways. The money the Hoyt Foundation raises goes directly to programs that help integrate handicapped people into everyday activities so they may live productive lives. Our team is run by volunteers and is able to support Easter Seals summer camp programs and Children's Hospital Boston. Through the assistance of so many people and corporations, we've been able to make donations to camps for the disabled and therapeutic horseback organizations. It's gratifying to see that, after all these years, Team Hoyt continues to move people with our motto: "Yes, you can."

Our favorite event is the Boston Marathon. We had 31

Team Hoyt runners participating for our 31st Boston Marathon. On Saturday, we distributed our Team Hoyt running clothes. Monday morning, we got up around 5:30, met in the hotel lobby for the bus ride, with police escort, to Hopkinton. When you get out of the bus, excitement fills the air. The beautiful morning was even more so as we did group pictures in front of our statue.

KATHY: It was so thrilling to have the team picture taken in front of the statue. Even though it's a huge marathon, it still feels small-town friendly. The entire area embraces the Boston Marathon. Everyone is a runner, spectator or supporter. For about a week, it's all about the Boston Marathon. It's kind of like Mardi Gras. It's the buzz around town. For all of us on Team Hoyt, the 65-mile drive from Holland to Boston is like coming back home again each year. Almost like a holiday.

It's a full weekend. We arrive on Thursday, the guys speak at the Expo and we are at our Team Hoyt booth for all three days. We also have a pasta dinner for our running team and families. It's always such a joyful time.

DICK: Rick and I started with the wheelchair division. It was a perfect morning and we were having one of our better runs. In fact, we were on a pace to finish about an hour and a half ahead of the prior year, the hot year.

When we got to the Mile 22 marker, about 3:05 p.m., I noticed more police activity than usual. I stopped and asked a police officer what happened. He told me, "Two bombs exploded at the finish line." For me, the Boston Marathon was over at that moment. I couldn't care less about finishing the marathon. My immediate concern was my family, most of whom were at the finish line. My youngest son Russell, his wife Lisa, and their two sons Troy and Ryan were in the bleachers, along with Kathy and her parents, and Rick's care attendant, Mike. Most of our Team Hoyt runners' families were sitting in the grandstands, too, very close to the finish line.

KATHY: We were in the higher rows of the middle grandstands and cheered as some of our runners finished and one had just crossed the finish line about a minute before the explosion. When it happened, we were looking directly at it from across Boylston, but I didn't think bomb. Maybe a gas explosion? I thought it was minutes before the next explosion because it was all in slow motion. The police were yelling, "Get down! Get down!" And then, "Get out!" I was nervous with every step. Like you can't breathe, not knowing where the next one would explode. Dick's son and grandson had gone down to use the restroom, but his daughter-in-law and other grandchild were with us. We were all dazed as we streamed into the Boston Public Library. My mother, who had a hard time walking because of her knees, kept saying, "Don't leave me." It didn't feel safe in the library and they took us out the back door. We then met up with some of our runners and families. We're a very tight group. Some of our runners have been with us five or six years. Everybody ended up connecting with other members of the group. We gathered in the lobby of the Sheraton and that was our station for the next five or six hours.

Dick: Even though the marathon was over, we kept running, hoping we could get closer to the Sheraton Hotel and find out the fate of our loved ones. One report I heard was that the grandstands had blown up! At the Mile 25 marker in Kenmore Square, the police stopped us and said we couldn't go any farther. Right on cue, our "perfect stranger," came out of the crowd. Mike Skiotos said, "Dick, I have a Jeep close by and you're welcome to take it, or I can drive you where you need to go." We were a group of ten, five of whom said they could walk to the Sheraton. Rick's wheelchair was too big to fit in the Jeep, so the walking five said they would take the chair with them. I picked Rick up, put him on my lap and we headed for the Sheraton. It took us over one and a half hours to get there. One and a half hours to go about two miles! The 51-year-old son got to sit on his father's lap that day.

Kathy: Dick didn't have a phone with him, and my phone wasn't working, so when I got someone's phone that was working I tried calling a couple of runners that I thought might be with him, but my calls were not going through. Then a text came in on my phone from Maureen Hayes, one of the team runners. She was with Dick and Rick and asked if we were okay. My phone wouldn't send texts, so I borrowed a phone to text her back to tell Dick that Russ and his family were fine, that they had been able to get to their car and drive home; that I was with my parents and Mike at the hotel and we were okay, and all the families in the bleachers were okay. This was over an hour after the explosions. It was a relief to hear from Mo, because while we knew they were okay because there no stories of bombs going off on the course, we didn't know where they were.

DICK: Before we got that text, the police stopped our car and Mike Skiotos told the officers, "Listen, I've got Dick and Rick Hoyt here and we've got to get to the front door of the Sheraton." The policeman waved us on. We got to the Sheraton and I carried Rick into the lobby, where we discovered that all of our Team Hoyt families were okay. We stayed in the lobby, waiting for all our runners to show up.

KATHY: When they arrived at the Sheraton, there were many tears and hugs.

DICK: It was very upsetting for Rick and he took it hard for about five or six days. We love the Boston Marathon and we were so concerned about the wounded and the families who lost loved ones.

KATHY: Within our group, it brought us closer because we helped each other through the chaos that day. Since that experience we've said to each other, "We felt like a family before, but we feel even more like a family now."

At the Sheraton Hotel, employees walked around the lobby the whole time offering towels, water and blankets. They were offering us comfort. They created calm at a very difficult time. We were all in the same boat that day and people, strangers, came through and really helped each other. People helping people.

Dick: Boston's is the best marathon in the world and the fans of the Boston Marathon are the best fans in the world. The crowds all along the way are just unbelievable. They are there right from the starting line, and every step along the way, just cheering the runners on. They will pick you up and carry you. And when you really need it, like at Heartbreak Hill, they will pick you up and carry you up those hills. And when things fell apart that day, the fans picked us up again and did everything they could to help others in need.

When the runners were stopped around Heartbreak Hill, people came out of their homes and took them in to warm them up. They cooked food for the runners and gave them comfort.

I'm grateful to the emergency personnel who helped minimize the trauma on that worst of days. The police were so calm and in control. It was an unbelievable experience for me.

They will pick you up and carry you. And when you really need it, like at Heartbreak Hill, they will pick you up and carry you up those hills. And when things fell apart that day, the fans picked us up again...

I did not know Mike Skiotos, our perfect stranger who gave us the ride. That's the way people are. We thanked him so much and later sent him a fruit basket and a gift card for dinner at a local restaurant.

Rick and I will be running the Boston Marathon 2014 to honor those people who were killed and injured. This marathon is so important to Rick and as we get older and slower, he says if we run only one race a year, he wants it to be the Boston Marathon.

*Dick and Rick Hoyt, and Kathy Boyer, appreciate the
continued support for the Hoyt Foundation, which
aspires to build the character, self-confidence and
self-esteem of America's disabled young people
through inclusion in all facets of daily life.*

*Inspirational and autobiographical books by Dick
(Devoted - The Story of a Father's Love For His Son) and
Rick (One Letter at a Time) are available at
www.teamhoyt.com.*

Courtesy Team Hoyt

*The 2013 Team Hoyt pre-race photo at the
Dick and Rick Hoyt statue in Hopkinton*

*Bill Iffrig, knocked over by the force of the first blast, being
helped up by one of his "perfect strangers"*

Bill Iffrig

Runner

Age 78

Retired carpenter

Lake Stevens, Washington

My son, Mark, called me from Seattle after the bombings and my fall. "Dad, you're all over the Internet and the TV news!"

Earlier in the day, my goal was to improve my track record in Boston. It wasn't the best. The first year I ran Boston was in 1985. I had just turned 50 and was still running 2:40, 2:50, but I came in at 3:11. Then I quit running marathons until a few years ago when the guys who I run with in Washington were after me to enter marathons again. I had run 45 of them, and they felt I should run more. I wasn't sure I wanted to, so I didn't tell the guys about it, and I ran the Seattle Marathon in 3:50, which was good enough to qualify for Boston. So they said, "Let's go to Boston!"

That was 2012, and I had trained hard for it. I was ready for a good run. When I got up race morning and opened the drapes, oh my God! The sun was intense and I knew it was going to be an awful day for running. When I got out there on the course, it was already too warm, 90 degrees, and after about three miles I didn't have it, no push or anything. It was crazy. By the halfway point, I was walking. It became hard just to stay on my feet. But I kept going. Slowly. It took me seven and a half hours to finish! Some of our friends were tracking me and were asking, "What happened to Bill? Where is he?" My wife was waiting and worried. The race officials even offered me a ride to the finish. But it was really important for me to finish on my own. There were no spectators left and crews were cleaning the finish line area. I was the third or fourth to last person to finish, but I did better than many. Over 100 runners were taken to hospitals that year.

I wasn't going to let that be my final time at Boston, so I came back for the 2013 marathon. I trained extra hard for four months and put in a lot of miles.

Last year, everything was perfect; the temperature was perfect. We arrived on Saturday and my wife and I planned to spend six days in Boston. We really like the city and wanted to see more of it. On the morning of the race, I was feeling real good, but the start at Hopkinton is kind of a mess for guys running back where I'm at. If you're going to use the restroom you need to go an hour before just to stand in line. I didn't start my race until ten o'clock and there's such a mob of runners you can't run the pace you'd like to and it doesn't open up until five or six miles. But I felt great throughout the whole race. I was passing a lot of people and was charging ahead when I got to the hills. I felt energized and thought, this is gonna be great!

When I came around the corner from Hereford onto Boylston and saw the finish line, I started to sprint a little. I was going for it. I was about 20 feet from the finish line, running on the left side of street and, oh my God, this explosion went off right in my ear! I was about 15 feet away from the curb when it went off. At the same time as I was trying to process what was going on, I was going down. I was thinking it might be a terrorist attack because I knew it had to be a bomb. My legs were wobbling uncontrollably and going all over the place and I was forced to the ground. Briefly, I was thinking that might be it for me.

The force of the bomb is what knocked me over. When I felt myself going down I was trying to fall so I wouldn't hurt myself, and kind of rolled to my right. I was never unconscious and I wasn't afraid because I hadn't comprehended what had happened. I lay there for a little while, on my back and kind of half-sitting and that's when three police officers were standing over me, guns drawn, and looking down at me. They asked if I was okay and I said I was. They moved on immediately, but not before a photographer took a picture of them and me. That shot that was on the cover of *Sports Illustrated*.

The sound of the blast was louder than anything I've ever experienced. I only heard the sound of the bomb and did not hear screams from the crowd. The smoke was coming over me and there were pieces of tin cans, or some kind of metal, flying onto the road. The second bomb went off while I was lying on the ground. I realized that everything was working and I wasn't bleeding, so I needed to get to the finish line. I still didn't know what had happened, but I knew one thing: I had been running this thing for four hours and I was gonna go for it!

A B.A.A. volunteer, who wants to remain anonymous, helped me up and another guy gave me a hand. After I crossed the finish line, another man told me to wait while he got a wheelchair. While I waited, I looked back and saw all the things that were going on and what had happened to the injured spectators. I was thinking to myself that I just want to get out of there. It was chaos. Smoke from the bomb had settled over the street, emergency vehicles were coming and people were running all over the place. When the man returned with the wheelchair, I told him there were other people hurting real bad and they needed the wheelchair more than I did. "I'm okay, I can walk." It was about six blocks to the Park Plaza hotel and it took me a while, but I got there. Along the way, another person stopped and offered to help, but I said no, thanks, that I would be okay.

My wife of 58 years, Donna, had decided to wait for me in the room. She'd watched me run marathons many times before. I didn't have a phone and wanted to get back to her as soon as I could. We hugged and talked about how bad it was. Donna had watched a little footage of it, of me falling, and couldn't wait for me to get back. She was getting calls from others who had seen me on TV. We called our son, Mark, who was back home in Washington. He filled us in on what he knew about the bombings, which was more than we knew at the time. That's when it started to sink in about how lucky I was to come away with minor injuries.

The pictures of me on the ground were already out there, everywhere. Reporters started calling our hotel room in no time at all. A CNN producer knocked on our door and asked if I would do an interview with Anderson Cooper. So I went with her, but I didn't know my way back and she disappeared. I hitched a ride with one of the other reporters. Cooper was a nice guy to talk to. George Stephanopoulos, too. We had a small hotel room and it seemed there were two or three reporters with us all the time. That went on for a day and a half! Finally, my wife and I just had to get out of the room, so we went walking. All the people in Boston were so good to us. Everywhere we went they knew who I was and they were so good, so kind.

I was able to retrieve my bag and got a finish medallion, but the B.A.A. didn't have me listed as a finisher, but they straightened it out. I didn't have a bad time: 4:03:47. That was fourth in my age group. The guy who won our age group, a man from Japan, was at 3:46:23.

I'm so grateful that I came out of it as well as I did. After I stood at the finish and looked back at the carnage, the people with blood all over their legs and faces, and later when I saw the TV coverage and how horrific the injuries behind the barricades were, I felt so lucky. I do have some hearing damage from it, but it's nothing, really, just something I have to live with.

The Boston Marathon has such a wonderful history and there are so many great stories. So many amazing races have happened at this marathon. It's so meaningful, and it's such an honor to run the Boston Marathon. It is just so hard to imagine what happened.

As for Boston this year, Donna and I need to talk about that. I don't think we're ready to go back yet. But I'm planning on 2015, when I'll have turned 80 and will be in the next age group.

Mark Iffrig

Seattle, Washington

Before I tell you about what it was like to be 3,000 miles away when the photo of my fallen dad went viral, please allow me to brag about him a little. He won't. He's far too humble. He'd never tell you he was a national championship runner. Or that he's been the fastest in the country in his age groups 30 to 40 times. He's an incredible runner. Until Dad turned 70, I was not able to beat him because he's so fast.

The 2012 Boston Marathon provided a dramatic backdrop to Dad's return for the 2013 marathon. As he described on the previous pages, the weather in Boston that day was miserably hot and he finished the race in seven and a half hours. I was in Seattle and had been watching his progress online and was getting concerned about him. Had something horrible happened? I called my mom in her hotel room, but she didn't know where he was or how to get in touch with anybody who knew.

Going to Boston to watch Dad run is out of the question because I'm a CPA and the marathon always falls at the end of my busiest time of the year. But I was watching Dad run the 2013 marathon online — rather, I was watching his stick figure, as the B.A.A. website allows. Because it was tax season, I hadn't talked to my parents for awhile. I knew my mom would be in the hotel room so I called her and we talked for 45 minutes as I continued watching my stick figure Dad run. I hung up the phone and a half-hour later I saw that my stick figure Dad had finished the race. I went on Facebook and proudly posted:

"My 78-year old Dad just finished the Boston Marathon in 4:03!"

A few people posted their congratulations, and then one asked, "Was your dad impacted by the bomb?"

Bomb? I knew nothing about it because I had just been watching the stick figures. Oh my God, I called my mom right away, and as soon as she answered, Dad walked through the door. He got on the phone, and it was funny because he's such a low-key guy. This is the way the conversation went: "Dad, were you affected by the bomb?"

He said, "Oh yeah, I got knocked over, but my time was good. I had a 4:03. But things are a total mess out here. I don't know what we're going to do for lunch. We'll probably have lunch right here in the room."

So I hung up the phone thinking that, well Dad got knocked down, but he was so casual about it and made it sound like other runners got knocked down, too, so I didn't think much of it. But I was curious about the bombings, so I went back to the Internet. After 30 minutes, I saw the video of a runner going down. I thought: that kind of looks like Dad!

I turned on TV in time to hear NBC's Brian Williams say, "Here's the iconic photo of the event." There was my dad, lying on the ground with three policemen standing over him! Thank goodness I had already talked to him and knew he was okay.

I called him back and asked, "Dad, were you in an orange shirt?"

"Yes."

"Were three policemen standing over you?"

"Yes."

I told him, "You're all over the Internet and the news."

He said, "Oh, maybe I am." Just his normal old self.

I finished that conversation with him and in 30 minutes my office phone started ringing off the hook. The first couple of calls were reporters and I made one or two comments. After realizing all of the calls would be from reporters, I stopped answering the phone. When I went home there was a TV news truck waiting for me. Actually, I'm a little embarrassed that anybody was even interested in what I had to say because our story had a happy ending. My heart breaks for those families who are dealing with the loss or critical injury of a family member.

It's great that my dad got a little attention because he's such a humble person, so even-tempered and has accomplished so much in his life. That he climbed back on his feet and staggered across the finish line was no surprise to any of his family and friends who have seen how he lives his life. He's a great role model for me and, by sheer chance, for many others.

As President Obama said at the interfaith memorial service in Boston: "Like Bill Iffrig, 78 years old — the runner in the orange tank top who we all saw get knocked down by the blast — we may be momentarily knocked off our feet, but we'll pick ourselves up."

Bill and Mark Iffrig encourage you to consider donating to the One Fund at onefundboston.org.

Photo by Linda McIntosh

Peter Sagal of NPR's "Wait Wait ... Don't
Tell Me!" waves as he guides William
Greer to the Boston Marathon finish line.

Peter Sagal

Runner/Guide

Age 48

11 marathons, including three Bostons, once as a guide

Host, NPR's "Wait Wait ... Don't Tell Me!"

Chicago

So William Greer was really hurting, in that very particular, very painful way known only to Boston Marathon rookies, the hurt that comes from taking the first half too fast and getting hammered by the Newton Hills, and he kept wanting to walk.

"How far is the 24-mile marker?" he asked. The 24-mile marker was about 20 yards ahead of us, but William couldn't see it because William is legally blind, and he was asking me because I was running next to him (or, just ahead of him and to the left, because he has some peripheral vision on that side) as his guide.

"Just up ahead," I said.

"I'll walk when we get there," he said. And when we did, he did.

It wasn't William's best day. He had hoped for a 3:45 finish, and if not that, better than his 3:50 PR, or at the very least under 4:00, and all three goals had slipped away between leg cramps and stomach cramps and general fatigue. I said to him, "William, it's your race, and it's your day, and it's your first Boston, so just crossing the finish line alive is a win. But I want you to try to run that last mile. The last mile of Boston is a great thing, and you don't want to be walking it."

And William, who had conquered a brain injury at 17 that robbed him of his sight and almost his life, and gone on to live and work and marry and run six marathons (sans guide) and qualify for Boston, gritted and walked and jogged and got himself to Mile 25, and started running, and started hurting even more, and as we approached the right turn onto Hereford Street, he said, "When we get to that turn, I'll need to walk again."

But he didn't. We turned onto Hereford and William didn't

stop. He danced around a traffic cone like a man sighted and took the left turn onto Boylston like a man reborn, and as we ran that famous interminable canyon to the finish I kept urging him on as I waved my arms to whoop up the crowd, shouting, "A quarter mile! Three hundred yards! Two hundred! Can you see it yet, William?"

"Yes!" he yelled, and we crossed the line in 4:04, and I was as proud of him as I've been of anyone I've ever known, and happier with this marathon — my slowest — than any other I've ever run. I told him he could stop running — he hadn't realized he'd crossed the line — and I put my arm around William and enumerated his praises and we shuffled, slowly, into the finishing chute.

"You need some water?" I asked William.

"I don't want anything," he said, "until I get that medal."

BOOM. An enormous noise, like the most powerful firework you've ever heard, thundered from behind us. We all turned to look, even William. Another BOOM. White smoke rose in a miniature mushroom cloud into the air, a hundred yards away, just on the other side of the finish.

"What the hell was that?" said someone.

I had just finished my tenth marathon, my third Boston, and I had never heard anything like that. Ever. Cowbells, music, cries of pain, sure, but never that.

"Keep moving, please," the officials shouted through megaphones.

I was curious. But I also had a very tired runner whose brain couldn't process the information his eyes gathered, and I was responsible for him, so I led him through the chute, helping him pick up snacks, sports drink, and yes, his medal.

The volunteers and officials looked fraught. Somebody told me it was a car bomb. Somebody told me it was in a building. Somebody else guessed it was an electrical transformer going up. By the time we exited the finishers' chute and headed to the rendezvous point for the rest of our team, we knew it was something bad. Ambulances and cops were racing through the runners' meetup area. Cops, clearly in the grip of an emergency, were screaming at us all to get the hell off the street, which we were supposed to own today. I got William to our meeting point safely, but his wife wasn't there. He started to worry. I started to worry. We tried to call her, but my cellphone wouldn't connect to anything.

Our team leader was hearing bad news. That it was a bomb. That there were injuries. That the race had been halted, leaving his runners — half of whom were blind — out on the course with nowhere to go. He was trying to organize rescue expeditions, get messages to lost runners. I got a call from my employer, NPR, asking me to go live on the air and describe what I had seen, what I could see now.

I walked down back toward the finishing chute, or where it had been. In the half hour since I had collected my medal, it had all been cleared away — no tables, no volunteers, no water trucks. Just the barriers, now intended to hold the media and the public at bay. I described to Robert Siegel the explosion I had heard, the smoke I had seen, the vast crime scene I was now seeing before me.

I returned to the meeting point. William was embracing Ellen, his wife, and in the mist of the growing chaos we posed for one last proud picture. They headed off to their hotel, and I started on my trip back to my uncle's apartment, normally a 15-minute subway ride or 30-minute walk away. That day, it took almost two hours.

As I left Copley Square, I came across an amazing and terrifying sight. Beyond the barriers the police had set up, keeping everyone — not just runners — away from the finish line area, I saw ambulances. Dozens of them, maybe a hundred, lined up, lights on, engines running, ready to go. It was the same terror you might feel seeing an invading army ready to launch ... except instead of promising horror to come, it demonstrated that a horror had already happened.

It only occurred to me, much later, as I viewed online videos of the bombing, how important William's gutsy last mile really was. We crossed the line at 4:04. The bomb went off as the clock read 4:09. Five minutes later. Which might well have been the five minutes that William would have needed to walk that last miserable mile, had he given in to the urgings of his hip, gut, and mind. But he ran the bravest and toughest mile of his life, not even able to see clearly what he was doing, just because he wanted to be able to say he did it, and by doing so, he crossed the line alive.

SAGAL RECEIVED THE FOLLOWING MESSAGE FROM WILLIAM GREER ON TUESDAY: "I HAVE REALLY SORE LEGS. I AM READY TO START TRAINING FOR THE NEXT MARATHON, AND I'M GOING TO HAVE A LOT MORE

LONG RUNS. I HAD THE SPEED, I JUST NEED TO REALLY INCREASE MY ENDURANCE. THANKS VERY MUCH FOR BEING MY SIGHTED GUIDE; YOU MADE THE MARATHON A GREAT PLEASURE. THE ONLY PROBLEM WERE THE BOMBS."

ORIGINALLY PUBLISHED APRIL 16, 2013 IN RUNNER'S WORLD.

Peter Sagal encourages you to support the Massachusetts Association for the Blind and Visually Impaired, at www.mabcommunity.org/massachusetts-association-for-the-blind-and-visually-impaired.

William Greer
Austin, Texas
Eight marathons, first Boston
Film Festival Coordinator/IT Specialist
Coalition of Texans with Disabilities

Ellen Whittier
Austin, Texas
Free-lance writer

ELLEN: Long distance running legend Steve Prefontaine once said, "A lot of people run a race to see who is fastest. I run to see who has the most guts." My husband, Will, knows a thing or two about guts. He's a legally blind long distance runner. Will started running about ten years ago as a hobby, then he began entering races: 5Ks, 10Ks, and eventually marathons.

WILL: I had run four marathons in Texas and decided it was time to do one in another state. I ran San Francisco and had a good enough time — 3:55 — to qualify for Boston. As I was thinking about running Boston, I realized that I'd never run a marathon with a sighted guide before. I had just relied on following the crowd, but I was a little bit nervous running San Francisco and in Boston, I wanted to concentrate on running the course and not on whether I was on the right path. So I decided to see if I could get hooked up with a sighted guide. The B.A.A. put me in touch with Team With a Vision, which is organized by the Massachusetts Association for the Blind. A few weeks after I registered, I got a call from M.A.B.

"Would you mind running with a celebrity guide?"

"No, of course not," I answered.

They informed me my celebrity guide would be Peter Sagal.

"I just love *Wait Wait ... Don't Tell Me!*" I said, "so that sounds like a heckuva lot of fun."

And it was. Peter could be incredibly funny. He told lots of stories about people that he had as guests on *Wait Wait.* A really interesting guy. Peter hadn't been a sighted guide before but was a veteran marathoner and did a great job. He talked a lot, and he told me things about parts of the course. Peter grew up in Boston and passed along some memories as we ran.

The race went well. I really did love it. I was struggling a little bit at the end and I wound up with a time of 4:04, which was slower than what I wanted it to be, but that's how it goes sometimes. I absolutely loved the marathon, though. I had heard about the Wellesley Wall where all of the coeds from Wellesley College are screaming so loud you can hear them nearly a mile away, and it turns out that's accurate! They are really loud, really enthusiastic about cheering people on. That was a heckuva lot of fun. It was just really something experiencing the course.

The hills were nothing, but I made a mistake. I ran the last hill, Heartbreak Hill, at a pace that I normally take on a hill when I'm running a 10K. That wound up hurting me about a mile later. I was having stiff legs and all sorts of problems and not having as much fun finishing the marathon as I usually have.

Crossing the finish line was incredible. Really great. One of the things really striking about the Boston Marathon: the sighted guide has to finish behind the blind runner. That's really notable. The first thing I said was, "Give me the finisher's medal!" I wanted the Boston Marathon medal before water, before bananas, before bagels; I wanted that medal.

I had done lots of reading about the Boston Marathon and one thing I dreaded was the long walk after the finish. First you have to run 26 miles, and then you have to walk another mile to get all of the things they give you after the race. We're walking and walking and I said, "Oh wow, this is an extra mile at the end of the marathon!"

Then we heard the first one go off.

Peter said, "I've never heard that before. I wonder if they're firing a cannon to celebrate."

Then we heard the second one. Where we were, we didn't see a lot of chaos. There were a couple of fire trucks and a police motorcycle that went by and I thought that maybe there was a problem with one of the buildings; maybe there was a fire. I had no idea what was going on. A race official told us not to stop, to keep walking. We didn't know, really, what was happening until we got to the team reunion area and people were checking the Internet on their phones and we started hearing reports about the bombs going off and the damage.

Meanwhile, Ellen wasn't with me and I was getting worried. I hadn't seen her along the way. All I knew was that she was alone and was going to try to see me cross the finish line. She had both of our cellphones. I didn't know her number, but I knew mine, so Peter and members of Team With a Vision were calling my phone to see if she would answer. The calls weren't going through. We couldn't connect. I was concerned. I didn't know where she was, whether anything had happened. I imagined all sorts of bad things that could have happened.

At one point, NPR called Peter and told him this was serious, and he needed to go report on it for *All Things Considered,* so he left.

ELLEN: I saw Will and Peter run by on Hereford at Newbury. I tried to get to the finish line, but the crowd was so thick, and I'm a little claustrophobic when it comes to crowds. Then I heard the explosions and saw the smoke. I had been tracking Will on a service from AT&T and I knew that he and Peter had finished, but that was all. I knew something bad had happened and I just turned into a robot: I must get to the family and friends area — I must get to the family and friends area. Instead of panicking, I felt like a heat-seeking missile. I just needed to get there, needed to get there, needed to get there. That's all I could think about. I don't know Boston all that well and I didn't have a map with me. I just had a rough idea of where it was and headed in that direction. I kept stopping people and asking, "Do you know anything? Do you know anything? Nobody did. I asked everybody I could for directions to the family and friends area. I ran into a guy who was on his phone, and I heard him say, "My wife was in the race. I don't know what has happened to her." I asked if he knew what was going on. He said he'd heard that there was an explosion, and that's all he knew. I asked, "Are you going to the family and friends area?"

He said, "Yes."

I said, "Do you want to walk with me?"

He said, "No, I can't think about anybody else right now. I just have to go." And he left, just like that.

My first thought was, gee, that's rough! And then I understood how he felt. He just couldn't process anything else.

So I tried to keep calm and kept walking, and the farther I walked, the more things started to happen and the more panicked I felt. The cellphones stopped working completely. I had Will's and mine. Neither one would work, and that freaked me out. Other people's phones stopped working, too. The police were closing off streets, and I still didn't realize what had happened. No one had said there was a terrorist attack or anything like that. I went up to a police officer who said he didn't know what had happened. I said, "Do you know where the runners are who crossed the finish line? Are they headed toward the family and friends area?"

He said, "Oh, no, no. They're putting them all on buses and getting them out of here as quickly as possible."

That was a tough moment. "My husband was one of the runners! I don't know where he is!" I hadn't started crying yet, but I was getting even more worried at that point.

The policeman said, "Well, what you need to do is go down to the family and friends area and they'll tell you where the buses are going because he's probably on a bus right now."

But the closer I tried to get to the family and friends area, the more streets were closed off, and it seemed like every time I tried to go down a street, it would get blocked. All the police would say is that they'd been told to block the streets. During the entire hour I was looking for Will, nobody could tell me what was going on; never a word about a terrorist attack, or fatalities and injuries.

By this time, I was really lost, and that was painful because I couldn't get to where he might be, if he was even there anymore.

Eventually, I ran into a woman who I'd call my first perfect stranger. She was a runner, still in her shorts. I said, "Do you know what's happened? I can't find my husband, I can't find my husband!" I was getting to the point where I was expressing my panic to others, as opposed to just keeping it to myself.

She said, "No, I don't know what happened. I finished the race and I'm just going to go home now. You should stop in at my hotel (where she stayed the night before), it's just right here. Ask the concierge for a map because he's really good at giving directions around Boston and he can help you."

Why I didn't think of that, was my immediate thought. I thanked her and went into the hotel. I told the concierge where I needed to go. He gave me a map and, "Okay, I'm going to draw the route for you on the map." And I said, "Can you draw two routes because one of them may be closed off?" And he did, and I used the map and made my way to where my husband may or may not be. I wish I could remember the name of the hotel and the man who helped me.

Back on the street, I started seeing police officers and soldiers with guns, like big rifles. I'd never seen that, even when I lived in New York City. I was like, "Oh, hell, what has happened?" I was praying, praying that nothing terrible had happened to anybody, much less my husband. I have great respect for the runners' culture, the marathon culture. It's a fantastic sport. It's a sport where people are truly supportive of each other, with the most supportive spectators. I was praying that nothing had happened to any of them, but to be honest with you, I was most concerned about Will.

I kept going, police everywhere, and still no one would tell me anything. I got closer to the family and friends area and an older couple stopped me. The woman was crying and said that she couldn't find her son. He'd been in the race and she didn't know where he was, and she was freaking out. I said, "You're welcome to come with me to the family and friends area and wait. I think it's about a block and a half." She said they had family that was looking for him, and that she and her husband had better stay where they were. I took her son's name and told her, "I'll ask around about him. If I hear anything, I'll come back and let you know." It was really rough seeing her like that, so upset. When I asked around about him, nobody knew who he was.

I walked another block or so and all of a sudden I heard someone shouting, "Ellen! Ellen!" It was Josh Warren, a fabulous guy who ran Team With a Vision. Will was standing next to him and I broke into a run, didn't say anything, and threw my arms around him ... just held on, not saying a word.

WILL: I started talking to her and she said, "Be quiet and hold me!"

ELLEN: I really couldn't say anything. I'm normally a really verbose person, but I could say nothing. Even, "I love you," would have been too much for me. I'd been looking for Will, and panicking, for at least an hour and there was just nothing to say. It was just ... here's my body, here's your body, let's hold each other, that's it. I was so relieved to see him. It was just such a weird experience. You just don't contemplate your husband being dead. And I hadn't seriously been thinking that Will was dead at that point, it would have just been too much. My head would have exploded.

WILL: I am registered for the 2014 Boston Marathon, so I'm going back in April. There's just something really important about going back and doing it again after that horrible attack. I just feel like it's something I have to do. I cannot miss a chance to do that.

ELLEN: I can't wait to go back. I'm excited to go back. I think it's important to go back. I feel it's critical for Will to run this race again, and I plan to be on exactly the same spot where I was watching Will and Peter go by last year. I want to be at the same spot along Hereford at Newbury. It's important to be there as a sign of life and as a sign of support for the runners and for the marathon, and to not allow that bombing to define a great event.

Will Greer and Ellen Whittier urge you to consider supporting the Massachusetts Association for the Blind, and its Boston Marathon running team, Team With a Vision, at mabcommunity.org.

Photo by Ramsey Mohsen

This "perfect stranger" brought orange juice and
bagels from his home across the street to
stranded runners Diana, left, and Ali.

Alison Hatfield

Runner

Age 27

Kansas City

Another runner walked up to me.
"Can I use your phone to call my mom?" he asked. "I
need to tell her I'm okay.
"Oh yes, please take it."
After he dialed, I heard him say, "Hi, Mom." And, standing
five feet away, I could hear her scream.

When my fiancé Ramsey Mohsen and I arrived in Boston the
Saturday before the marathon, the first thing I wanted to do
was go to the finish line. When I saw it, I immediately got choked
up and was struggling to talk. It was so emotional, it really set in. I
get to run this race and I get to run across this finish line. I was going
to run the Boston Marathon! It is the dream and goal of so many.

The rest of our group, my parents, my friends Stacy
Scalfaro and Diana Stauffer and their spouses, arrived in the afternoon. We were staying at the Copley Square Hotel, which is
about a block from the finish line. That evening, we went to a bar
on Boylston Street, had a few drinks and had so much fun. Normally, I would not drink beer before a race, but I wanted to soak
in every moment of this experience. We were not running this race
for time; just to finish and celebrate. On Sunday morning, we went
on a run and saw all the 5K runners. We got coffee and walked over
to the Expo. What an amazing experience! I picked up my bib and
got tears in my eyes just seeing it. We took pictures in front of the
course map and visited all the booths. We wanted to see everything!

Sunday night, we went to dinner on Newbury Street and
stopped by the finish line on the way back to the hotel. It was just
buzzing with people; everybody was taking pictures and there was
such a feeling of excitement mixed with anxiety. We had our Bos-

ton Marathon jackets on and took funny pictures at the finish line. Everyone was excited to run, and if they weren't running, they were excited for the people who were. Wherever we went people would ask, "Are you running tomorrow?" "We are!" Everything revolved around the race.

On race day our plan was in place: My parents and fiancé planned to watch me around Mile 24-25, and Stacy's husband was bringing our clothes and meeting us at the family meet-up. My dad bought champagne the night before for the first part of our celebration, a toast on the street. We would then go back to the hotel, shower, relax and go for fish and chips and my favorite wine at Legal Seafood that night. We made the reservations six weeks earlier.

Stacy, Diana and I ran together. The weather was perfect. Although we didn't have a specific goal, we wanted to finish in less than four hours. I was carrying a cellphone because I write a blog and planned to take lots of pictures and document everything. One of my great memories is running through some of the towns where there were crowds from every angle, screaming and cheering for us. It was so loud, so wonderful. Stacy had run the race before, but Diana and I had never experienced anything like this. At one point Diana grabbed my arm, tears in her eyes and yelled, "This is amazing!" I yelled back, "I know!" There were a bunch of kids jumping on mini-trampolines and dancing to the Gangnam Style song. And running through the college towns was pure happiness! We saw our families at Mile 25. Things were going as planned.

As we were running into the city and approached the Mass Avenue bridge, Diana got really bad stomach pains. The three of us slowed to a walk and by the time we came out of the tunnel, she was fine. We started running again and from there on, it was eye on the prize. Get to the finish line! We ran the race side-by-side and were going to finish it together, no matter what. A right on Hereford and left on Boylston, and it was so loud we couldn't talk as we ran down the street. We soaked it all in; I can still remember everything about it. Right before we finished, we grabbed hands and threw our arms up. It was a great moment!

Our clock time was 3:54:35, about 30 minutes before the explosion. We got our blankets, got our medals, grabbed some snacks and took pictures. We met up with everyone else in the family waiting area, a couple of blocks from the finish. I hugged them and said, "I need my clothes. I'm freezing." My dad was holding me up and my mom was helping me get my clothes on. I threw my jacket and gloves on. We took a few more pictures. I had taken a picture at the start of the race and wanted to post a picture of me finishing the race. As they got ready to take a picture of me holding my medal, we heard the first explosion.

Photo by Ramsey Mohsen

When it went off, it got eerily silent and everyone had a nervous look on their faces. I remember a woman next to me start to cry. Then the second one exploded. I was feeling panicked and saw panic all around me. My dad said, "Okay, let's go." He put his arms around my mom and me and we started walking. My friend Diana said it was probably cannons for celebrating, someone else thought it was scaffolding falling. But I saw police officers running and in an instant it went from so happy to panic mode. I thought bombs were dropping out of the sky and I wondered where the next one would explode. My dad thought we should move away from large groups of people and we walked across a bridge into a quiet neighborhood and wandered around. I pulled out my phone and checked Twitter and read about the bombs. OMG, two bombs near the finish line! Stacy began crying. We reached out to our family and friends to let them know we were okay. My brother was having a hard time; his entire family was in Boston. I updated my Facebook to let everyone know I was okay.

Dad called the hotel and they said we could come back, but I was uneasy about going back to Copley Square because it was so close to the explosions. I really felt anxiety walking back there. We got into our rooms, but were only there for about 10 minutes before the hotel evacuated everyone. "Grab your possessions and leave!" Stacy remembers: "It was one of those moments when you think of what to take. I grabbed my ID, credit cards, phone and wedding ring. This sounds awful, but I wanted to have my ID in case something really bad happens. Yes, I think of the worst sometimes, but this was like nothing I have ever experienced." We went across the street to the Westin but couldn't get in because it was in lockdown. We didn't know where to go, so we sat on the street in front of the Westin. My dad remained calm, our voice of reason. My mom reached out to everyone and told them we were going to be okay. There were so many runners walking around with their heat blankets and medals looking for someone they knew. One female runner appeared to be lost and all of a sudden a man screamed her name. He ran to her, hugged her and they both just started sobbing. I promised myself I would never run without my cellphone.

We were ordered to move from our spot in front of the Westin. We tried the Marriott, but they wouldn't let us in either. We wandered a few blocks into another neighborhood; no businesses, just brownstones. There were a ton of runners and others sitting against a wall. Residents started coming out of their homes to help and offer their support. I remember seeing Carlos with the cowboy hat walking by us, covered in blood. At that time, we still didn't know how many people had been hurt or killed, but after seeing Carlos, we said, "Oh, God. This is bad." While we were sitting against the wall, our "perfect strangers" started appearing. A man named Peter brought us orange juice and bagels. He lived right across the street and was having a marathon party. A woman brought out blankets. We were so cold and so grateful for that. We just kept thanking the many people who were being so kind to us. Another woman and her eight-year-old daughter were telling people they were welcome to come into their home to warm up. We declined, thinking we wouldn't be there much longer.

But we were, and sometime later a woman, Margaritte, walked up to us and asked, "Are you okay and do you need anything? I just live around the corner in a brownstone. Would you like to come to my home?" We were freezing and we all nodded yes. All eight of us followed her. We still had the blanket and Stacy gave it to this poor, shivering guy who was wearing just his running clothes. When we reached Margaritte's house, we had to walk up the most insane staircase to get to her front door. That's when it kicked in how sore I was. Once inside, her home was so warm. We sat down on the couches and the floor. I charged my dead phone. Margaritte apologized for not having very much food, and then brought out chips, chocolate and cheese on serving trays. It was so elegant. We would've been happy just eating chips right out of the bag. Diana kept saying, "These are the best potato chips I've ever eaten in my life!" And Margaritte brought warm Heineken beer, which was awesome! We called the hotel and were told it was okay to go back. Margaritte gave us her phone number and told us to call if we needed help. She said, "You can spend the night if you need to. I have a couple of air mattresses you can sleep on." It was hard to leave there, I felt so safe. We hugged and told her how grateful we were.

> *"Are you okay and do you need anything? I just live around the corner in a brownstone. Would you like to come to my home?" We were all freezing and nodded yes.*

Back at our hotel and watching TV, I finally got the magnitude of what had happened. The images! Ramsey gave me a hug and we just sat there for a long while, watching it together. I said,

"I think I smell." He said, "Yes, you do." We cleaned up and went downstairs for dinner around 9:30.

I couldn't sleep that night and just needed to write about what happened. I remembered everything so vividly at that point and I posted on my blog.

We flew back to Kansas City the next day, and then it all hit me. It was non-stop crying for five days. Non-stop feeling sad and being in a daze. I made the mistake of going to work right away. I wasn't ready to focus on budgets and reports and wound up with tears pouring down my face.

That was the moment when I knew I wasn't yet right. When people would be having a normal conversation about other things, I would be wondering how they could talk about normal happy things.

I didn't understand why I took it so hard. I finished the race, found my family, didn't get hurt and didn't see any of the destruction. Why was I so upset? Crying? Angry? I soon found out I wasn't alone. There were 75 of us from Kansas City who ran Boston. After the race, the organizer sent out a note checking in with everyone. From that, we created a kind of support group. Occasionally, I would get an e-mail in the morning saying, "Having a hard day today. I hope everyone else is doing okay today." It was so helpful knowing someone else was feeling what I was feeling.

I still tear up and get upset, I sometimes feel less secure when traveling and being among large groups of people. Loud noises startle me more than they used to.

Boston changed me, but for the better. The experiences there allow me to see things in a different perspective: I no longer sweat the small things. My priorities are different. It reinforced how precious life is. Boston will forever be a part of me.

Ali Hatfield urges you to consider supporting the One Fund at onefundboston.org. You can read Ali's blog at mileswithstyle.com.

*Jacqui Sager being helped out of a locked-down zone
by a couple of her "perfect strangers"*

185

Jacqueline Sager

Runner

Age 27

Education/Management Consulting

Boston/Chicago

"**G**o Izzy!" spectators were yelling at me. "Go Izzy!" Since that wasn't my name, it took me a while to realize their shouts were meant for me. I was "WUN-ning" for the charity Wake Up Narcolepsy, and the t-shirt the organization gave me read:

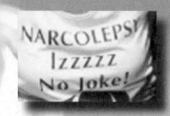

And, as spectators do when they see a name on a shirt, they shout encouragement. "Go Izzy!"

That was one of the funny moments of what had been a really good day for me. I had trained harder and trained well for this race. I felt stronger than at any of my nine other marathons. I took this race very seriously. The past year had been really rough for me around job stress. And I had hesitated about signing up for the race; so much training and the daunting task of raising $3000. Did I have the time and energy to commit to running the Boston Marathon? But I went for it with an "all in" philosophy!

Because this was my 10th marathon, I sent an e-mail the night before to friends, family and acquaintances. It was a note of gratitude and reflection and I sent them my bib number and instructions on how to track me. As an educator, I had stayed connected with many of my American and international students and they were among over 100 people tracking me in the 2013 race. Just overwhelming support. I was so excited!

Race morning, I did not feel well. A shin splint that was acting up and I had a slight fever. But I was grateful that the weather wasn't as miserable as the 2012 Boston and, after all, this was the Boston Marathon, the Holy Grail of marathons!

I stayed back for the first mile and the pace felt good. I wasn't worried about pushing it at this point, just maintaining. My mom was at the top of Heartbreak Hill with some family friends. I missed seeing my mom but saw the others. My dad was at home and tracking from there. My brother, sister and a few handfuls of my best friends were scattered along the route.

My shin splint pain had vanished and my legs were feeling strong, which is exciting to feel at Mile 20 after the hills. I passed one of my friends and she yelled out, "You're ahead of time!" I didn't have a watch with me, but I realized that I was running faster than I thought. Maybe I'm doing really well! And I started running faster. I was passing people right and left, weaving between them. I was feeling so happy and strong. When I got to the Kenmore area, I expected to see my brother, sister and my friends, but didn't at first and was a little disappointed. Then I saw these huge photos of my face. They were the size of my entire torso! Ten enormous versions of me with my tongue hanging out, making a goofy face, each carried by one of my friends. They were running along, trying to catch up and yelling, "You're too early, you're not supposed to be here yet!" They'd been taking a

Photo by Brian Sager

187

group picture as I ran by. I was laughing so hard and was running backwards at this point to see them, still amazed at the sight of all of my huge heads. I thought, this is so great and I love these people so much!

As I went under the bridge and turned right onto Hereford, I thought I was going to finish sub-4:00. Wow! This is so exciting! Just a week earlier, I was intent on just finishing the race; nothing else mattered. But as the finish line was nearing, I became overwhelmed with the symbolism of running Boston and about all the past marathons and the support and encouragement I had gotten from so many people. As I turned left onto Boylston, I was laughing to myself. Just giddy. I was looking down when there was a loud sound. I thought, that sounds like a bomb. And my second thought was, that's crazy! Who would bomb this? Maybe it was a cannon or fireworks. No, that doesn't make sense. Maybe something fell. I ran another block and was in front of Whiskey's when the second explosion went off about a block ahead.

> *I had given up rest, food and, really, everything for this moment.*

My mind, not the sharpest after four hours of running, was thinking that whatever was going on, it wouldn't stop me from finishing. But, wow, that really sounded like a bomb. I tried to reason it out in my head for a few seconds. The cloud of smoke is getting bigger and I can't see the finish anymore. Everyone is still running and I'm in full sprint mode because I was hyper-fixated on finishing. I had given up rest, food and, really, everything for this moment.

The smoke was getting denser; it got eerily silent, followed by screaming. But we're still sprinting. As we got closer to the second bomb, a policeman ran out into the street and put out his arms to stop us. He bellowed, "Everyone stop! Everyone stop!" Most of us did, but some runners bolted past him. He was pushing the rest of us to our right, to the Prudential Center side of Boylston. Runners started piling up and those of us at the front were yelling for the runners behind us to stop. By the time I turned around, the police and volunteers had already pulled the spectator gates across Boylston. It was a stunning moment. What is going on? I want to finish the race. I'm so close to finishing under 4:00! I thought, you've got to let me finish!

As soon as they stopped me, my quads began shaking. You can't run 26 miles and just stop dead. It's like slamming your body into a brick wall. I needed food and water. My body was running on adrenaline. I started shaking and I stumbled. I made it to a light post and railing, hanging on, shaking and feeling confused. Ambulances and police trucks are flying by us. Spectators were screaming and running towards us. More smoke drifted our way. One hysterical young woman was running in our direction and yelling, "Don't go that way. Whatever you do, don't look and don't go that way!" That's when we began to realize that something terrible had happened. We're not finishing the race. This is over. Then there was a mass exodus; people with marks, powder or dirt on them. Stunned looks on their faces. They were hopping and crawling over the barricades into the runner's space. Everyone run! The city is under attack! I didn't know where to go. Some spectators were saying there was another bomb near the Prudential Center. I saw people dropping their bags and running; people running with just one shoe on. So much confusion.

One of the spectators handed us a bottle of water and 20 or 30 runners shared it — taking a sip and passing it to the next runner. That little sip was so crucial. Another female runner and I had collapsed along the railing and were sitting on the street. But there was a sense of urgency to move away from more danger. Flight or fight. I stood up, but there was no flight because I couldn't move. My legs were trembling, like Bambi trying to stand for the first time. I stumbled and fell and as I was going down, I experienced a vision, or hallucination, I guess. I saw all the friends with my big heads, saying "We love you!" And I saw people from other parts of my life, like thumbnail photos. My life didn't flash before my eyes, but the people in my life did. Then I hit the ground. I couldn't move. Wow, I thought, this is it.

A police officer scooped me up. It was so swift; one arm under my legs and one under my back, and he ran with me for about 50 feet. He squeezed us through a barricade and put me down. A middle-aged couple, two of my many "perfect strangers," were hurrying by at that moment and saw that I was shaking. They each put one of my arms around their shoulders and helped me walk. They asked, "Do you have a phone?" I did, but had not been able to get in touch with anyone. My body was going into shock and I hadn't had any food or water, other than that sip. I'm shaking and they are trying to keep me up. "How can we help you?" "Who are your emergency contacts?" "Keep walking, keep walking because we are not out of the danger area yet." They were carrying all of my weight. My face was tingling, my vision was blurry and I couldn't speak, at least coherently. I couldn't get a thought out. My clothes were soaked in sweat, my lips were blue and I had an overwhelming need to vomit. I was doubling over, but they wouldn't let me stop walking. Finally, they let me sit down on a curb. I put my head between my knees. They were rubbing my back and shoulders and told me, "It's okay, honey." They saw a police officer nearby and called to him, "She needs an ambulance!" They were amazing. Thank you, whoever you are.

The officer said, "I've got her," and told the couple to leave the area. And they were gone. He bent down, picked me up and took me to an ambulance. I kept trying to say, "I'm going to be fine. I just need a blanket, water and some food. There are far worse things happening and I'll be okay." But I couldn't get the words out. The EMTs were looking at my pupils and doing some tests. They took my phone and looked at the back of my bib to get my emergency contacts.

They called my brother and sister and released me. I took a few steps and started swaying again so another officer picked me up and ran me across the street. As he did, my head was by his shoulder, right next to his radio. I heard, "Send SWAT!" Send this team, send that team. That's when I realized how big this was. People around us heard his radio, too, and another couple told him, "Go on, sir. We'll take care of her." He handed me off to my second "perfect stranger couple." They were talking to me, telling me I'd be okay, and the woman had her arm around my waist to support me. I managed to tell them my brother was coming. They said, "Okay, but we've got to get you out of this area." It was still crazy, people were screaming and running past us. That couple was so amazing as they just kept telling me, "You're okay, you're okay." They're the ones pictured in the photo at the beginning of my story. Thank you, again, whoever you are!

We got across the street and I looked up to see my brother Brian and sister Annie plowing through the crowd to get to me. They took me from the couple and Annie kept saying to them, "Oh my God, thank you so much!" She had tears streaming down her face and my brother was shaking and crying. He picked me up and ran me across the street. He put me down and I'm crying by then, too, so happy to see them. There were other runners there and we were all shaking uncontrollably. Brian took off his jacket and gave it to me; somebody else gave me their jacket and hat. Before I knew it, I had a jacket on my shoulders, one covering my legs and a hat on my head. I was hyperventilating and having difficulty breathing. A woman kneeled by me and kept a watch on my breathing. In a calm voice she told me, "Breathe, Jacqui. I said breathe."

All of the runners suddenly had three or four people around them. And they appeared to be random spectators, more perfect strangers.

All of the runners suddenly had three or four people around them. And they appeared to be random spectators, more perfect strangers. Someone arrived with a case of water. Others were giving out sports drinks. Some were taking off and handing their coats and sweatshirts to others. Others were walking around asking, "How can I help?" and were offering their phones. It was almost like a trauma treatment area.

We were finally able to get to a friend's house about four blocks away, but before we left the street side trauma unit, we thanked as many of the perfect strangers as we could. The fluids were working and the fog was lifting and I was beginning to process the ordeal. I had an intense need to look at my phone. There were so many texts checking on me. My family was freaking out, especially after my sister's boyfriend called her from his naval base saying he had seen me on TV, being carried out. Thankfully, Annie had sent mass group messages to let people know I was okay.

The support the next couple of days was unbelievable, and the city really came together. On the next Monday after the marathon, my dad was shopping at Staples when a statewide moment of silence was to be observed for the bombing victims at 2:50 p.m. A sales associate, after hearing my dad choke up a bit explaining that he was about to observe the moment, said he would be honored to share it with my dad. They stood there together silently, then exchanged a few words, and went their ways. My dad couldn't stop talking about how much the random sales associate had meant to him. Small things, but so significant.

I don't really remember the rest of April after the 15th. There are many accounts of weird things I did or said and I found that I just simply was not myself. I woke up for a month seeing the chaos on Boylston. When my body recovered enough to start trying to run again, it felt weird, and I had anxiety about running alone. I want to acknowledge the incredible offer of therapy that was made to runners. My volunteer therapist, Joann Pomodoro of MGH, was specifically reaching out to athletes to help them get past the fear of running again. She helped me process the vulnerability I felt about both running and being near the Back Bay. Joann and others like her put time in months later without regard to insurance and ability to pay. She exhibited such kindness, compassion and empathy. Without her, I wouldn't have started running alone again for months more. On April 21st, I'll be running the Boston Marathon again.

Marathon Monday in Boston was marred by senseless violence and I grieve for the victims and their families, but it was also a day marked by great acts of heroism, human kindness and selflessness.

Jacqueline Sager encourages you to support Wake Up Narcolepsy at www.wakeupnarcolepsy.org.

Sarah Pakstis

Runner

Age 35

Product Manager

Cambridge

W ho knew it would be so hard to find someone in Boston who had a charger for an iPhone 5? My search for one led me to my "perfect strangers."

T his was my first Boston Marathon — my first marathon. I had run a half-marathon at Disney World and that went okay. I did it mostly because my brother was gung-ho on running Boston, so I figured I'd run it with him. Then he changed his mind, but I de cided to keep going. I had worked so hard and went through all the craziness that comes with training for a marathon: blizzards, ice, snow, rain, fatigue, aches, pains and doubt. I was never an athlete in school and never really considered myself a runner, but I felt if I did this marathon, I'd have accomplished something; something big. I knew it would be a slog, I am not fleet of foot by any stretch, but I felt like my body, which I had (and have) such a love-hate relationship with, could do it. As I got stronger, running changed the way I viewed myself.

There's so much anxiety leading up to this race, it's so intimidating. I'd done the training and felt confident, and was mostly concerned about the weather because April in Boston, you have no idea what it's going to be. But the forecast was for a per-fect running day, and at the start in Hopkinton, it was perfect. Dry and cool, but not too cold. The atmosphere was great. We did a moment of silence for the victims of the Sandy Hook shootings in Connecticut. Then we walked over to begin the race. I had my iPhone with me and took a bunch of pictures and did some Face-book posts, and then we were off.

The crowds were amazing. All along the way, people

were cheering, really supportive and into it. They made some of the best signs, very funny, inspiring signs for us to read. Once you leave Hopkinton and you cross into Ashland, there's a big biker bar along the route where the people were going nuts. It was awesome. By the time we got there, the marathon had been going on for about an hour, but they were still out there cheering like crazy. I'd read that a veteran runner had advised high-fiving as many kids as possible, so that's what I was doing. The girls at Wellesley were wonderful. There were live bands along the way; one in Framingham was so good I thought, wow, it would be great if I could stop and listen to them. They were awesome.

I spotted my family at Framingham and I was having a good race. I was hoping to do just under five hours. I still wasn't sure I could run a marathon, but I felt really good. At Mile 23, I was going to meet my boyfriend Bryan and then he was going to hop on the T to meet me at the finish with my family. I high-fived him as I ran by. I was definitely feeling fatigue at that point, but knew I was close enough to finish and was going to finish as strong as I could. But, about five or ten minutes later, I saw Bryan again. At first, I was really annoyed because the way the T runs, I was going to beat him to the finish.

"What are you doing here?" I asked.

"I don't know if you want to hear this, but there have been explosions at the finish."

That was all he knew. It didn't really register with me being in such a haze of grit and focus, because people around me were still running and just ahead, the B.A.A. volunteers were still handing out water and cheering people on. So I kept going, I was going to finish. Not much farther, there was a guy standing in the street waving and saying, "The marathon's over, go home!" I thought it was a cruel joke; maybe it was someone who'd had too much to drink. Even though I heard what my boyfriend said, I had no idea how serious it was so I kept running and made it as far as Kenmore Square, where the police had closed the street and told everyone to go home.

I wasn't sure what to do and where to go. I had nothing with me: no money, no keys even if I could get home. I was supposed to meet my family at the finish, but I couldn't get there and I was worried about them. I reached for my phone. It was dead.

I'd been GPS-ing myself through the race and the battery died. I decided to walk back to where I'd last seen Bryan. Along the way, I was trying to find someone with a charger, but I had the iPhone 5, which has a different plug than the previous iPhones.

Some people living along Beacon were outside and offering phone chargers to runners and spectators, but they weren't iPhone 5 chargers. People offered me the use of their phones, but I didn't know anyone's number. They're all in my phone's memory. I kept walking, focused on finding a charger, and noticed that there weren't any more runners coming toward me, the street was empty. I looked around, and it was pretty much deserted. Then emergency vehicles — police, fire and ambulances — were using the marathon route, so I got off the street and used the sidewalk, still searching for someone with an iPhone 5.

B.A.A. volunteers were handing out heat sheets near Kenmore Square, so I was wrapped in one of those as I continued walking along Beacon, freaking out a little more each minute as I wondered about my family. Outside an apartment building, some college kids were hanging out on a stoop, smoking and drinking. I was hysterical and crying. They could tell that I needed help. Once they saw me and took me under their wing, they seemed to sober up a little. I spotted an iPhone 5 in a guy's hand.

"Please tell me you have a charger."

"No, not with me. I don't live here. But maybe someone has one upstairs."

So, we walked up three flights of stairs to an apartment. I must have been running on adrenaline because the stairs didn't bother me.

"Hey, does anyone have a phone charger?" he shouted.

Again, there were iPhone 4 chargers, but none for a 5.

They felt bad that they couldn't help because they could see how desperate I was. And they were all apologetic about the smoking and drinking, and I said, please, I'm invading your space. They knew something had happened, but weren't really paying attention to the coverage. They didn't turn on the news or anything, which was a good thing for me in the state I was in.

The guy who was helping me decided we should go back to his place to use his charger. He, his two roommates, both women, and I started to walk a few blocks to their place. They were offering to call a cab for me, but I said, "I have no money, and you guys are college students, you can't even afford food."

"No, no," they insisted, "we'll get a cab." But, there were no cabs, and we kept walking, finally reaching their apartment. Along the way, they kept talking to me about everything but the marathon to keep my mind off what was going on. One of the girls was a senior majoring in music and wanted to move to LA. I'd lived in LA, so she was asking what it was like to live there. She kept me talking.

We got to their place and I plugged in. They were asking me what kind of music I like and just having a conversation. Do you want a sweatshirt? How about a shower? Gosh no, I was already sitting, all sweaty, on their couch. They were apologetic about the size and condition of their place, but I told them that just letting me inside to get warm and plug in my phone was so great.

It felt like an eternity for my phone to get enough of a charge that I could use it. Finally, I was able to get through and found out everybody was okay. My family was at the finish, and were ushered into a store on Newbury Street; some really generous employees locked them in the store so they could hunker down while the confusion sorted out. So if you are looking for some nice outdoor gear, Barbour has some good stuff and some really kind employees; a heartfelt thanks to them. I got in touch with Bryan and told him where to find me. While I was waiting for him, the kids kept offering me things.

"Do you want something to eat? Something to drink?"

During the marathon, I kept thinking that, gosh, once I'm done, a beer is going to be really sweet. "Well, you know, if you have a beer, that would be awesome."

But they'd been partying most of the day and had run out!

"We'll go out and buy you a beer," they said.

"No, no, that's okay," I said. Again, these were college kids and they'd done so much for me already. They insisted that getting me a beer was the least they could do. So I told them I'd really like to have a Harpoon IPA. One of them went out and got a six pack, and I really appreciated that beer. What my perfect strangers did for me, they probably thought was pretty minor, but it sure helped me out when I really needed it.

Shortly after that, my boyfriend showed up and took me back to Cambridge. We rendezvoused with my parents, my brother, sister-in-law and nieces.

I don't consider myself a victim just because I didn't get to finish the race. I know I'm lucky, but I didn't get to make that right onto Hereford and left onto Boylston. When you're training for four months, doing those long 20-mile runs, that moment is the only thing that keeps you going. To have that taken away doesn't feel good. But I'll have my moment this year.

I just feel awful that this happened to those wonderful spectators, the people we rely on so much. I'm sure most of the spectators aren't runners and don't understand how important they are to us. That's what was so gut-wrenching about the bombings, that they attacked the crowds. The crowds are what lift you. The crowds are really the soul of the marathon. They know what runners need; they're handing out tissues and orange slices and water, they're shouting support at moments when you really need it. They were my legs when mine were like cement, my focus when mine was a mess, my determination when I felt like I was ready to quit. They cheered me on, telling me I inspired them. I was just a runner, but to them, I was a marathoner.

> *The crowds are really the soul of the marathon ... They were my legs when mine were cement, my determination when I felt ready to quit.*

My heart aches for the people who were killed, their families, the people who were injured and will have to live with it for a long, long time; it's so sad.

In the months since, the massive outpouring of support has been incredible. The way the city came together has been amazing. I'm so proud to be from Boston.

Sarah Pakstis encourages you to donate to the One Fund at onefundboston.org.

The marathon used to be a man's only race.
And then came

KATHRINE SWITZER

Photo Mike McMaster

Halina McMaster with the original "Marathon Woman," Boston Marathon legend Kathrine Switzer at the 2013 Expo

Halina McMaster

Runner

Age 45

Business Relationship Manager, Microsoft

Bellevue, Washington

"Good times never seemed so good — so good! so good! so good!"

Neil Diamond's "Sweet Caroline" was the last thing I remember hearing before we were stopped. Someone in the brownstones along Beacon Street was blaring the song and people were singing (yelling) along to it. Pure joy.

Anyone who has run marathons dreams about Boston. It's a bucket list race! I started running years ago as a release, a moving meditation. I got hooked. There's something about the combination of physical and mental challenge to distance running that attracts me; working toward a goal, competing at my own level. I ran four marathons in my early 30s and then stopped running after struggling with Achilles issues. About three years ago, I found a trainer who helped me get back to running again. I spent a year building up to my first full marathon in more than a decade — the San Diego Rock 'n' Roll Marathon in June of 2012. My husband, Mike, was determined to qualify for Boston for the first time at this race and I had hopes to eventually do the same. I would test my speed at San Diego as a new baseline.

Instead, I was a spectator cheering on Mike, my foot in a CAM walker boot after tearing my Achilles during an early morning strength circuit workout in January of 2012. By June, I was cleared to jog short distances and worked my way up to a half marathon in October. Mike qualified for 2013 Boston. We began planning our trip to Boston. It had been hard to be the spectator at races that I had intended to run and didn't want to be on the sidelines for Boston. I was accepted to run with Dana-Farber's Marathon Challenge team. It would be perfect — the challenge of raising money for a great cause and the opportunity to join Mike in running Boston. It would be my post-Achilles tear marathon comeback!

It was chilly the day before the race when we went to Fenway to watch a Red Sox-Rays game and rest our legs. So on marathon morning I layered up. I wore a long sleeve tech tee with my Dana-Farber singlet over it, my race number pinned to my singlet. The sun came out early and it warmed up quickly. By Mile 9, I was overheating. I stopped to attempt to shed a layer but nearly ripped my race number with the timing chip attached to it. So I gave up and kept going. But in the second half my pace was dropping off. I was really hot. At each aid station after sipping my water, I was pouring another cup or two on myself.

Finally, at Mile 16, I couldn't stand it any longer and found a spot to step off the road and carefully shed my long sleeve shirt. I lost a few minutes but by this time I had slowed down enough to where I knew I would miss the four-hour mark, so it didn't matter. I tied the shirt around my waist, vowing to just ditch it if it bothered me. Twice along the course later I thought about tossing that shirt as it blew in the wind a little on the Newton hills, but it wasn't chafing me or anything and it was a nice shirt so I kept it on.

marathonfoto.com
It was a beautiful morning.
Halina and Mike at Hopkinton

The energy as we ran into Boston was so great. A local woman we met the evening before when we went to dinner in the

North End told us that she had run Boston three times and that it was the most amazing marathon we would ever run; that there was nothing else like it and that the energy in any other race will never compare. She was right. It was such an amazing and joyous day. People were cheering and generally having a big party along the course. The crowd noise was echoing off the brownstones. I had passed the Citgo sign and knew I was almost there and could not wait for the finish line experience. Mike would be waiting for me to cross. It was incredible.

My last thought before we stopped was about food. I was hungry with the late race start. I should have eaten more than usual before this race. My Garmin said 25.8 miles when about 15 people in front of me stopped all of a sudden. Police were stretching a rope across the street and blocking us. I heard sirens and was trying to process what could have possibly happened.

I had two thoughts: first, maybe there was a car accident. But, no, it must be a horrific car accident for them to block the marathon course in Boston. Second was, did a runner just die on the course in front of us? But the sirens kept going. The crowd of runners behind us was swelling quickly and the mass of people started to surge, not knowing that we were stopped. We yelled back, relaying a message to stop pushing, that we were stopped. But we still didn't know why. We'd been standing there for about 10 minutes when a runner turned to me, looking at his watch and asked, "Do you think they're going to adjust our times for this?" I told him I didn't know but we needed to find out what happened. We started asking through the crowd. A few runners and some spectators had cellphones and had gotten word that there had been an explosion at the finish, that it was really bad, that people had died. Total shock. The growing crowd, in the thousands by then, got strangely quiet. It was absolutely surreal, it didn't compute.

My first thought was about my husband. Mike had started in the wave ahead of me and would be waiting for me at the finish line. Oh my gosh, could he have died? Could he have lost a limb? How horrific to come and do this race — his dream, our dream — but then lose your life. I was hoping for the best but trying to prepare myself for the possibility that he might have been affected. And I wasn't alone in my worry; nearly every runner had someone waiting for them at the finish line. We had no idea what was going on. We were all in shock.

After Mile 20, you typically aren't thinking the clearest anyway. The shock, that feeling of disoriented fearfulness, is still hard to describe. What could have happened? I didn't think about terrorists at first. I wondered about a propane tank or restaurant-related explosion. I was so worried about Mike.

About 30 minutes into this, "perfect strangers" began appearing. I was standing in the street with tears streaming down my face. A woman walked by offering tissues and the use of her cellphone to runners in need. I was so touched by her kindness. I took her up on both. We tried Mike's number three times. The first two times, all circuits busy. The third time it went straight to his voice mail. I left him a voice mail letting him know that I was all right, I was being held on the course, and that I loved him and hoped he was okay.

I stood there myself, walked a few paces back and forth. The feeling of hunger was gone, replaced with shock and concern. It was shady on the road between the brownstones. I was glad I had held onto the long-sleeve shirt but it was very thin and not much help. I was shivering uncontrollably. A few times someone had yelled that they would try to get blankets to us, but they never arrived. And from the sirens we were still hearing, there were clearly bigger issues to deal with than our impending hypothermia. A spectator nearby saw me shaking and told me to take his jacket. I looked at him and his wife, both bundled up, and said, "No, trust me, I'm covered in sweat and you don't want me to wear that." He insisted and I finally took his coat. Later, some neighbors came out with large rolls of trash bags offering them to us for warmth. I took a trash bag and gave the man his jacket back, thanking him.

Other residents were starting to come around with bottled water and a few other offerings, but I declined. While my body clearly needed water and food, it just wasn't my mental priority to take anything in — my focus was elsewhere. I kept scanning the area looking for Mike, wondering if he was able to walk over and find me, still hoping against the worst.

It was a little over an hour before someone came out yelling to us via megaphone that the race was closed. They would try to get buses for us or we could start walking and detour around the finish to gear check if we absolutely needed to get to gear check. Like many others, I was so cold and feeling so helpless that the prospect of walking and making immediate progress toward Mike was the clear winner. A huge group of us walked several blocks over, relying on each other to recall the directions we had just been given, not thinking the most clearly to say the least.

I walked part of the way with a female runner from Canada. I don't have her name and wish I did. Having someone to talk with helped, although she told me an eerie story about how she had actually worried about something happening at the race after so many gun violence episodes in the States. It was her first Boston, too.

When I finally got to gear check, things were so chaotic and most of the volunteers had been evacuated, so it was a struggle to find the special bus with the Dana-Farber bags on it. Once I did, I spotted a friend from Seattle who also ran — Meredith Buffington. Besides Mike, she was the only runner I knew who was racing that day and I was really glad to see her alive and well. Finally, I found my bag, and my phone — I could try to call Mike again! Just as I grabbed for my phone, a policeman yelled for us all to move down two blocks past Arlington, that there was another suspicious package. Crap, it hadn't occurred to me that more terror could unfold. Strange in hindsight, but your mind just doesn't compute — or want to compute — something like this. I broke into a run and once I was past Arlington, finally got through to Mike — he was safe and alive! I cried tears of joy. I am extremely grateful for all the little things that led to our timing being so lucky that day. And I am so sad for those whose timing was equally unlucky.

After getting back to the hotel, I sat down and started returning e-mails, texts, and phone calls. I did that for two hours before Mike suggested that maybe a shower and some food would be a good idea. We were staying alongside Boston Common, near the crime scene. The employees at our locked-down hotel did the best they could for their captive group of hungry, shaken guests, but Mike and I couldn't get into the restaurant until 8:30 that night. There were helicopters circling all night and two false evacuation alarms made sleep elusive.

I wish I had been thinking clearly enough to get the names of my perfect strangers: the woman with the phone and tissues, the man who loaned me his jacket, the person who gave me a trash bag for warmth, and all of the other help given to those of us shivering from shock, exhaustion, and fear. It was such a stark contrast that day — experiencing humanity at its worst and then immediately experiencing strangers expressing such kindness — people at their best. I'm so grateful for the kindness of strangers that day and so touched by everyone who helped me and helped each other. It's reaffirming after such an atrocity.

Since the race, I've been fortunate to connect with other runners who were there and experienced the event. We have vented to each other, shared thoughts, and helped each other get through it. I am so grateful for my new friends who understand as someone who wasn't there never could. They are a silver lining — a true blessing.

On my shoe is a charm that I got at Kathrine Switzer's book signing at the Expo. It says 261 FEARLESS. I drew energy, strength, and inspiration from that charm on that day. Until 2:50 p.m., it was truly the most amazing race I've had the honor of running. Thanks so much to the B.A.A., volunteers, fans, first responders and the people of Boston for putting on such an amazing, class-act event. I am extremely grateful to the B.A.A. for the chance to come back and finish what I started, show the terrorists that they can't stop us, and run in memory of the victims. It is going to be an extremely emotional right on Hereford, left on Boylston this year.

Halina McMaster encourages you to support the One Fund to aid victims and their families (onefundboston.org), or one of the many great charities like Dana-Farber Cancer Research (rundfmc.org) that works with the marathon each year. Pick one that moves you.

*Kathy Glabicky at Mile 23, about 10 minutes before
she and thousands of other runners were stopped*

Kathy Glabicky

Runner

Age 39

Marblehead, Massachusetts

Certified Personal Trainer, owner of Chakra

I felt like I was 10 years old. I was scared, crying, freezing, didn't know what was going on, and felt so alone standing in the middle of Beacon Street.

"Do you want to stand with us?" asked a kind, grandmotherly woman standing at the curb with her husband and son. "Have you been able to talk to your family?" I hadn't talked to my father for 11 years. His death from cancer was one of the reasons I was running Boston. I knew Dana-Farber was a charity sponsor, so I applied, but was surprised at how difficult it was. I went through three rounds before they accepted me. Dana-Farber is a huge organization and had 500 runners. We raised $4.7 million and 100% of the Boston Marathon money goes to cancer research.

I had run some half-marathons, but this was my first attempt at a full one. It was unbelievable. The tone was so much different. First, the size of the crowd was huge. At the start in Hopkinton, people were screaming, there was a band blaring, there were flags waving; the energy was out of control! That energy continued all along the course and while some areas had more, it was crazy throughout the whole marathon. That is what gets you through. It's a serious race and it is not easy. I didn't know exactly where the dreaded hills were but I knew they were coming up after I'd passed 10 miles. I knew I was going to have to dig deep. At this point I was running 9:15 miles and was on track for my goal. I had a watch to track my pace and I was scheduled to come in at 4:25.

A woman I knew from Marblehead ran with me the first 10 miles, but I lost her when she stopped to use the bathroom and I kept going. I was feeling good and I knew I had a friend waiting at Mile 12 and had family waiting at Mile 16. When I saw my mother, sisters and their kids, I stopped for about a minute to talk to them. I was so excited and thought, okay, I'm at Mile 16 and I knew that once I got to Mile 20 I was going to be fine. I knew I could do it.

Then I hit Heartbreak Hill and thought, Holy Crap! But I didn't stop and went for it. The crowds at Boston College were the best! The college kids had their hands out and I was high-fiving them and thinking, oh, I needed that so badly! When I think back now, I think of these kids and how happy they looked and how important they were to me.

At Mile 23, I saw Jonathan, one of my best friends who planned to meet my husband John and me at the finish line. I was so psyched and yelled to him as I went by, "I've done it!" But as I got to the end of the street where the route turns onto Commonwealth, the runners were stopped. Then, as I slowed to a walk, I saw that the crowd was silent and I just didn't know why. I thought someone might have passed out and people were helping. Then I heard sirens and saw the police cars and fire engines and thought, what the hell happened? Everyone was asking, "What's going on?" and someone said, "There was an explosion." "Was it a gas line?" "Maybe it's a terrorist attack!" We just didn't know. I'm hearing more sirens and I'm getting nervous. Some of the spectators started to panic. Someone said something about a bomb near the finish line. "What? My husband and friend were at the finish line!" I was planning to meet John as I turned onto Boylston. In my head I said, "Please, God ... !" If John kept with the plan, I was going to look for him on the right side. I hoped he stayed where he said he would be.

Within a minute of stopping, I was freezing. It had been a perfect day for running, but not for standing still after you'd run 25.2 miles. I had no phone or anything. There was a hotel right at the turn, Hotel Buckminster, and runners were trying to go inside to warm up, but the hotel was locked down. The hotel staff was handing out some blankets, but there were so few. Several runners were sitting on the ground, huddled together, sharing blankets.

Other than worrying about where my husband and friends were, I kept thinking of 9/11. If this was a terrorist bombing, I thought the John Hancock and the Prudential were about to blow up. It was like Boston was being attacked. I was petrified, the scariest thing I've ever experienced. Not only did we not know what had happened, we didn't know what was coming next. OMG! Were more bombs going to go off? I wanted to get the hell out of there, but to where? Not knowing the devastation just a mile ahead, a number of the runners had become angry and were demanding, "Let us through!" The police yelled back, "The race is over!" We runners are thinking, what the hell are you talking about? We're so close, we're almost there! We'd just been running for four hours, we were exhausted and we knew we were almost done. And this was a race I trained so hard for. Don't stop me!

Slowly we're starting to realize something really bad happened and we're starting to panic. Runners are asking spectators, "Can I use your phone?" I remembered that Jonathan saw me at Mile 23 so he knew I was close to this spot. He'll find John and tell him he had seen me. I was waiting and was so scared. Should I stay where I am? We couldn't walk forward because the police wouldn't let us. I didn't know what to do.

My "perfect stranger" emerged at that moment. I was still standing where I stopped, in the middle of the street. There was an older lady standing at the curb with her husband and son. She asked if I needed help, and then offered me her phone, and her son gave me his jacket. It was so nice of them. I stood with her and was almost cuddling with her, getting warmed up. It felt like she was my grandmother. I was so alone and so worried about my husband. It felt so good to be standing next to someone who cared.

I used her phone to text John and Jonathan. "This is me. I'm okay," I wrote, and gave them my location. I texted another friend who had been in the same area with my husband. She wrote back that they had separated after the second bomb and lost each other. She didn't know where he was.

In about half an hour, Jonathan ran up to me yelling, "Kathy!" I was so happy to see him. I asked him if he had talked to John. He had not, but assured me that we would figure it out.

It turns out John was on Boylston near the Mandarin Hotel, about halfway between the turn from Hereford and where the second bomb went off in front of the Forum. He was on the "right" side as we had planned. My friends were across the street from him, a little closer to the Forum, by the Crate & Barrel. When the first bomb went off by the finish line, they thought maybe it was fireworks. When the second one went off, people on the jammed sidewalks panicked, jumped over the barriers onto Boylston, and ran. John was running away from the finish line and toward where I was. He had been tracking me and knew I was close. My mother and sisters, who had seen me at Mile 16, were already home at this point and were beside themselves. They knew I was due to get in between 4:00 and 4:30. They couldn't reach John because his phone was dead. They were seeing the coverage on TV and people were calling them to see how I was. But they did get through to Jonathan before he found me. They begged, "Please find her!"

My other friend who had texted me did find my husband and eventually we all found each other. Exhausted, we just wanted to go home, the T wasn't running, and our next best option was a friend's house, about two miles away. I could barely walk, I was in so much pain, so John and my friends had to help me. One friend's husband is a police officer who brought along a group of teenaged girls. They had been in the bleachers near the finish line and were upset and still in a state of shock. When we finally got to my friend's house, we waited it out and planned our route to drive back to Marblehead, a journey that took three hours.

All these months later, I still say to John, "I can't believe I ran the Boston Marathon and there was a terrorist attack. This can't be." It's unfathomable. I've watched the coverage on TV and couldn't believe I was there.

As for running this year, I am! I'm going to finish. But, I'm a little bit scared and I know it's gonna be crazy!

Kathy Glabicky urges you to consider supporting the Dana-Farber Cancer Institute in Boston: dana-farber.org.

Kielo Sauvala at the starting line in Hopkinton

Kielo Sauvala

Runner

Nine Boston Marathons

Physical Therapist

Citizen of Finland

Residence: Glenview, Illinois

Y ou could say that I was running the Boston Marathon because of a bet; the one I accepted 25 years earlier in my home city of Helsinki, Finland, where a friend bet me I couldn't run the Helsinki City Marathon. Thirty-seven marathons later, I was ready for my ninth Boston.

April 15th was a cool, crisp day, perfect for running. Everyone at the start was in a happy mood. Four hours later, my run had gone well, but not my best. I hadn't trained as much as I should have. But I didn't walk and I was happy with that.

As I was running toward the finish line on Boylston, I saw the first bomb go off, and I thought it had something to do with a Patriots Day celebration at the finish line. Maybe it was because I'd been running so long and my brain wasn't working anymore, but it didn't occur to me that it was a bomb. I heard people screaming, but I thought that was just part of the excitement.

When the second bomb went off, I knew right away what it was. I was directly across from it, and shrapnel was flying at the other runners and me. Luckily, I was running toward the right side of the street, opposite from the blast. I didn't know until later what hit me, but one ball bearing buried itself in my skin a few inches above my left ankle, and another one left a hole as it grazed my leg. The air pressure from the bomb nearly knocked me over. The guy running next to me did lose his balance, and I can't say I was any kind of a hero because rather than help him up, I went into survival mode. I wanted to get away, and was wondering, was there a third bomb? A fourth one? I was in shock. It seemed like time was moving so slowly, but I knew that within a matter of seconds the police and volunteers in yellow jackets were pushing us back, making us turn around. That was fine with me because that's the direction I wanted to go.

The Mandarin Oriental Hotel was about a half-block back up the street and it let a lot of people in. That's where my "perfect strangers" appeared. Hotel employees gave me towels so I could clean my leg and bandages that I put on the wounds. The ball bearing that was in my skin was bothering me and it wasn't that deep, so I used my fingernail to dig it out. The hotel had water for us, and because we were freezing, they wrapped us up in a bunch of curtains that had been hanging on a nearby laundry carrier.

But our moment of refuge didn't last long as the hotel staff pushed us upstairs into an adjacent shopping mall. They were concerned about us being so close to the glass windows on the Boylston Street side of the building. Once we were in the shopping area, a race spectator let me use a cellphone to call a friend and leave a message for him that I was okay.

The next morning, the Finnish Embassy in Washington, D.C. called me. I'm still a citizen of Finland and the embassy was contacting all 17 of the Finns who had been registered to run.

The day after the bombings, I went for a walk and saw the memorial that was piling up, but I didn't cry. I must have stayed in shock the whole time I was in Boston. It wasn't until I got home to Illinois that I was able to cry. I tried to follow the coverage of the bombings on TV and in the newspapers, but it was too much, too traumatic.

I've run races since then, and as I neared the finishes, I had flashbacks to the bombings. It's a horrible feeling, that fear, but I can't let fear rule my life that way.

In October, I finished my 40th marathon, my 15th Chicago, in 3:49 which qualified me for the 2015 Boston Marathon. I had already qualified for Boston 2014 and I'll be there. It will be a healing process for me to run it and finish it, although it didn't bother me that I couldn't finish; I was more interested in running from danger.

Kielo Savaula urges you to consider supporting the Dana-Farber Cancer Institute in Boston: dana-farber.org.

Erica Newman Nash

Runner

Massage Therapist

36 years old

Bellevue, Washington

There have been many perfect strangers in my life, especially in Boston, the city that saved me. From the age of five, I began making trips from my family's home in Providence, Rhode Island, to Tufts/New England Medical Center/Floating Hospital to see the amazing "Dr. G." (Dr. Michael Goldberg). "Dr. G." and his team in Pediatric Orthopedics believed in me and my potential to beat the statistics for kids with cerebral palsy. More importantly, they helped me believe in me.

There were many reasons I shouldn't have even been standing at the starting line of the Boston Marathon on Monday, April 15, 2013, let alone running. Here's the short list:

- I was born 10 weeks premature to a 16-year-old mother. She may not have been able to keep me, but she entered a home for pregnant teens to get care and education for the duration of her short pregnancy.
- Within a year and a half of being adopted, I was diagnosed with CP. My parents were advised to institutionalize me. Thankfully, they didn't believe that was right.
- In order just to walk, I had multiple spine, foot and tendon surgeries.
- I wore leg braces until I was 10.
- At the age of 14, I had advanced arthritis in my feet.
- By age 22, I had no disc left at L/5-S/1.
- 2009 brought a year-long battle with kidney cancer.

In the fall of 2010, in an effort to get fit after surviving kidney cancer, I started running. During long walks, I began running in 15-second intervals. I ran my first 5K in December of 2010, my first half-marathon in June of 2011 and my first full marathon in February of 2012. Unfortunately, though, this body was not designed for walking, let alone running. A stress fracture in my right tibia confined me to a wheelchair from April through August of 2012. I thought I had rid myself of injuries by the autumn of 2012, but in the 10 weeks prior to the 2013 Boston Marathon, bad posterior shin splints kept me from running at all. I trained on an Alter-G, reverse gravity treadmill.

So there I stood at the 2013 Boston Marathon start line with 14 other mobility-impaired runners. It was a cold morning and my blood was pumping with excitement. I was prepared and all I wanted to do in that moment was to cross the finish line. Admittedly, I made a common rookie mistake: I took the first 10K too fast. It was hard not to pick up the pace (around mile 5.5) when passed by elite runners, such as Shalane Flanagan and Kara Goucher, whom I idolize.

By the time I entered Newton, I was running 10 minutes slower than my goal pace. My projected finish was 2:50 p.m. but, luckily, my heart told me to stop and hug my husband, kids and parents on my way up Heartbreak Hill. Then, inexplicably, my body told me to slow down after Heartbreak Hill.

The last clear memory I have is passing the "one mile to go" mark. Then, with the Citgo sign in my sights, I knew I was going to finish. All of the rehab had worked and I was going to cross the finish line with my hands in the air and a smile on my face that would energize me for years to come! I remember calculating my plan of attack so I could finish on a run interval rather than a walk. As I entered Kenmore Square, there was a runner to my right who had gone down. That's not unusual at the end of a marathon. But then the crowd in front of me quickly thickened. Within a minute, I realized we were barricaded in. We couldn't go forwards or backwards. I was at a dead stop after nearly six hours of running and walking.

We were held at mile 25.7 for over an hour. People were lending phones and sweatshirts to stunned, shivering runners. It remains an utter blur, almost as if I were watching an old movie through a window screen. It didn't seem real. I sat on the curb near the tip of the park in the middle of Kenmore Square — stunned, confused and virtually paralyzed.

By the time we were allowed to leave the area, I was vomiting, had hypothermia and major spasms in my legs. According to the wonderful runners and bystanders around me — my "perfect strangers" — I was blue and shaking uncontrollably. They acted quickly, and I didn't understand why everything seemed so urgent to them. Some wrapped me in garbage bags, while others ran for help. One woman, who I met on a Facebook support group, remembered taking off her yellow face shirt and waving it in the air to gain the attention of the medics who were trying to make their way through a sea of 5,000+ people to find the injured. I hadn't realized until then just how intense that moment was for everyone involved. The EMTs found me and rushed me to Mass General, where my legs continued convulsing for seven hours. I spent two days there getting my pain and spasms under control.

The perfect strangers who helped me get medical attention, selflessly stepped up to save me in life and body. There were a few other instances, though, of perfect strangers reaching out to heal broken hearts and bruised souls. These acts of giving must not go unnoticed. Helping someone smile in the midst of tragedy is a beautiful act of loving kindness.

The marathon day Bruins game was supposed to be the first NHL experience for my hockey fanatic children. Understandably, it was cancelled. In an effort to help my family heal, my sister-in-law, who lives in Newton, asked a season ticket holder if he knew of a way to get affordable tickets to the Wednesday game against long time rival Buffalo. By some miraculous good fortune, our story made it all the way to Bob Sweeney, former Bruin, and current executive director of the Bruins Foundation. He called us as I was being discharged from the hospital, and invited my husband and kids (I was in no condition) to be guests of the Bruins Foundation in a suite.

My kids were thrilled to think about something other than the bombing. Not only did they get their first NHL experience, but they attended the game that is now known for its beautiful communal rendition of the national anthem. During the game my husband and children were gifted with Bruins swag, and were visited by none other than Ray Bourque, idolized by all in our family. Yes, this was pulled off by upper-level folks, but they didn't have to do it. Even though Boston lost to Buffalo that night, my kids told my husband, "it was the best night of the worst week of their lives." It was much more than a game.

Then there were the most random small acts of kindness by strangers. I always forget the airport story; I was really out of it, but it was so meaningful to my husband. When we were leaving Boston, I saw a *People Magazine* at the kiosk near our gate. My husband was about to buy it for me, but they called for assisted boarding. I was in a wheelchair, feeling very sick from meds, so we had no time to buy it and made our way to the gate. As we handed our tickets to the agent, a woman tapped on my husband's shoulder. "For you," she said. "Have a safe trip." She handed my husband the *People*. I never realized, until writing this piece, how much that perfect stranger's small act meant to us in the grand scheme of all that happened on that trip. As I sit writing this, bawling in the warm room of my son's hockey rink, I realize how much it really did matter.

At that point, injured physically and emotionally, I thought Boston 2013 was going to be my last full marathon. I was sure of it. Being a slow runner adds significantly to my training hours and is very hard on my body (and my family). But the emotional scars have been far harder to overcome than the physical injuries. Anxiety, panic, lengthy bouts of crying and deep feelings of confusion and sadness have plagued me since the marathon.

Life changed after we returned to Seattle. After recovering from my physical injuries, I decided to scale back my massage practice and return to the non-profit world, focusing on working with the special-needs community. In July, I started working for the Friendship Circle of Washington, a nonprofit organization that provides respite, therapies, education and activities for families, children and teens with special needs. Witnessing terror, and benefitting from the random kindness of strangers, made me want to work to make the world a better place for everyone.

Nonetheless, even though I have a new focus, some days the only thing that keeps me going is the feeling that I can never stop until I finish what I started on April 15, 2013. I have the chance to train harder and get stronger and finish all 26.2 in 2014; the chance to change how the story ended last year. How many people actually get the chance to change the end of a story like that? Mind over matter, the concept of never stopping until you finish, is a huge part of success in endurance sports, especially for a novice, let alone a novice with a permanent musculoskeletal disability. So, I will train, and I will never stop until I cross the finish line on Boylston on April 21, 2014.

I am not only a runner, a marathoner, or a Boston marathoner, I am a survivor.

Erica Newman Nash urges you to consider supporting Friendship Circle of Washington, which extends a helping hand to families who have children with special needs and involves them in a full range of social experiences.
www.friendshipcirclewa.org

Gratitude

Gratitude is not just saying thank you — it has a much broader definition. Gratitude is wonder and appreciation. It is savoring instead of taking things for granted. It is looking on the bright side of setbacks. It is fathoming abundance and counting blessings. It is an antidote to negative emotions, a neutralizer of envy, avarice, hostility, worry and irritation. Gratitude involves a focus on the present moment, on appreciating your life as it is today.

— Sonja Lyubomirsky, Ph.D.

Photos courtesy Lacey Cumming

A young marathon fan celebrates with Lacey Cumming.

219

Lacey Cumming

Runner

Age 23

Boston

Works at Boston Children's Hospital

"**H**ave you seen my dad?"
I worried about my dad, Jack, who, at 67, is a crazy
running man. He had run three Bostons in a row, but it
still makes me nervous for someone his age to be running that far.

"Have you seen my dad?" I asked the Boston Children's
running coaches who, all race long, ran up and down supporting
our team as we hit the Newton hills.

"Yes, he's ahead of you, but he's not having the best day."

A few minutes later, another coach told me, "He's not
having a good day; you'll definitely catch up to him." I did catch
him at about the Citgo sign, Mile 24. I tapped him as my running
partner Amy Wagner and I kept going because we were feeling
good and he, although he wasn't doing great, seemed focused and
in a zone. Less than a mile later, we started hearing ambulances.
Of course, I immediately thought, "Oh goodness, I hope it's not
my dad!"

Amy, who was my roommate at Bentley University, and
I passed the "one mile to go" sign. We looked at each other and
smiled. "We're doing this! We're going to finish!" We were just
moments away from what every runner looks forward to the most:
right on Hereford and left on Boylston. All of our best friends
from school were going to be on Boylston to see us. But, just as
we were about to go under the Mass Ave bridge before Hereford,
we were stopped.

Someone said, "There's an explosion at the finish line."
I thought it must be an electrical explosion. There was so much
electrical stuff going on at the finish, that must have been it. I
didn't really think much of it and imagined that we would be run-

ning again soon. I had worn a Camelbak and had thrown my phone in at the last minute. When I turned it on, I saw that my mom had sent a group text message to my dad and me saying, "Explosions at the finish line. Are you guys okay?" I still didn't panic, because I knew my mom and sister were okay, and soon heard that my friends were okay. And I knew my dad would be catching up to us soon.

When Dad arrived, he didn't look well.

"Are you okay?"

"I'm fine," he said, but wasn't very talkative. He sat down and I stood behind him so he could lean on me. I was stressed about him, plus we'd been standing for several minutes and were getting cold. Friends had been tracking me on a GPS app and knew exactly where we were. They had been waiting nearby at Hereford and Boylston but when the bombs went off they headed toward Comm Ave. They spotted a door to an apartment building that was open and saw they would be able to charge their phones. One friend came to find Amy, my dad and me, and when they saw that we were freezing, suggested we go there to warm up.

I spotted a girl I went to high school with a few rows ahead of me, Jacqueline. Her parents had jumped in and run the last several miles with her. I asked them if they wanted to come with us to warm up, and her mother looked at me and said, "Well, Jacqueline kind of wants to finish."

I was, "Well, I do too, but we're going to go stand inside until we get moving again." None of us understood the severity of what was going on, and we felt we were going to get to finish the race.

When we got to the apartment building, some of my friends were crying. We're all hugging, and I'm asking, "What's wrong?" I had just run 25 miles and wasn't on top of my game.

Some guys who lived upstairs — our first "perfect strangers" of the day — came down and saw we needed help. They were bringing us water and whatever pieces of clothing they could grab. I wound up wearing some boy's flannel pajama pants. My dad put on a flannel shirt, covered by a Reggie Bush football jersey and a scarf. Just random pieces of clothing. We stayed there for a while. I looked outside and noticed the runners were moving.

I said, "Dad, let's go, we're probably going to get to finish." I still wasn't thinking clearly.

We thanked the boys who had been helping us and I returned the pajama pants, but my dad was still wearing the Bush jersey so we told them we'd send it back to them. One of the guys told my dad, "Don't worry about it; I don't even like Reggie Bush anymore, just keep it."

When we got outside, the runners were being ushered one street over away from Comm Ave, and then we were on our own. Volunteers were handing out the heat sheets, and I wrapped up my dad in a couple of them to try to keep him warm. One of my spectator friends, Julia, insisted on coming with us, worried that we weren't in the best of shape to be wandering around. After that, we went back on Comm Ave and were walking toward Boston Common. Several blocks later we were glad to see that BarLola was open. We sat and texted and drank water. My dad had his credit card with him so we ordered some food, but the fire alarm went off before it arrived and we had to evacuate. My apartment is in Boston, but my roommate was already headed out of the city with some of our friends, as her aunt and uncle came to pick them up shortly after the bombs went off, and my keys were at the Mandarin, which we couldn't get to. Plus, my apartment was three miles away and we were in no shape. So we kept walking along Comm Ave and made a right on Arlington where we tried to get into the Taj Hotel. But it was locked down and they wouldn't let us in.

About then, we started seeing army tanks and soldiers, and that freaked me out, because as we're walking around, looking for a place to go inside, we were about the only ones around. If there is someone out there with a gun, we're going to be the first to go. We called a couple of more hotels and were told they had no rooms and couldn't let us in. We walked another few blocks to the Park Plaza. They were more than accommodating and let us in. There were no rooms, but they let us into the lobby.

A woman who'd been sitting there walked up to us. She introduced herself: Ashley Gilreath from North Carolina. Ashley was our second "perfect stranger" of the day.

"Are y'all trying to book a room?"

We said, "Yes."

I must not have looked very good because she looked at me again and asked, "Are you okay?"

I lost it, broke into tears and sobbed, "No, I'm not!" She gave me a big hug as I told her we'd been walking for over an hour and no one would let us in until the Park Plaza did.

She said, "Come up to my room, I'll let you shower." Her husband, Jim, had run the marathon. She took me upstairs, and I'm still crying. Ashley, who I found out later was a kindergarten teacher and had two children of her own, was so comforting. While my dad and I are very close, at moments like that, you want your mom, and I hadn't seen mine yet, so just having someone motherly like that to talk to and take care of me was amazing. It felt good to shower. Ashley gave me a long-sleeve shirt to wear, and it felt good that she was there for me.

We hung out downstairs in the lobby with Ashley and Jim for about an hour and a half until my mom and sister got there. They had been watching the race across Boylston from the Forum. They ran into the Mandarin, then were evacuated into the Prudential and

Safely inside our perfect stranger's hotel room, my dad is still wearing another stranger's football jersey and my friend Ally's scarf.

then out of there, too. They wound up in the South End where they got in a restaurant. My mom's a runner and had trained to run Boston three times, but one year broke her ankle two weeks before the marathon; in 2012, she bowed out because she's Irish as they come and she knew she wouldn't last in the heat, and before 2013 she was injured again. 2014 will be her year.

Late that night, we made it to my parents' home in Sudbury. The next morning, my dad lay down on my bed with me and we were watching TV and trying to process what had happened. Until then, it had been such a blur, it hadn't really sunk in. It wasn't until later that day we were allowed to go into the Mandarin and collect our belongings, and I was able to go back to my apartment.

I never lose sight of the fact that I was a lucky one. Yes, it was stressful, but I came out okay. My family and friends are fine. My heart breaks for the three people who died, their families, and the dozens of people who survived the bombings but were left with lifelong challenges. I admire how strong they are in their re-coveries, and the response of the people of Boston has continued to be amazing; Boston Strong!

Ashley and I became Facebook friends and we're making plans to get together in Boston this year. Jim will be running the marathon again. My dad and I would like to do something to show our appreciation for their kindness, but she and Jim have humbly declined our offers. For now, we'll have to be satisfied knowing that they know how their kindness impacted our lives, that there is goodness in the world and they personify it.

Lacey Cumming urges you to consider supporting the great work being done at Boston Children's Hospital, which not only responded to victims of the bombings, but on a daily basis provides loving care and hope as its researchers make amazing discoveries that change children's lives: giving.childrenshospital.org.

Kelley and Kay Huemoeller at the finish line on Sunday, April 14, 2013, excited about the next day's race

Nicole Maneri, who became a perfect stranger on Marathon Monday

Nicole Maneri
Perfect Stranger
Age 30
Medical Sales for Medline Industries, Inc.
Boston

Kay Huemoeller
Runner
Age 62
Greenwood Village, Colorado

Kelley Huemoeller
Spectator
Age 29
Denver, Colorado

NICOLE: I've gone to the Boston Marathon almost every year since living in Boston. I worked here every summer while attending college and when I moved here full time in 2007, I didn't realize what a big deal it was. It was a social event; maybe go to a friend's house for a party. But then it became more important. Many of my friends ran it, and I went to watch and cheer for them.

KELLEY: The Boston Marathon 2013 was going to be so much fun. My mom was running the race for the second time and my good friends Eliza Deland, Kelli Briggs and Erica Broadwell were coming to support my mom. It was going to be a great weekend. We shopped, went to the Expo and our larger group of friends went to a pasta dinner in the North End on Sunday night. The only two runners at the table, my mom and our friend Katie Montiel Vidaillet, were anxious, but the rest of us were in the best of spirits and had a great time. Our plans for Marathon Monday: we would all watch the race and meet at 3:15 at Stephanie's on Newbury Street to toast our runners and celebrate their accomplishments. It was going to be a great afternoon!

KAY: I've been running since college. I love to eat and drink beer and running allows me to maintain my weight but what it does for me mentally is my true motivation. It almost does more for me mentally than physically. My goal was to run one full marathon. I chose the Rock 'n' Roll in Phoenix in 2007, which turned out to be the coldest race in its history. But I had a good one and I was surprised to learn that I had qualified for Boston. Well, how do you not run Boston? In 2008, I did. My husband, Jim, and our daughter Kelley came to watch me. It was a difficult experience. The race was grueling because I ran with an injury and I missed re-qualifying by two minutes. Adding to the difficulty was Jim's unusual behavior, which I found out later might have been caused by the rapid onset of dementia. But I knew I had to run the Boston Marathon again someday.

Jim passed away in 2011. In his honor, Kelley and I ran the 2012 Chicago Marathon. I didn't tell anyone, but my personal goal was to re-qualify for Boston. I did, and made plans to run the 2013 Boston. It was going to be closure for me in many ways. It was time to move forward from my husband's death. The training was difficult mentally and physically, but I knew I could do it. The 2013 Boston Marathon would be my last marathon.

KELLEY: On Monday morning, Mom was super nervous and I helped her get all her stuff together and walked her to the VIP tent to meet Katie for the bus ride to Hopkinton. Erica, Kelli, Eliza and I went to a long brunch and then headed over to Hereford and Commonwealth to watch the race. We were looking for my mom and finally saw her. As she ran by, we started yelling and screaming, but she didn't hear us.

KAY: I get pretty nervous before a race, but getting together with our friends on Sunday was a good distraction for me. We had such a great time at the Expo, brunch at Trident and a pasta dinner in the North End that night. The race was not one of my best, but once I got over Heartbreak Hill, I felt like I was going to make it. I will finish this race and this would be it! And I would have closure. Kelley and her friends were watching the race and I thought they would all be at the finish. I saw the "one mile to go" sign. That's when I turned it on; I had all this extra energy. I felt excited that I was going to finish and then meet everyone for the celebration after. And I would have a beer!

NICOLE: Monday was a beautiful day. I went to the Red Sox game that morning and hadn't planned to go down to the race. But my friend Damian invited me to the game and he had never been to the marathon so we decided to go. As we left Fenway after the game, we stopped in Kenmore Square to watch the runners, and then headed to the finish line to see my friend. We got to Boylston Street and were right across from the convention center. The crowds were huge and everyone was cheering. We made our way to the front of the barricade and were standing in the front row. We were watching the runners take their left on Boylston, and the first bomb went off. I saw it, smelled it and felt it. There was a fireball and then smoke mushroomed into the air.

KELLEY: Right after we saw Mom run by, we heard the first explosion. At first we thought it was a cannon. Then there was another one. Everyone along Hereford continued cheering as if they were just part of the festivities.

KAY: As I was running down Hereford, I remember hearing a boom that sounded like fireworks and thought, I don't remember them doing fireworks in 2008. What a neat addition to the Boston Marathon! But why would they do it for the third wave? We were the slower runners. At this point, I was still focusing on finishing. I was hauling and was going to finish with a pretty good time.

As I turned the corner to go on to Boylston, I saw a female runner on the ground. She had her hand over her face and was kneeling down. The police were yelling, "Stop!" I did, but, really? This runner is injured and you're making me stop running the marathon when I can see the finish line? The police said, "Something happened at the finish," and they kept pushing us over to the side of the street. But it didn't occur to me that it was something horrible. My first feeling was anger toward the policeman. I'm a competitive person and I wanted to finish! It was all kind of surreal. I looked around there was only one other runner near me. There was a lot of confusion and I saw people on their cellphones and crying. It was so chaotic. I looked down Boylston toward the finish and saw smoke. But nobody had told me what had happened yet.

KELLEY: We were far enough away that we didn't see or smell the smoke, and I said, "Let's run and meet Mom at the finish." We headed up Hereford and as we hit Boylston, suddenly everyone was running at us. They looked afraid; it was fear and chaos all of a sudden. People were yelling, "Get away! Get away!" and "Go toward the river."

It was all happening so fast and the girls and I just stopped. Behind us, I saw the police stopping runners. Then we knew it was a bomb. It was so crazy. I was just trying to process what was going on. I talked on the phone to our friend Diane and she said she was looking for her daughter Katie. I just thought: this isn't real. All of a sudden, people were running everywhere and the four of us started running down the alley between Newbury and Boylston. It was just chaos, people were screaming as they ran. We saw four cops running toward us, but they were not able to tell us what was going on or where to go. My brother James called from Philadelphia to see if our mom had finished the race. And I told him, "James, turn on the TV, tell me what's going on!" He asked, "What are you talking about? Is Mom slowing down?" He had no idea what happened. I said, "James, there are bombs going off and I don't know where Mom is." And then my phone cut out and I'm sure he panicked. I was beginning to panic myself. I didn't know what to do and I didn't know where my mom was.

NICOLE: My friend Damian asked, "Do they have fireworks at the marathon?" I said, "No. Something's not right." And I looked at the police officers lining the interior of the street and they had their heads to their shoulders, listening to their radios. I said, "I don't think that was supposed to happen." The next explosion went off and it was even closer to us. And that's when people started running. The cops were yelling, "Get out of here!" We backed up against the wall, just taking it in and waiting for the crowd to stampede by. We then walked back up to the guardrail. And then

Kay appeared, all of a sudden, right in front of me.

KAY: I saw Nicole, my perfect stranger, standing at the barricade, holding a cellphone. I hadn't seen Kelley and the girls on Hereford where we planned to see each other, so I assumed the worst, that they were by the bombs. I asked her, "Can I please use your phone? My daughter is down at the finish line."

NICOLE: I told her, "Yes, of course." I gave her my smart phone. She looked at it for a moment and said, "I don't know how to use this."

I got her to the right screen, but she was shaking so badly that she couldn't type in her daughter's number. I typed it in, but the service was down.

I told her, "We'll keep calling her."

The police were now telling us to get out of the area and pushing everyone back to the Charles River. She said she wasn't from here and didn't know her way around. She was shivering so badly, I gave her my coat.

She said, "No, I don't want to take your coat."

And I said, "You've just run a marathon. Please take it."

I don't even think I knew her name at this point, but Kay reminded me of a friend of my mom's. She's so petite and I just wanted to pick her up and throw her on my back and take her home. I wanted to make sure she was okay. I grabbed her hand and said, "Follow me."

KAY: Nicole kept saying, "I'm not going to leave you until you find your daughter."

NICOLE: Kay was just in shock and kept asking, "What happened?" I told her I thought it was a bomb. She was so worried about finding Kelley. And Damian and I were scared, but I just thought we have to help this woman. We must help her find her daughter. We couldn't leave her, not knowing if Kelley was okay.

KELLEY: I had no idea where my mom was but I was convinced

she was in danger. She would've been so close to the explosions. A woman ran by us, hysterical, with blood on her shoe, and I went into a state of shock. I couldn't really talk and I was having a panic attack. I didn't know what to do and I didn't know where my mom was. I just stood there. I was probably more hysterical than I remember. I felt responsible for inviting my friends to come to this and I didn't know if there were more bombs. Are they in trash cans? Are they in buildings? I was so scared. Eliza was crying and no one knew what was going on.

My friend Kelli stayed pretty calm and kind of took control as she and my friends were trying to console me. Kelli said, "We need to make ourselves safe." All I could think about was going after my mom. But I knew it was not a good idea to go back to find her. We needed to get to someplace safe and then figure out a way to locate her. We didn't think that being in an alley off Newbury was a safe place to be, so we ran to Commonwealth Avenue.

NICOLE: Kay and I started walking toward the Charles River and the Boston Common area. I kept dialing Kelley.

KELLEY: A call came in, but it was a number I didn't know.

NICOLE: She answered the phone and I said, "Hi Kelley, my name is Nicole and I have your mom. Where are you? Are you okay?"

KELLEY: I just broke down in tears. Mom got on the phone and kept telling me, "I'm okay. I'm okay." She said she was with Nicole. Mom kept saying, "I need to come find you." And I said, "Mom, stay where you are. We are safe." I knew she was determined to find me and I was worried that she would do something irrational to get to us. We were trying to tell her where we were and she didn't understand directions.

KAY: Kelley was crying hysterically and I thought she or one of her friends had been injured. And then I realized it was because she thought something had happened to me. My focus was on getting to Kelley. I'm so grateful I had Nicole.

NICOLE: I got back on the phone and Kelley told us where they were and where they were heading. I told her we were two blocks away and said, "Stay where you are."

KELLEY: Nicole said, "I will not leave her until she finds you." So we waited, and I called my brother and told him, "Mom's okay!" I was getting so many texts from people so we posted on Facebook: "We are okay."

NICOLE: It took us 30-45 minutes to find Kelley. Kay was so anxious to get to her, and at one point said she couldn't believe this was happening to her. She told me about her husband's passing, and how the marathon was going to be a special event for her and Kelley. When we got to the corner where Kelley told me she was standing, no one was there. I asked Kay, "Do you see her?"

KELLEY: We were standing on the corner, and I saw my mom across the street. We ran to each other, we hugged and we just kept hugging and crying and hugging each other.

KAY: I didn't want to stop hugging her. It was such a sense of relief.

KELLEY: And then she was hugging my friends. My mom was wearing Nicole's jacket. I was crying and telling Nicole, "You're so wonderful. Thank you so much!"

NICOLE: When Kay and Kelley found each other, I observed the love between a mother and daughter; how they would do anything for each other. Just the way they ran to each other, hugging and crying. It was almost like they couldn't believe they found each other in the midst of thousands of people. It was a bond that only a mother and daughter have. I'm very close to my mother and I knew that if I was in that situation, all I would want to do is see my mom. And I just wanted them to find each other.

They all thanked me and I asked if they needed help in getting somewhere. I told Kay to keep my phone number, in case they needed my help. I wanted her to keep the jacket, but she wouldn't. And then we parted ways.

KAY: When we left Nicole, I told her how grateful I was. We all hugged and she told us to call her if we needed help.

KELLEY: The girls went back to Eliza's and headed to the airport. I asked my mom if she needed to eat, but she's so hardcore; "No, I'm fine." We walked all the way to the Park Plaza Hotel. I was too nervous to stay there; especially after my brother called again and said there were rumors of more bombs and that he wanted us out of the area. The lobby was packed with runners and spectators, and I just wanted to get out of there.

KAY: When I run that far, I'm a little out of it and some of this was a blur. As Kelley and I walked back to the Park Plaza, I was starting to feel peaceful about everything. But Kelley was nervous and said, "I don't think I can spend the night here."

KELLEY: Mom showered and we packed up and left for Eliza's in Beacon Hill. I felt like there bombs everywhere, and as we pulled our suitcases behind us, it was so strange; the streets were empty.

KAY: On the way, I told Kelley I still really wanted to have a beer, so we stopped in a liquor store.

KELLEY: We continued to Eliza's. I felt bad for her; Boston is her city and this was very personal and difficult for her. After we settled in, we all walked to a restaurant that was across the street from Mass General. Ambulance after ambulance was arriving.

KAY: And we could see SWAT teams and armed soldiers swarming the area, but I was actually calmer than I thought I would be.

KELLEY: We were to fly out early the next morning. Mom hadn't gotten her race bag, so we went to pick it up at four the next morning. It was so eerie; it was still dark with police and military everywhere. There was confetti, but barricades and areas roped off. It was this odd mashup of great celebration and great tragedy. Mom had to run up an alley and soldiers were there to hand out the bags.

KAY: It was amazing how organized the bag pick-up area was and it took only a few minutes to get mine and we headed to the airport.

KELLEY: One of the terminals had police surrounding it. Everything was normal except for authorities at security asking if we had been at the marathon. Do you have photos? Do you have video? I just wanted to get out of Boston and told my mom, "I don't think I can do this again."

NICOLE: I was glued to CNN the days after and my world just kind of stopped. I kept in touch with Kay and Kelley over the next several days. I was so shocked by what had happened. I couldn't believe it was close to us. In the weeks after, I felt a little guilty about not running to help one of the injured. But my mom reminded me that I helped Kay and Kelley.

KELLEY: I was in touch with Nicole the entire night and the whole next week. She updated me on everything. Once we were at home in Denver, I went back to work the next day and everyone wanted to hear about it. But then they went on with their lives and I wasn't ready to. That was hard. People felt sad that it happened, but it happened far away. I wished that they had more of an understanding of what had just happened. And other times I would think, this didn't just happen! I can't believe I was in a bombing.

NICOLE: A month or two after the event, Kay called me and had some questions. There were so many things she didn't remember. "Where did you find me?" "What was I doing?"

KAY: It makes me sad to think about my son James that day. He was at work in Philadelphia, just finding out about the explosions and knowing that Kelley and I were there. That was so difficult for him; his mom and sister, all the family he had at the time, and he couldn't get to us. It breaks my heart to think about that.

NICOLE: All this time later, it still hits close to home for me. Boston as a city, proved itself to be stronger than I ever thought it could be. I never realized how much good can come from something so horrible. Am I going this year? Oh, yes!

KAY: I'm really looking forward to the Boston Marathon this year. It's going to be an amazing experience. When I see stories about the injured and their families, I am so inspired by their strength. I think running down Boylston is going to be so special and I will be full of emotion.

KELLEY: I feel terrible for the injured and killed. That isn't something you easily forget. But there was such an outpouring of love and Boston did the best it could to recover, and it was an amazing recovery.

This year we will meet at 3:15 p.m. on Marathon Monday at Stephanie's on Newbury Street with our group of friends — now larger with the addition of our perfect stranger, Nicole — to toast our runners and celebrate their accomplishments. It is going to be a great afternoon!

Nicole Maneri urges you to consider supporting One Fund Boston at https://secure.onefundboston.org.

Kay and Kelley Huemoeller encourage you to consider supporting the James L. Huemoeller Book Fund, which supports law students in the purchase of textbooks at the University of Wyoming.

Ella Pittman

Runner
Ran for the New England Patriots Charitable Foundation
Age 21
Medfield, Massachusetts

Studying to be a veterinarian at Mt. Holyoke College

After outrunning a stampeding mob of frightened runners, volunteers and spectators, I found myself at the corner of Newbury and Arlington, outside the Burberry store. That's where I lost it. As I was standing there bawling, my "perfect strangers" appeared — two women, probably in their 40s, quite motherly, which was just what I needed at that moment because my parents hadn't found me yet.

It was my first marathon and I was really excited to run a 3:59. I didn't quite expect that, and it really didn't get to sink in before the bombs went off. I had just crossed under the big blue arch and was being handed a bottle of water from the first group of volunteers in yellow jackets when I heard the boom. At first, I thought it was fireworks, and then I realized that we weren't anywhere near the harbor, and they only shoot fireworks off at the harbor. I turned around and saw the smoke emanating from the area in front of Marathon Sports and when I saw the fire from the second blast, it was immediately in my mind, this is a terrorist attack!

I frantically tried to get in touch with my parents — I always run with my cellphone because I usually train alone — the call finally went through and they were safe and in the family meeting area. I told them I was okay and would be there soon. It was so chaotic as I was trying to leave the post-finish area. There were people in yellow jackets running toward the finish line, and other people in yellow jackets telling the other finishers and me to keep going, just keep going, that everything was okay. Obviously it wasn't, but they were just trying to get us out of there.

I'm sure I was in shock because in spite of everything going on around me, I got my medal, I got my blanket and I got my food bag. I was picking up my gear — my drop bag from the school bus — and as I stood by the bus and was zipping up my coat, a mob came running at me — some runners, some volunteers, some civilians — yelling, "Run!" And it was the kind of mob that I knew if I got caught under it, I was going to get killed. I think that freaked me out more than the bombs. I didn't know if there was another bomb, if there was a sniper; I didn't know if there was a fire, and so I took off running. It didn't matter that I was exhausted and my legs were dead, I didn't want to get trampled. We ran smack dab into barriers and people were clamoring to get over each other to get over the barriers. It occurred to me at one point that we don't really know what we are running from, and we don't really know what we're running to. The mob had come from the general direction of the family meeting area, where my parents were. And that freaked me out even more. I kept running.

So there I was, a shivering 20-year-old woman bawling like a little girl at the corner of Newbury and Arlington. The fatigue and fear had overwhelmed me, I didn't know what was going on and I didn't know where my parents were. Up walked the next best thing at that moment, two women who both wrapped their arms around me and gave me comfort. One saw I was shivering and offered her jacket, but I was not cold, per se, just in shock. They checked to make sure I hadn't been injured, wasn't bleeding or anything, and helped me call my parents again. I wish I had gotten their names because I really would like to thank them.

As my perfect strangers waited with me, my parents finally made their way to us. I've never hugged them so hard, I almost knocked them over.

As soon as I hugged them, some of the first words out of my mouth were, "Did I break four hours?" It's a little embarrassing to admit that in such a moment of crisis, I was worried about my time. My half split was 1:59:57, and everyone had told me beforehand that with it being my first marathon, "don't do a time …" But I'm very competitive and I kind of hatched the idea two weeks prior that I could break four hours. So I ran that second half really, really hard. I was having watch problems, so I didn't know how I was doing. I knew I was close to 4:00, maybe a little under or over.

Trying to get out of the city was a nightmare. My parents had parked their car by Cleveland Circle, about five miles away, and had taken the T the rest of the way. The T was shut down and my mom has really bad knees, so walking that far for her was too much. They'd already walked a lot trying to find me. But we didn't have a choice and started walking.

After a couple of miles, we were in Brookline, where we took a break near some apartments. My mom was trying to call people to arrange a ride when a woman walking her dog stopped, and when she heard our predicament, offered to take us to our car. She pulled her car around and drove us, which saved us from having to walk about three miles. Another "perfect stranger!"

A residual effect of the bombs is noise. I went to a Patriots' game where they fire a musket every time the Patriots score a touchdown and that freaked me out a little bit. I was at a concert with fireworks and that got to me. And I was at a fair and it was one of those things where I was looking around and thinking, this would be a really great place to bomb because no one is really checking security, and how am I going to get out of here? So, it has come back in weird ways that I don't necessarily like, but I'm grateful to have my hearing and my legs.

All these months later, I'm still bothered by guilt. I was getting a medal while there were people bleeding in the street. Reconciling that guilt and grief with the pride about what I accomplished is still something I'm struggling with. Even within my own charity team, I know that I earned my time because of the way I trained, but there were many other people on my team who trained just as hard as I did, and fund-raised as hard as I did, but didn't get that moment I did, because I was 20 and could run faster. I still feel somewhat uncomfortable with that.

Am I running Boston this year? I wouldn't miss it!

Ella Pittman urges you to consider supporting the New England Patriots Charities at patriots.com/community.

Jeff Pflanz
Runner
Boston College Student
Age 21
Clive, Iowa

Sue O'Brien Lynch
Spectator/Perfect Stranger
Middle school English teacher
in Braintree, Massachusetts
Age 42
South Boston

Erin Joyce
Spectator/Perfect Stranger
Seventh-grade math teacher in Braintree
Age 35
Weymouth, Massachusetts

JEFF: Before I tell you about my perfect strangers, I want to describe what a magical experience running the Boston Marathon is, especially for a Boston College student. I first experienced the marathon as a spectator in 2011 when I was visiting BC as a prospective student during Admitted Eagle Day. It was such an amazing atmosphere and, as a runner in high school, I knew that I wanted to run the race someday, whether I wound up going to BC or not.

As I ran the 2013 race, I was greeted all along the route by high fives and smiling faces, children handing out oranges, live bands, thousands of enthusiastic and possibly inebriated college students enjoying their day off; all 26.2 miles are surrounded by people, and they aren't there just for the elite runners, but for the amateur and charity runners hours behind.

My campus, Boston College, is located directly after arguably the most demanding part of the course, Heartbreak Hill (which as any first-time runner sadly discovers is really the last in a series of four hills). It is such a lift after getting over the hill to be greeted by all your friends and family cheering along the Boston College campus. As over 100 of us run for the Campus School, it is not unusual for students to hop the barricades and join their friends along a stretch of the campus, if not the remaining five miles. In this case, my lanky, completely sober roommate Jon had starting jogging along beside me with our friend Christina. She had dealt with knee issues for many months, and it was clear that she was in tremendous pain. With five miles to go, I found myself with a decision to make: I could keep running on my second wind and finish at or near my goal, or I could stay back with Christina and Jon. I chose the latter.

My pace slowed as the three of us jogged and even walked all of Mile 23 and a section of Mile 25. Just after we passed the "one mile to go" sign, we were stopped. There was mass confusion. We were only a couple rows back from the first runners stopped. I remember pushing my way up trying to figure out what was going on. Within view, nothing was wrong and we hadn't heard anything. I was anxious, looking at my watch frequently, trying to figure out what was denying us the finish line.

Then we started hearing rumors. First, of an accident. Then we heard rumors of an explosion. I checked CNN on Jon's iPhone, but nothing was there. Then we began hearing about two explosions at the finish line.

My thoughts shifted immediately to contacting my girlfriend and friends whom I thought were waiting for me at the finish line.

Jon and Christina decided to go back to campus as I tried to make my way to the finish line to find my girlfriend. I didn't get far, of course, before being stopped by police and, as much as I wanted to get by them to find my girlfriend, I didn't fight them. I knew they were doing the right thing.

The next two and a half hours were a blur. My phone had died because I had been taking photos with it while I ran. Amid all of the chaos, my perfect stranger entered the picture. A spectator saw that I was in distress, probably looking dazed and desperate. She walked up, told me her name was Sue, and offered to make calls from her phone. Sue didn't leave my side for the next two hours.

SUE: The term "perfect stranger" is amusing to me; as if I could be perfect at any point in my life! What we did for Jeff was not unusual. Everybody was helping each other.

I've been going to the marathon nearly every year since college. It's so heartwarming to be at the corner of Hereford and

Boylston and see people who are near exhaustion after running four or five hours get a surge of energy as they near the finish.

My friend, Heather Wojcik, and I were meeting up with other friends who had gone to the Red Sox game. Another friend, Sheila, was running and we were hoping to see her go by. We popped into Dillon's, a bar next to the fire station, to grab a bite to eat. When the bombs went off, we thought maybe we felt something, but it took a minute to process that we actually did and then seeing it almost immediately on the TVs in the bar confirmed it. We were like, "Oh my God, this is happening right now!"

I got a text almost instantly from my friend Erin Joyce.

ERIN: My sister, Christine, and a few of her friends were watching the race on Hereford Street between Newbury and the turn onto Boylston. When I got out of work at Fenway, I ran over to where my sister was in hopes of seeing my friend's fiancé run by. But he had already finished by the time I got there at around 2:10 p.m. Christine was still watching for a few friends who hadn't run by yet, so we stayed there.

When the first explosion went off, I said, "I didn't know

they were doing re-enactments." It sounded like a cannon, and that was the conversation around me, too: why are they firing a cannon? Then the second bomb went off and we knew exactly what it was. The police ran up the street and sent all of the runners who were on Boylston back up toward Hereford. My sister and I were trying to help people over the police barriers. A police officer and I pulled a barrier down so that people could go west on Newbury.

SUE: Heather and I started walking, eventually wanting to head toward my home in South Boston. We were directed onto the sidewalk along Comm Ave, and as we looked at the runners, many of them just wandering in a daze, we said, "Oh my God, look at these poor people! They just ran 25 miles and they don't even know where they are."

And then we saw Jeff. He looked young. I mean, he's 20, that is young, but he looks younger. And he just looked bewildered and so vulnerable. "Can we help you in some way?" I asked. And there was a moment of hesitation when he looked at us and I thought he was going to say, "No," but instead, he said, "I don't even know what's going on."

I told him, "We don't necessarily know, either, but at least we have each other." Maybe it was the teacher in me, but I knew that in that type of unsettling situation I wouldn't want to be alone, so we took on the role of protector. Jeff told us his girlfriend was at the finish line and he was worried about her.

I suggested that he call his mother in Iowa, in part because I have a mother who would be freaking out if she heard or saw what was going on. (And she did. I got a text soon after that from my sister: "Mom can't reach you. She is so worried!")

JEFF: From her phone I was able to contact my mom who, back home in Iowa, was unaware of the unfolding events. I gave Mom my girlfriend's number, hoping she might be able to get through before I could. Imagining similar concern from my friends and family, I impulsively sent a message to a friend at BC with my Facebook e-mail and password so she could put out a message that I was fine. After that, with Sue monitoring me, I just continued wandering, resolving to 1) find my friends, 2) try a few more desperate calls, and 3) barring success in finding them, go to the nearest hospital, hoping it would somehow provide answers.

SUE: Jeff kept trying to reach his girlfriend but couldn't get through. In fact, the call to his mother was the only one that got through. Texting was the only thing that was working. Heather and I were with him for a good hour when Erin texted me again. Along with checking on Heather and me, she was looking for our running friend, Sheila, and another friend, Stacey, who was supposed to meet me at Dillon's, but didn't make it.

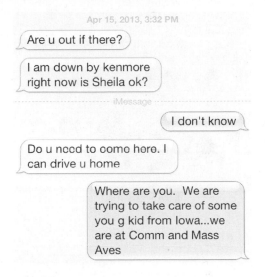

Apr 15, 2013, 3:32 PM

Are u out if there?

I am down by kenmore right now is Sheila ok?

iMessage

I don't know

Do u need to come here. I can drive u home

Where are you. We are trying to take care of some you g kid from Iowa...we are at Comm and Mass Aves

JEFF: I had remained relatively calm for 30-45 minutes, but after that I was, frankly, borderline catatonic. I was exhausted from running, my short night's sleep and the extreme situation. Sue gave me water and forced me to wear her coat.

SUE: It wasn't that cold of a day, but he was in a t-shirt and shorts and was sweating after running 25 miles. I said, "You must be freezing, why don't you put on my coat?" He didn't want it. I put it on him anyway. I don't think he knew what he needed. He was in shock and didn't know what he was feeling at that point. He was just worried about his girlfriend.

People along the route were just so good. These kids,

college kids, were bringing out sweatshirts, trashbags and pitchers of water with the red Solo cups, which took on a different purpose that day. There was one girl who was like Molly Pitcher, just walking around, not saying a word, filling people's Solo cups.

We got Jeff some water and then sat for a bit, thinking that maybe his friends would find him, when Erin texted again.

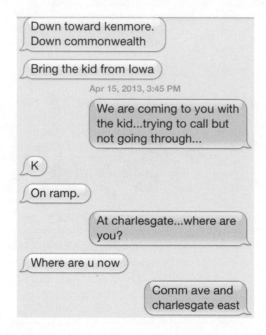

> Down toward kenmore.
> Down commonwealth
>
> Bring the kid from Iowa
>
> Apr 15, 2013, 3:45 PM
>
> We are coming to you with the kid...trying to call but not going through...
>
> K
>
> On ramp.
>
> At charlesgate...where are you?
>
> Where are u now
>
> Comm ave and charlesgate east

SUE: We started walking toward Erin and found a marathon Red Cross tent, where we got him some trash bags to wrap up in, which were probably warmer than my spring coat.

Erin: Sue, Heather and Jeff found me on the ramp to Charlesgate where it goes over the Mass Pike. We were with Jeff for about another hour walking up and down the street, helping him look for his friends, calling his friends and trying to find out if his girlfriend was safe. We didn't want to stray too far from where Sue had found him. He was kind of in shock, plus exhausted after running so long, so we didn't want to make him walk very much.

We were trying to be positive, even though we didn't know much at that point either. We heard that three people had been killed, but we were just trying to stay positive, keeping him talking, holding his hand, hugging him a little bit, just making sure that he was okay, and that the other runners around us were okay as well.

JEFF: I was beginning to fear the worst and thinking things I'd never want to think again. Out of desperation, I attempted to turn on my phone again. It had just enough power for countless text messages to flood in. There was a message from my mom, who had been trying to call me back but didn't know I'd used Sue's phone to call her. Mom told me she had gotten through to my girlfriend. She was safe, and I found out later that the credit goes to one of our friends who had failed to wake up on time, so the group of them was unable to make it to the finish line. Instead, they had been watching from Kenmore Square, where we didn't see each other. I can't even begin to describe the wave of relief I felt.

ERIN: Jeff broke down in tears. It was just joy, he was overcome with joy and relief.

SUE: Two of Jeff's friends, a couple, found him. They had talked to Jeff's girlfriend and told him that she was back at her dorm. The girl's father was driving in to pick them up and she was trying to give him directions on where to meet. There was a police officer nearby and he told us the Fenway area was still open to cars. We told her to have her father meet us at Fenway, and we would walk them over there.

JEFF: I knew my girlfriend's dorm was now within a mile. Erin offered to drive us back to campus, but I just wanted to get to her. I thanked Sue and Erin as much as I could and left on foot. I wish I had asked for contact information so I could have, at the very least, thanked her more than I did.

ERIN: So Sue, Heather and I walked Jeff's friends back to Fenway where her father picked them up. My car was there and I drove Sue and Heather home.

JEFF: Not overlooking the sadness and trauma that occurred on April 15th, there's something magical in experiencing tens of thousands of people supporting complete strangers struggling through the most physically demanding event of their lives. Perfect strangers like Sue and Erin took that support to an even higher level. I can only hope that I would display such courage and generosity under similar circumstances.

SUE: I think helping others is innate. And, I believe that there's way more good in the world than not. It's ironic: in the following days we were under lockdown and shelter in place while the police were spending so much time and manpower looking for who did this, looking so hard to find the evil; but you didn't have to look for goodness because it was everywhere. That reminds me of one of my favorite quotes, from Mr. Rogers: "When I was a boy and I would see scary things in the news, my mother would say to me, 'Look for the helpers. You will always find people who are helping.'"

Jeff Pflanz urges you to consider supporting the Boston College Campus School, a non-profit, publicly funded, special-education day school for students ages 3-21 with multiple disabilities. (http://www.bc.edu/content/bc/schools/lsoe/campsch.html)

Sue O'Brien Lynch urges you to consider supporting the Boston Bruins Charitable Foundation in memory of Daniel J. O'Brien. Checks can be sent to: Boston Bruins Foundation, 100 Legends Way, Boston, MA 02114.

Erin Joyce urges you to consider supporting The Jimmy Fund at www.jimmyfund.org, working toward a world without cancer.

Jennifer Anstead

Runner

Age 38

Registered Nurse, Mass General Cardiac Surgery Service

My first memorable marathon experience was when I was about three years old. I grew up in Cohasset, a suburb of Boston, and the marathon has always been huge. Our little town holds a "marathon bike race" for school-age kids and my older siblings, who were seven or eight, were participating. My mom brought my tricycle along and I rode around the little duck pond off to the side of the big kids' course. The local paper took a photo and did a story about me pedaling around the pond with the headline, "Is this another Rosie Ruiz?"

I was not. I have run five marathons, and there were no short cuts. 2013 was my third Boston, and I ran the Marine Corps in 2006 and the New York Marathon in 2013. When I finished the Marine Corps Marathon, I thought it was awesome that I got to run it with a girlfriend, and it was so inspirational seeing the service members running in full gear, and running past all of the national monuments was awesome, but personally, it was a little anti-climactic. I felt it was selfish; that I should've been doing it for something bigger. I decided that the next time I ran a marathon, someone besides me would benefit from it.

I moved home to Boston in 2009, and a friend and I went to Boylston Street to watch the 2010 marathon. It was so inspiring and I said to her, "I'm going to run this next year!" I thought it would be fun to run where my friends and family could be along the course. I applied to the Mass General Pediatric Oncology Unit charity team for the 2011 race, but there were no spots available. In February, I was notified that a girl on the team was injured and I was able to take her spot. I had eight weeks to raise $3500 and train. Luckily, I had been running all winter and I was able to raise the money in time. The marathon was, as I had expected, an awesome time and I applied and was accepted for 2012, and then again for 2013.

As I ran in 2013, there were some friends scattered along the route cheering me on, and my parents were at Mile 24. After the race, a group of friends were going to meet me at the Forum. Mass General has gym privileges at Fit For Life, so my plan was to cross the finish line, go to the gym, take a shower, get a massage and a bite to eat, then meet my friends at the Forum.

One of my friends saw me run by at Kenmore Square and texted our friends at the Forum: "I just saw Jen and she's about a minute away. Get your cameras and get out there to take pictures." As two of my friends headed out onto the sidewalk, I had just hit the "take a right on Hereford and a left on Boylston" area. When I could see the finish line I thought, "I'm almost done! I'm doing it!" As I passed Crate & Barrel, the first bomb went off. It sounded like a cannon, and I wondered why they were shooting off a cannon for a race that was won over two hours ago. But then, I stopped. I knew it was a bomb. The advantage I had was that I was standing in the street and had an unobstructed view. People in the crowd couldn't see much more than what was right in front of them. I had a panoramic view and saw all the smoke and debris blowing onto the street. It's strange; I wasn't confused and I knew exactly what was happening, and I knew it was bad.

When you are running down Boylston to the finish line, the police are normally facing you with their backs to the finish line. I'd stopped in front of two police officers who were facing me. They turned to look at the finish line and then turned back and looked at each other as if confused. I thought, this is not good. They would know if the race officials were shooting off cannons of celebration at the finish line. You could hear a pin drop on the street as soon as the bomb went off and that was the eeriest thing. When you are running down Boylston Street, the crowds are cheering so loudly, it's like they are going to bust an aneurysm. But they went silent after the first bomb. And then the second bomb went off right behind the police officers! Instantly, four policemen stood together, spread their arms and pushed us back. It looked to me like a mailbox or trash can had blown up, like a bomb was in them. As I looked around, panic was starting to set in. I saw lampposts and mailboxes; I didn't know where to go. Would there be bombs going off every ten feet?

I didn't have my phone, money, ID, credit cards, not even the keys to my apartment. I had nothing. Just what I was wearing. My only identification was my bib because I had written my name on it. What was worse, I only knew my parents' home number, and they weren't home. I couldn't remember their cell or the numbers of my brother and sister because they're stored in my phone.

The last few friends who'd seen me run were back a few blocks at Kenmore Square and their plan was to head to the Forum after I passed. So I decided to walk back that way to find Matt, Jen and Carolynn. I couldn't find Matt but saw Jen and Carolynn sitting on the side of the road. They were crying and hysterical. They had been getting the text alerts tracking me and were waiting for them to show that I had crossed the finish line. But my times weren't refreshing and then they heard the bombs go off. They thought I was there.

They didn't see me walk up. I said, "We need to get out of here. There are bombs going off."

They both started screaming, "Oh my God! Jenny! We were so worried about you!"

I was the calm one out of the three of us, but it must have been because I was in shock. One of my friends had been communicating with her dad, who found a number to the hospital where my sister works as an ER nurse. I got her on the phone, told her I was okay, but told her, "Two bombs went off at the finish line and you need to call Mom and Dad right away and tell them I'm okay. They're going to think I'm dead."

In the meantime, one of my friends called her husband but was so hysterical she couldn't talk, so I took the phone and told him, "We're going to walk to the river to get to Mass General." I don't know why I thought the river was safer but I thought that if we could get to Cambridge we'd be out of the city.

I was just grateful that I was with my friends at this time, because while I had nothing but the clothes I ran in, I had them. I heard stories about runners who were around Mile 17 and were knocking on doors. Residents invited them in, let them use their phones, get warm and get something to eat. And they gave them blankets to take with them. It's just amazing how people opened up their hearts to everybody. I was feeling fine physically, but I was cold and my friend had given me her jean jacket so I was wearing running shorts and a jean jacket.

Outside the Forum, my friends had crowded along the fence to watch the runners. Sabrina was leaning against the mailbox and was shielded from the blast. Roseann wasn't and lost her leg above the knee.

Roseann is like the girlfriend every girl should have. She has an easy phone number and out of all my friends, hers is one of the few I know in my head. I just kept calling her that day and left messages saying, "I'm okay and I hope you're okay, too. Call me as soon as you can." I had seen blood in the streets and people screaming and running toward me. It was horrific and it did occur to me that my friends could have been hurt. But I'm really an optimist and I thought, she's okay, she's okay. Roseann hadn't answered my texts and the phones had gone dead. We have a mutual friend in Florida named Katy. She used to live in Boston and was friends with many people at MGH. Katy was the only one I was able to get in touch with. So I was getting all my news from Florida. Katy was my Command Central!

We found out from her that Roseann was hurt and had been taken to MGH. So I got on the phone and dialed the Cardiac OR where I work and asked to talk to the evening charge. When she heard my voice, she started yelling, "Everybody, it's Jennifer and she's okay!" And I heard everyone erupting in the background. They'd been tracking four of us runners from the department and when they saw that I hadn't finished, and they hadn't heard from me, they were worried. And then they got the emergency alarm at the hospital that bombs had gone off at the marathon and to be prepared for casualties. So they all thought I was going to be a casualty.

They didn't know at this point that Roseann was a patient. They were so overrun with casualties and they were just naming them, "Trauma 1 Male," "Trauma 2 Female," "Trauma 3 Male," and so on. I did find out from Katy that Roseann was having surgery. In fact, one of my cardiac team members was operating on her but didn't know who she was. I wish Roseann hadn't come to the marathon and that she wasn't injured. And that is a guilt I'm trying to work through. There's so much of it that stays with me and it's every day.

Everything is a blur after that day. I didn't sleep for two

weeks. Although I feel so lucky to be okay, every single day something will happen that will trigger a feeling. Over the months, I've gotten used to some of the triggers. In the beginning, it was the train. The first week or so I was adamant that I was not going to change my schedule; I took the train and bus as usual. But there were times I would get on the train and in my head I'd be saying, so many people, get off! Loud noises bothered me, too.

I was never angry about not finishing the race, but I have so much guilt and sadness about it. My heart was broken. I was angry at the terrorists. Why did they do this when the first trickle of charity runners were coming in? These people are not going to win money or even qualify for the next race. These people are running for a charity or a person they care for. They probably have a full-time job and a family and carved out all that time to train. It was pure will and determination and their belief in themselves and a cause. They and the spectators were out there for something so much bigger than themselves.

It tainted something that was so good. And I can't believe it happened here. It just broke our hearts. But guess what? I'll be at the starting line this year and I'm dedicating my race to Roseann.

Jennifer Anstead encourages you to support the Mass General Marathon Team in raising money for the "Fighting Kids' Cancer, One Step at at Time" program. Learn more at http://give.massgeneral.org/marathon/our-causes.

Courtesy Andrea Hadfield

All smiles before the marathon, Andrea "Haddy" Hadfield and some of her Boston Children's Hospital teammates. LEFT TO RIGHT: *Jennifer McNamara, Andrea Hadfield, Amanda Welsh Rossetti, (who was crossing the finish line when the bomb went off; it made her watch stop.) Lauren Hayes, Marcy Rebello, Emily Kahn, Lauren DeFranzo and Kate Kennedy*

Andrea Hadfield

Runner

Age 30

South Boston

Works at Dana-Farber Cancer Institute in corporate and foundation relations and fund-raising

T hey were closing the course already? Oh, my God, had it already been six hours? I knew I was having a bad day, but didn't know it was that bad! My stomach hurt; I wasn't running well; I walked at every water stop. I struggled every step of the way to the finish, which came for me at Mile 23 when B.A.A. volunteers were blocking the street and diverting me and the other stragglers off the course. The B.A.A. closes the course after six hours. I purposely hadn't brought a watch because I didn't want to be constantly reminded of how badly I was doing. But six hours? Really?

Then I started hearing people talking about explosions. Off to the side of the street, I saw the parents of a fellow runner who'd been watching the race, huddled around their phone, and they were crying. I heard someone say Copley Square had been blown up. What did that even mean? My friends were supposed to wait for me at the finish. Were they okay? Then someone else said a bomb went off in front of Lord & Taylor. Oh, my God! That's where my mom and dad were supposed to be waiting for me. That's when I began panicking.

I knew Mom was keeping her cellphone turned on in case I needed help, and I'd warned her there was a good chance I would. I didn't feel well race day morning. I'd been having a really hard year of training. Boston had a long winter with countless blizzards and cold, rainy, icy weather. I was also working crazy hours, long evenings and I wasn't getting the training in I wanted. I just wanted to get through the marathon. I did not feel ready. I'm normally a very lighthearted person, but I was worried. I thought

I'd finish, but it would really be painful and I'd never do it again.

As I looked around for a phone to borrow to check on my parents, SWAT vans were flying down the road. I could hear sirens all over the place and combined with the very little I had heard, I began to fear that I had led my parents and friends to their deaths.

This was my second Boston Marathon running for Boston Children's Hospital. My mother's brother, who's 44 years old now, wouldn't be here if it hadn't been for the excellent emergency care he received there at birth. Any amount of money I can raise by running goes toward a debt that can never be repaid. One of the great things about running for Children's is that the tent it provides for us at Hopkinton is next to the elite runners. We get to see them warming up, and there's something about realizing you're on the same trail as all these amazing athletes; it's kinda cool.

I take every Patriots Day off from work; it's my favorite day of the year in Boston with the marathon and the Red Sox game and just how everybody is so happy. I was inspired to run after cheering on my neighbor and high school friend Lauren DeFranzo in 2011. In the days before the 2012 marathon, B.A.A. was putting out advisories because of the expected hot weather. At a team breakfast two days before the 2012 race, I found myself sitting next to the father of one of the runners, who was a medical volunteer for the race.

"What are you most worried about?" I asked.

He said, "The heat. When people get disoriented and suffer from heat exhaustion, we have to put them in an ice bath."

"Sounds awful."

"Yeah, and we have to take their temperature rectally, because it's the only way to get an accurate reading."

That was a shocking bit of information. So all during the 2012 race, the only thing going through my head all day was, "Don't get heat exhaustion!"

There were no invasive thermometer worries in 2013. It was a cool day with a light breeze. Perfect for running, but not for overheated runners who found themselves suddenly battling hypothermia. The first of my perfect strangers was a spectator who let me use her phone. I dialed my mom's number, expecting to hear her reassuring voice telling me everything would be okay.

It went to voice mail. My mind immediately jumped to the worst case scenario: I thought they were dead. For 45 minutes I was sure they were dead.

Still not aware of the tragedy at the finish line, I lost it. Looking back, I would have loved to have behaved differently, but I was so erratic and borderline aggressive. The B.A.A. volunteers were a godsend. I don't think they knew any more than anyone else, but they were so friendly, comforting and helpful; so positive, and they weren't panicking at all. They seemed to know what they were doing. I can't say enough about those volunteers.

As we walked along, wandering, almost everyone along the street was asking, "Do you want water? Food?" I turned all of them down, even though my body could have used them. I had a one-track mind: get to the Westin, where I had made pre-race plans to meet my parents. I ran into another guy on our team whom I didn't know. I recognized him from our training runs, but we hadn't met. He had just passed his wife and 10-year-old son when the race was stopped, so they were standing together. His wife was so nice, so lovely. She basically treated me like a child, which was what I needed. She comforted me, got me water, bought me chips and, most importantly to me at that moment, let me try her phone every few minutes to try to reach my mom. Voicemail, again and again!

I was still wearing just my singlet, and another woman walked over and put a towel around my shoulders. I'm sure I was freezing and bordering on hypothermia, but I told her I didn't need it. I turned down offers of coats from at least five other people. I wasn't looking for anything except how to get to the Westin and finding out if my parents were alive. Fortunately, the woman with the towel insisted I take it. There were many other perfect strangers on the backside of Boylston whose help I unwisely rejected; residents of brownstones who were inviting me and other runners in, offering warmth, clothing, coffee, food and more. In retrospect, it was amazing, but at the time, I wanted none of it. I wanted my mom and dad.

Everything changed when, finally, after 45 minutes of trying, my mom answered her phone. I burst into tears; I didn't think they were alive. Mom told me they were okay and she, my dad and cousin Stephanie Bliss, a therapist at Spaulding Rehabilitation

Hospital who later worked with many of the victims, were in the Westin. I eventually got there, but couldn't get in because it was locked down. And my parents and cousin couldn't get out. We could literally see each other through the glass doors, but I couldn't touch them, and I really needed to hug them. By that time, the shock had worn off enough so that I could feel the cold. I was shivering, even with the towel. Stephanie, who's the most mild, quiet person in our family, essentially bullied a cop into letting them out of the Westin to come over to help me.

My parents' car was locked in the Westin garage, so we walked the two or so miles to my Southie apartment. Stephanie brought my phone and I was on it almost the whole time returning texts or posting on Facebook and letting the people who'd been trying to reach me know that I was okay. Until that day, Facebook was not much more than a diversion. It's fun to keep up on what my friends are up to. But on that afternoon, it was essential. I found out that my friends had been walking along Dartmouth to the finish line when the bombs went off. They were with a friend who had been in the Army, and when he heard the explosions, he said, "Those aren't cannons, those are bombs. Run!" And they ran all the way to Southie.

> *Until that day, Facebook was not much more than a diversion ... but on that afternoon, it was essential.*

I will probably never be able to properly thank most of the perfect strangers who helped me — or tried in vain to — along the way, but I want them to know how grateful I am. I did have the chance to meet one of them, though. Bob Catinazzo, the Children's team member whose wife, Caroline, took such good care of me, was at a gathering that Children's threw about a week and a half later for its team members and volunteers. It was at the Whiskey Priest in Boston and was just a chance for all of us to get together and acknowledge the good that was done that day, the money that was raised for Children's.

I told him, "I'm so thankful I found you and Caroline because I was in the worst state of mind, having the worst moment of my life. Things are still blurry but I feel like I was swearing in front of your child and carrying on like a crazy woman, yelling at the cops. I feel terrible! That's really not the person I am."

Bob said, "No, no, Andrea, you were totally calm."

"I was?!"

"No!" he laughed. "You were freaking out!"

"Oh, my God, I'm so sorry!"

"It's okay, really, it was a terrible day; you didn't know where your parents were. I'm sure I would have been the same way."

Bob's exemption aside, I feel badly and guilty about how I reacted. It was purely fueled by emotion. I wish I'd been able to keep it together a little more.

April 15th was heartbreaking, but watching how the city responded in the months since, I have never felt so proud to be from Boston. I've noticed a change in how people treat each other. I think every person in the city was affected in some way, either on that Monday or the following Friday when we had shelter-in-place. I think everyone became more sensitive to each other and kinder, much more than I'd ever experienced. Over the last two years when I went on training runs through South Boston, people would heckle me. I've had some hilarious encounters in Southie. It's such a strange neighborhood, but I love it. Since the bombings, though, people are different; they seem nicer.

The B.A.A. had a little fake finish line set up at one of the offices where you could pick up your medal and bag. It was remarkable how emotional that was, getting my medal and stepping across the line. They had therapy dogs there, which really helped. The B.A.A. was remarkable; I can't say enough about how the organization responded.

Andrea Hadfield encourages you to consider supporting the Dana-Farber Cancer Institute (dana-farber.org), and Boston Children's Hospital (giving.childrenshospital.org).

Photo by Nicole Maneri

That's me, bib number 20505, just off the right shoulder of the policeman with his back to the camera. At that early moment of confusion I, and those around me, were wondering why we weren't being allowed to finish the race.

Gail M. Burgess

Runner

Age 61

Running since age 15

Triathlete for seven years

Toronto, Ontario

I got into marathon running while training for my first Ironman a few years ago. I qualified for Boston in my first marathon in 2010 and did the epic race for the first time in 2011. Qualifying for 2012 in that race was a bonus. I deferred in 2012 (the "too hot" race) and so was in Boston last April on that deferral.

The weather on race day was perfect — cool, sunny and just about the best race conditions you could want. Tens of thousands of people lining the route were a welcome diversion to the commentary coming from my body (aches, pains and the usual "Why am I doing this?" conversation). I remember just turning onto Boylston thinking that I was slower than I wanted but I would still easily qualify for 2014. Knowing the finish line was a couple of hundred meters away was a wonderful feeling. When I heard the first bomb go off, I thought that maybe it was a natural gas explosion or something like that. However, I had a clear view of the second blast and knew there was a problem. The police had stopped us by this point but like true runners many of us (not realizing how serious things were) were trying to figure out how to get to the finish line.

As we watched the long line of EMS vehicles and police on motorcycles roar by us up Boylston, we knew it was a big deal. When I finally realized what was happening (we saw a young man with shrapnel wounds on his face and burns and tears all over his jacket), I immediately thought about my husband. He was not at the race, which was fortunate because he would have been at the finish line, but I knew he was tracking me online. I desperately needed to reach him to let him know I was okay. If he didn't see that I'd finished he would think the worst. There was a gentleman with a large camera on the side of the road (professional or amateur, I don't know). I approached him and asked if he had a phone I could borrow to call my husband. I remember apologizing for it being a long distance call. My kind stranger pulled out his phone and because I guess I was a little shaky, dialed the number for me. He also stayed close by to make sure I was able to communicate to my husband that I was okay and that I didn't fall apart on the phone. I remember him nodding his head as I told Paul I loved him and that I'd call him later from the hotel. This perfect stranger's kindness enabled me to turn my brain to thinking about getting back to the Ritz without worry about what was happening at home. My husband was, as it turns out, inundated with calls, text, e-mails and people dropping by at his office. My stranger's kindness not only put Paul and my minds to rest, but dozens of friends and family as well.

Shock and post-race cooling off was beginning to hit me and I had to get moving. I knew I had to circumvent the finish line and made my way over to Newbury Street, encountering many people who wanted to know what had happened. I also saw people from the finish area walking in a daze, some of them injured. Paramedics had fanned out to the side streets to find the injured and get them help. My own problem was the cold. I knew I was nearing hypothermia and still had a long walk back to the hotel.

As I walked up Newbury, an American Apparel store was open. I went in, looking for anything that I might buy to keep me warm, but with only $20 in my pocket I knew chances were slim. A member of the staff (a young man) approached me and asked what had happened at the finish line. I gave him the short version (I really didn't have a lot of details) and then pulled out my $20 bill and asked if he had anything I could buy to provide me with some warmth. He disappeared into the back room and returned with a wonderful black hoodie that actually fit me. He then absolutely refused to take my $20. Little did he know what an incredible act of kindness that was. My second perfect stranger. I honestly don't know how I would have made it across Boston Common and back to the hotel without my (now cherished) hoodie. The whole way back I was composing my thank you e-mail to American Apparel in my head. It was one of the first things I did after getting back to my room.

My friend, who had finished and was almost back at the hotel before the explosions, and I stayed in Boston that night glued to the television. Tuesday morning we joined other athletes at the airport, heading home. We all had our stories, we all had our memories but the overriding feeling was one of gratitude and heartfelt thanks to the people of Boston for their calm compassion during what must have been an emotionally wrenching time for them. They truly took wonderful care of their guests.

The two seemingly small acts of kindness amid such human misery have remained huge for me. I still feel guilty that I not only ran into such kind strangers but that so many spectators and their families' lives were so tragically altered that day while I escaped unscathed. B.A.A.'s and Boston's quick establishment of the Boston One Fund was one way for me to express my gratitude. Running in a 10K race in Toronto six days after Boston, wearing my Boston gear, was another. Running Boston this year will give me a chance to say a proper thank you.

Gail Burgess encourages you to support the One Fund to aid victims and their families: onefundboston.org.

Photo by Nicole Maneri

*The spot on Boylston Street where the marathon ended for
me and thousands of others. The look on my face tells it all.*

Tammy Hartje

Runner

Age 48

Surgery Scheduler

St. Charles, Illinois

"Well, that's not good." My perfect strangers weren't prepared for my answer when they asked me which hotel I was staying at: "I can't remember." That inability to remember such a basic detail speaks to my state of mind after running four hours and being stopped by police just short of the finish. I met George and Robert at a Dunkin' Donuts. I was having my post-marathon snack at a Dunkin' Donuts! Nothing against Dunkin', but I had expected that I'd be getting Gatorade, a banana and my medal in the finisher's chute.

I love to run, I've always been good at it, and I became addicted to it. I make the time to run every day, no matter the weather. It makes me feel free. I do my best thinking when running and always feel better after running. My social life revolves around it and I've met so many nice people. There is an instant bond among runners. There were many years when I wasn't able to run because of parental responsibilities raising my children, Tyler and Heather, but they are now among my inspirations for running.

When I hear the words "Boston Marathon," it sends a chill over me. Just finding out that I qualified to run Boston was such a big deal for me. It was one of the most exciting things I've ever done. Some runners feel like the Boston Marathon is a victory lap: you earned it. It's just icing on the cake.

I first qualified for Boston in 2012. When I arrived in the city the day before the marathon, I was so sick with the flu that I couldn't run. Even though I could have used the heat deferment B.A.A. offered runners, I felt the need to re-qualify for 2013, which I did.

I was excited and very nervous as three of us from my running group flew from Chicago to Boston on Saturday. Angie, Jeanine and I shared a hotel room at the Hilton. We had so much fun at the Expo where we picked up our packets and visited all the booths. As we were going to bed the night before the marathon, I said, "Do you realize what we're doing tomorrow? We're running the Boston Marathon!" I got a little sleep that night, but would feel an electric jolt every once in a while. Nerves and excitement.

Before races, I always give my gear bag a kiss before handing it over. In it were my phone, credit card and ID. The only thing I had were mittens, hat and a headband underneath my hat. I had all my favorites on; I was running wearing the things that make me feel the best. And I did feel good, even though I wasn't at my best. Right after I re-qualified in 2012, I fractured my pelvis, which took three months out of my training schedule. So I wasn't running at top speed and was just taking it all in and enjoying the event. There were enthusiastic spectators on both sides of the street. It was truly the most fun marathon I've ever run.

As I made the turn onto Boylston, I recalled an e-mail from one of the race directors that read, "When you're running down Boylston, remember that you are the spectators' hero. Look to the left and look to the right and notice all the country flags." That's what I was doing at the time of the explosions. I could see the finish line. The ground shook. I thought they were celebratory and I didn't understand why the police had stopped us. I said to an officer, "Please, you don't understand. I need to cross that finish line." He said, "You do not want to go down there." What should I do? Should I try to sneak around the officers so I could finish the race? Instead, they made us run in the opposite direction. I didn't want to get too far in case they resumed the race. Then I saw a young man running by with blood on his face. The scene became more chaotic and the police told us to get off the street. But go where? Oh my God, I had nobody and nothing.

A woman pushing a stroller came up to me and asked if I needed to use a phone. I did, but I couldn't remember anybody's number! I went into a Dunkin' Donuts, but as I mentioned, I didn't carry cash. One woman offered me a piece of her bagel, but I couldn't eat. I was thirsty and I needed to sit down. That's where my perfect strangers, George and Robert, entered the picture. They were from New Jersey, runners who had been stopped, too, but they had money and phones. I finally remembered my daughter's number and George handed me his phone, but I couldn't figure out how to use it. Then the cellphones weren't working for calls, but he was able to text my daughter that I was okay, and she let everyone else in our family know. I was so cold and George gave me his sweatshirt saying, "Here, you have no body fat, you need to put this on."

That's when Robert said, "Let's try to get you back to your hotel." But I couldn't remember its name! We needed to get our bags, so we started walking to the buses and I saw mine on the street among a bunch of other bags. A woman looked at my bib number and gave me my bag. George and Robert went in another direction for theirs but said, "Don't leave this spot. We're going to come back for you." And they did. I changed into warmer clothes from my bag and gave George back his sweatshirt.

The guys were so good to me. They walked me back toward where the finish line was, hoping I would remember the name of my hotel. Robert distracted me from the horror of what had happened by telling me stories about a reality TV show that one of his relatives was on. Since I couldn't remember the name of my hotel, they tried Googling hotels in the area to see if I could recognize the name. I couldn't. They said, "You gotta help us out here. Do you remember anything?"

All of a sudden I saw J.J., a member of my running club. He was like a mirage. We ran to each other and hugged; J.J. said it was the biggest hug he's ever gotten. J.J is one of the leaders in our running group and is a huge inspiration. I was so scared. He said he'd been looking all over for me and wasn't going to leave Boston until he found me. I always tell him how much that meant to me. We went through a life-changing experience together.

I said goodbye and thank you to George and Robert. They were so wonderful to me, and I've stayed in touch with them. J.J. and another fellow runner walked me to our hotel. Things started to click for me as we were walking.

Angie and Jeanine were waiting at the hotel, and Angie got me some food. She, and the rest of our group, had finished the race. Being the only one who didn't finish was a weird feeling for me. It almost felt like a failure on my part. The others were happy about completing the race but were sensitive about showing their medals around me. Elena, a member of our club, placed first in her age group. At a gathering celebrating everybody's accomplishments, she gave me her medal and said, "I want you to have this." That was such a kind gesture. I did receive a medal in the mail weeks later and returned Elena's medal to her.

I may not have finished the race, but I did run the full marathon distance when you count when we were ordered by police to reverse our course and run.

The people of Boston were so wonderful to us runners. As my perfect strangers and I wandered the streets hoping that I'd recognize my hotel, residents were coming out of their brownstones asking us and other runners if we needed to go in to use their bathrooms or to get warm. And the staff at Dunkin' Donuts was so kind. In fact, the manager, suddenly faced with a store full of cold, thirsty, hungry runners who had little if any cash, was giving product away.

I couldn't watch the news coverage of the event when I returned home. I was there and I lived it. I wasn't injured but it's something that hits you emotionally, and I had my ups and downs in the months since. I'm not running this year. I'm okay, but I'm not ready to go back. I will return someday.

Tammy Hartje encourages you to support the One Fund to aid victims and their families at onefundboston.org.

Patricia Hazelton

Runner

Age 35

Teacher in Lynnfield, Massachusetts

One of the rewards of running the Boston Marathon is spotting your friends and family cheering for you. In 2012, I missed seeing two of my friends, so last year we made plans to meet at a specific spot, just after the left onto Boylston Street. I stopped, we took pictures, and I was on my way toward the finish. When the first bomb went off, I was still far enough away that I thought it was some sort of an electrical issue and I kept running. When the second one exploded, just behind me and over my left shoulder, it was clear that the marathon was over. Panic set in as runners and spectators scattered, screaming.

Exhausted and delirious after running 26 miles, I was quickly headed toward hypothermia, was disoriented and didn't know where I was and where to go — were there going to be more bombs? My post-race plan was to meet my brother at the Westin Hotel, and I immediately tried, but failed, to reach him by phone. I didn't know how to get to the Westin, which was a measure of my brain function — the Westin was maybe two and a half blocks away. I was so shaken up, and I was alone. Cold and weak, I was sitting on the steps to the Prudential Center when two boys, college boys, descended the steps and they appeared fairly together in a moment of chaos. I started crying and just looked up at them and asked, "Can you help me ?"

They said, "Yes, what do you need?"

I told them I needed to get to the Westin and didn't know where I was. Each boy took one of my arms and helped me up. They put a jacket on me, asked me my name, calmed me down, put their arms around me and started walking me to the Westin.

I asked them where they went to school, just making conversation, trying to keep my focus and keep in a conscious state.

They said they attended Northeastern. I said, "I'm so glad you're here." I'm a teacher, and they reminded me of some of my students who had graduated, just so sweet.

They held my arms all the way to the Westin, and did not leave me for about 15 minutes until my brother arrived. When they left, I gave them a hug goodbye and they were on their way. It was such a crazy day and when all was said and done and I was more lucid, I could only remember one of their first names. I don't know what I would have done had they not shown up to help me. And they seemed to have no regard for themselves, their own safety. I needed to find them, so I e-mailed Northeastern with my scant clues as to their identities.

A contact person at Northeastern, who was so nice and helpful, got back to me and said, "Patricia, we went through our whole database, and with the information you gave me, there's just no way we can locate them."

I was devastated because I felt this debt of gratitude and I just wanted to thank them. But more than that, I wanted to tell their parents — their mothers — what nice boys they raised.

Patricia Hazelton urges you to consider supporting
Mass Mentoring Partnership at massmentors.org.

The grace this tragedy exposed is the best of who we are.

*Massachusetts Governor Deval Patrick, at an interfaith
memorial service at the Cathedral of the Holy Cross
in South Boston, April 18, 2013*

OTHERS, PERFECT STRANGERS
IN THEIR OWN WAYS

The final pages of this book are a collection of stories, ideas and thoughts from a diverse group. We begin with Steve Silva, the man whose video of the finish line bombing was seen around the world. An eyewitness to the horror, he felt a responsibility to do his job in a manner respectful to the casualties and their families, while still providing a frame-by-frame record of the events as they unfolded.

Therapy, as you've read in the previous stories in this book, played an important role in the healing. Whether provided by humans like LICSW Joanne Pomodoro, or by the Lutheran Comfort Dogs, the events of April 15th created complex feelings that many of us needed help sorting out.

Blooming yellow daffodils, symbols of rebirth and new beginnings, will — with help from Mother Nature and thousands of volunteers — line all 26.2 miles of the race course this year.

We end with thoughtful essays about how runners can process what happened and, why, after such an attack, running still matters. Finally, from *Lowell Sun* writer Katie Lannan, a beautiful piece about why the Boston Marathon is everything that's right with the world.

"The smoke billowed into the air and people started moving in all different directions. Some runners were still heading for the finish line, some people were moving away and some were moving right to it." — *Steve Silva, Boston.com*

A frame of the Boston Marathon finish line video shot by Steve Silva that was viewed over 60 million times online and on broadcast, cable, and satellite television.

Steve Silva

Senior Sports Producer

Boston.com

Brighton, Massachusetts

The marathon is the biggest one day event for Boston.com and the *Boston Globe,* and it's the signature event for the city and region. It's so many things — news, sports, culture, travel and community. Everyone from Boston knows someone running in the race, and even the first-time charity runners can boast that they competed on the same course along with some of the world's greatest marathon runners. All eyes are on Boston that day.

My day began in Hopkinton where I was responsible for hosting our live webcast from the starting line, doing live interviews with runners and race officials, then back to the city and the finish line around 10:30 a.m. My credentials allow me to be right at the finish line and I arrived in time to shoot video of the elite winners from ground level. It was great to get the first reaction from Shalane Flanagan, an elite and Olympian from Marblehead, after she crossed the finish line in fourth place.

After the elites and the American favorites come across, there is always a brief lull, followed by a sea of very good runners from all over the world who are often attempting to run their personal bests. But it doesn't make for great video for me because those finishers are typically not struggling, emotional, or performing any antics as they come across the finish line.

It gets more interesting as the afternoon goes on when the bulk of the charity runners and first-timers finish. That is when you see the raw emotions of the runners, costume-wearing runners and runners doing cartwheels or push-ups at the finish line. Just a year earlier, the excessive heat during the 2012 race made for compelling video of exhausted runners crossing the finish line. In 2013, the day had been pretty uneventful heading into the afternoon. The temperature was perfect. There were no world records, no American or Boston Marathon course records set. But my plan was to stay at the finish line until around 5:00 p.m. My batteries were charged, the camera was in my right hand and a microphone in my left as I settled in for the next three hours. Up to that point, it was an extremely uneventful Boston Marathon.

Then at 2:49 p.m. ... Boom! The first explosion went off 10 yards from me and my body immediately rocked back. I looked in the direction of the explosion through the lens and I started moving toward it. What just happened? I saw a fire ball and heard a weird, dull thud sound. Not the loudest sound I've ever heard, just the strangest. I don't remember being scared. My father was a police detective and I just have a natural curiosity and a need to investigate what is going on. I didn't immediately think something bad happened, but just that something weird happened. I knew it was going to affect the race. What was the fire? What was the noise? Was it an accident or a cannon? The smoke billowed into the air and people were moving in all different directions. Some runners were still heading for the finish line, some people were moving away and some were moving right to it.

As I got closer to the source of the explosion, the smoke was heavier. And then there was a second blast. I had a headset on so I was hearing everything through my microphone, and when the second bomb went off, my mindset changed immediately: This was something planned and deliberate. It was not an accident. Was it a terrorist attack? Then everything seemed to get really quiet and things were moving fast and slow. A police officer told me to get back from the fence. I did a quick roundabout but went right back to the frontline again. And I said into my microphone, "We've had an attack." There was nothing else that could have caused this. And then I kept saying, "Oh my God." It was me reacting to what I was seeing and the massive amount of blood on sidewalks and people badly injured. I was looking at it and looking away at the same time. Recording and deleting it in my mind. I made a decision, conscious or subconscious, to lift the camera so it wasn't pointing down at the injured. I was up close and didn't want to focus on victims, which I thought would be insensitive and inappropriate for their families. I wasn't comfortable putting someone on the video with a leg or other body part missing. I would never want the person or their family to see that. Some of these runners and families are friends and neighbors. Boston is a small town in that way. My friends are among the runners and spectators on Patriots Day. They're in the restaurants and bars along Boylston Street. I socialize in this area and the marathon is a local race for me, not an international event. I've run it twice and I know the significance of it. So it was personal for me. We're all connected. These were innocent people, just watching the race, enjoying the day.

I kept getting pushed out and was asked to leave by police several times as the scene unfolded. I knew I didn't want to get too close because I'm sometimes like a bull in a china shop and I didn't want to risk doing something to get in the way of the responders. I didn't want to be the guy climbing a fence to get a picture. But I wanted to do my job as a videographer and I continued to roll, but I also wanted to be out of the way. And I didn't feel that I needed to drop the camera to get in there and help because I witnessed so many first responders on, and rushing to, the scene. My job was to show people what happened because I was right there and recording.

Nobody knew what was going to happen next. My gut reaction to the injuries was that I wanted to know what happened to those people, but I wanted to forget. I was horrified at the injuries and thought about how awful this was for these people. While recording, I also took a picture and posted it to Facebook and Twitter so that people who knew me would know I was okay. I posted the caption, "God help us."

About five minutes after the blast, I was being pushed out of the area. As I slowly walked back across the finish line, I finally reached my editor, but my first words were just grunts; it was just the raw emotion of what I had seen. It took me about three tries to speak with a normal voice. As I was standing on the side of the street just beyond the finish line talking to him, I watched wheelchairs and stretchers going by with the seriously wounded — including seeing Carlos Arrendondo and other heroic first responders rushing the badly injured Jeff Bauman to the medical tent.

I knew the event was going to be a big story, the first domestic terrorist attack since 9/11. But it was also a community story. We're Back Bay people and it was very personal. I get very

Steve Silva
God help us
Like · Comment · Share · April 15, 2013 near Boston, MA

tied into the moment. When I see a child with a disability, I get choked up and wonder why it happened to them. My heart breaks. So as I assessed the scene, I thought about the injured; these innocent survivors who are going to go through the rest of their lives missing limbs, and the hardship on their families. This is going to affect a lot of people and I thought of the unfairness of it all.

Once I got to the media center and realized that no one else had any finish line footage of the explosions, I got nervous. I knew I had to get it processed and uploaded to Boston.com quickly, but it uploaded very slowly. After the video went out, my phone started ringing. First came an interview with CBS radio. Then MSNBC had me on the air and wanted to know what I saw. I felt I was calm and could speak clearly and intelligently about what happened and what I shot so I continued to take the rapidly incoming requests. Next thing I knew I was on the phone with Brian Williams during NBC's breaking news coverage; next came CBS with Scott Pelley. And it just ballooned from there. I did 40 interviews over two days with media outlets all over the world. But what was most memorable was an e-mail I received

eXTRA

extratv.com

Steve Silva with Maria Menounos, one of the dozens of interviews he did on April 15th and 16th

from a soldier who had been stationed in Iraq, complimenting me on covering the story the way I did by not going in for the gory shots in the video.

It was also gratifying when Boston EMS synced their emergency radio transmissions with the video for use as a training tool. I am proud of what I shot, but I'm prone to second guessing especially after seeing the magnitude of the event. Between the online and television audiences, there were over 60 million views of the breaking news video.

I'm still a bit uncomfortable about being acknowledged for the work I did, because the story is only about the injured and their families and those who lost their lives. Because of where I was, I happened to be part of the story. I was at the right place at the wrong time.

On April 21, 2014, I'll be back in Hopkinton, but this time as a runner. The Boston Athletic Association issued a special invitation for those "personally and profoundly impacted by the events of April 15." Of 1,200 applicants, I was one of 467 chosen. I'm honored for the opportunity to run on behalf of the survivors and families affected by the events of that tragic day.

boston.com

Steve Silva encourages you to support the One Fund to aid victims and their families: onefundboston.org.

Joanne T. Pomodoro

LICSW, Sports Psychology Consultant

East Boston

B oth of my brothers run toward danger. That's implied in their job descriptions. Brian Pomodoro, who has been with Boston EMS for over 30 years and whose story is in this book, was at the finish line when the bombs went off. So was my older brother Frank Pomodoro, a Boston detective. Brian helped the injured, and Frank helped establish order amid the chaos. I, too, am a first responder, although not in the same "run toward the danger" sense as Frank and Brian. I'm a member of the PTSD Critical Incident First Responder Group. We help people who have difficulty coming to terms with traumatic and violent events and counsel them on how to manage emotion, grief and stress.

A memory from April 15th that stands out the most is the silence. When they shut the city down after the marathon bombings, the silence was deafening. Streets that should have been bustling were deserted. The only other time I experienced that in Boston was on 9/11, and that was the last time I worked a mass-casualty incident. After the planes flew into the towers, I and some of my first responder trauma group went to Logan Airport and worked with airline staff, including the gate agents and ground crews who closed the doors on the flights that were hijacked.

The Boston Marathon bombing affected people in so many different ways. I work at Mass General and have a private practice on Commonwealth Avenue. Many of my clients live in the Copley Square area. It was common for patients who came in after the marathon to be feeling angry, depressed or anxious. When I would ask them, "Were you around the marathon?" the answer was often, "Yes." For some, it may not affect them now, but it may affect them down the road. One procedure I use is called Eye Movement Desensitization and Reprocessing (EMDR). It can alleviate the symptoms of post-traumatic stress disorder by neutralizing and desensitizing triggers.

As part of the mental health program that B.A.A. put together, I volunteered to work with the runners. As an athlete — nationally ranked in racquetball — I understand other athletes; there's a connection. Runners train so hard and look forward to this race. And in a moment everything changed. Thousands couldn't finish, which in light of what was going on down the street, seems inconsequential. But considering their mental and physical exhaustion after running for four hours or more and the amount of energy they invested in just getting into the race, not finishing became a recurring issue among the runners I saw. As did the fear of running; fear of just going out for a run. Fear of loud noises and large crowds. It was all very understandable and helping the runners cope, to varying degrees, was the resiliency they develop over time as they deal with everything from injuries to lousy weather.

This year, among the issues facing some people, will be anxiety and fear because there will be thousands more spectators. Just returning to Boston may trigger feelings among many runners. But that shouldn't keep anyone away. Security will be unprecedented. It will be therapeutic for runners and spectators to come back and there will be lots of services for anyone who needs help, and just the positive energy will carry others through it. There's nothing like the strength of the human spirit and the power of a community helping each other.

The fact is that no matter where you were that day last year, we all came together as one city, one nation, one heartbeat.

This Marathon Monday, I will be running my first marathon. I was selected to be one of 40 runners for Massachusetts General Hospital's Emergency Response Team. I am truly humbled to represent and fund-raise for such an amazing team of professionals: first responders, surgeons, doctors and social workers. They save lives everyday and everywhere they are needed.

Joanne encourages you to go to http://www.crowdrise.com/ joannepomodoro. All funds raised go to victims of last year's bombings for medical and social service care.

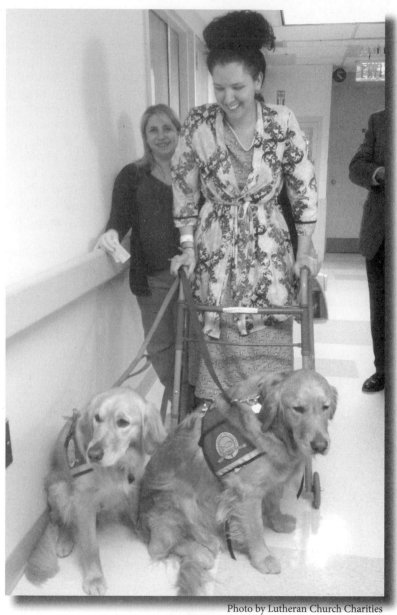

Photo by Lutheran Church Charities

Maggie and Luther raise the
spirits of a bombing victim.

The Furry Little Counselors

Richard & Dona Martin

Co-Directors

Lutheran Church Charities K-9 Comfort Dogs

Addison, Illinois

"**P**lease bring the dogs." The pastor of the First Lutheran Church of Boston, Reverend Ingo Dutzmann, and the New England District Lutheran Church president, Reverend Timothy Yeadon, contacted us shortly after the marathon bombings and asked for the help of our golden retrievers. We left Illinois for Boston early the following morning with Luther, Ruthie and Isaiah and two additional handlers. In addition, Addie and Maggie and their handlers from Connecticut met us in Boston. After the Sandy Hook shootings, we placed Addie and Maggie permanently in the area. Addie is at Immanuel Lutheran Church in Danbury and Maggie is at Christ the King Lutheran Church in Newtown. Both continue to provide comfort to the Sandy Hook community.

The work of our Comfort Dogs began quite by accident or, more accurately, by natural disaster. After Hurricane Katrina began flooding the New Orleans area in 2005, the president of Lutheran Church Charities, Tim Hetzner, got a call from a pastor in Metaire, Louisiana, who had a problem: People whose homes were in danger of being swallowed by the storm surge weren't evacuating because they weren't able to take their pets with them. So Tim arranged to buy three boats and get them equipped with gear necessary for search and rescue. Teams of volunteers rescued people and their furry friends. What we saw was not only the unbreakable bond between people and their pets, but how important that bond was in helping people cope with disaster.

Tim also noticed how people are attracted to dogs, even

neighborhood pets out for a walk. So Lutheran Church Charities began the K-9 Comfort Dogs program. When the shootings at Northern Illinois University happened in February of 2008, the campus pastor called us in. Students immediately gravitated to our dogs. Many students have dogs back home and miss them while away at college. We were given full rein to go anywhere on campus so the students could be with the dogs for comfort. We saw how the dogs facilitated the healing process and brought comfort to the students and worked well with counselors and first responders.

We use golden retrievers exclusively for a number of reasons: they are approachable and have that cuddly look to them. We refer to them as the Furry Little Counselors. They are non-aggressive, non-threatening and have the perfect temperament for what we ask them to do. The dogs learn quickly and they want to please. Children and adults love them and are attracted to them. Goldens are traditionally "leaners" and will often lean into people in need. Over the years, we've discovered that the dogs are very intuitive to people's needs and seem to seek out those individuals who need it most. Sometimes, the dog will be in a "with me" position and will gravitate to somebody and handlers just have to go with what the dogs are feeling. After seeing our dogs do that so often, we realize they're picking up on something we're not. Although some handlers have a background in counseling or pastoral care, the biggest part of their training is just learning to be quiet and let the dogs provide an outlet for those who are hurting to express themselves.

Over the years, we've realized there is a lot of need out there. We only go where we are invited and where there's a need. Unfortunately, we've been needed many times; from natural disasters like tornadoes in Missouri, Oklahoma and Illinois and Super Storm Sandy, the Prescott wildfires and the Colorado flooding; to the man-made disasters like the West Texas explosions and the school shootings at Sandy Hook and in Colorado, and the Boston Marathon bombings. As we've become more experienced, we've recognized the many needs early on and started to place dogs in churches and schools for their own community outreach. Of our 70 dogs, 30 have been placed in churches and schools in

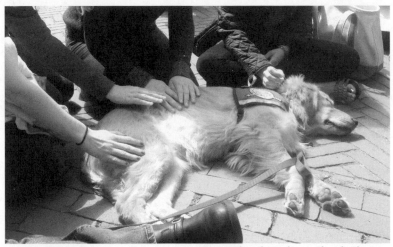

Photo by Lutheran Church Charities

10 states. We've also started a "train-the-trainer" program to meet the future demands.

The dogs provide an immediate calm and comfort for people. You'll often see pictures of our dogs lying down in what we call the "A-1" position (shown above) because it allows people to approach them, hug them, cry on them and tell them their stories. When people ask us if the dog is sleeping, we tell them, "No, he (or she) is just waiting to give comfort." Just as we never go where we aren't invited, our handlers are careful to let people approach the dogs instead of vice versa, in case anyone is afraid of or allergic to the animals. There is a difference between our dogs and service dogs. While petting a service dog is discouraged, our comfort dogs have "Please Pet Me" printed on their vests. People usually get down on the floor and hug the dogs. Our dogs are trained not to growl or lick.

Somewhere in everyone's life, there's an experience with a dog. Most of the time it's a good experience and we think that's why the dogs usually provoke a positive response in people. In disaster situations, our dogs are sometimes the only feel-good story. The idea of using a dog to help a grieving person might seem too simplistic. But that's why it works. When humans provide affection, it can be complicated with expectations and judgments, unspoken or not. But with our dogs, it's a very uncomplicated. They are silently non-judgmental and give unconditional love. They keep whatever they're told confidential, and they don't even take notes.

Our dogs often bring out emotions in people in the most unlikely places and at the most unlikely of times. In late 2013, we were coming back from Denver and as we walked through the airport concourse, people would just drop to their knees and pet the dogs. One woman began sobbing as she petted our furry little counselor. We visited a nursing home and one of the residents said it was the best day of her life. As handlers, we see time and time again the positive (pawsitive!) impact our dogs have on people in grief, but it's been scientifically proven, too, that when people pet a dog, good things happens. Levels of stress hormones can decrease, breathing becomes regulated, and blood pressure is lowered. Also, research has shown that petting a dog releases oxy-

Photo by Lutheran Church Charities

Ruthie and Luther, bags packed and ready to leave their Addison, Illinois home for the trip to Boston

tocin, a hormone associated with bonding and affection, in <u>both</u> the human and the dog.

When the dogs are vested, they know they are working. We tell them, "We're going to work now," and we get them prepared for what their work will be for that day. The dogs do take on a lot of emotion as people pour out their hearts to them. We always watch our dogs closely at events and position them right in front of us. The dogs are always in a protected area, whether lying between our feet or seated between our legs. We want the dogs to know that we always have their back. We do guide small children in their interaction with our dogs. Most of the time people will ask if they can pet the dog, but it's important for the dogs to know that we are always in a position where we can monitor how people approach and interact with them. The handler's main job is to make sure the dog doesn't get burned out, which means taking off the vest and going on a break to play ball, or give them a massage, or let them nap after about two hours of work. The dogs hit the reset button quickly and bounce back faster than humans, but we still have to watch for their stress signs.

Of course, we handlers aren't immune to stress. There are a lot of emotions when you go into a disaster area and we also feel that emotion and connection with the people in need. We watch each other closely as a team. Each day includes breakfast, devotion and a debrief session in the evening. Nobody ever goes into a disaster alone and we have counselors on hand for us 24/7.

In the midst of all the disasters, we see the good. The worst of all events has brought out the best in people. Goodness always wins. Sandy Hook's motto is "Love Wins" and Boston's is "Boston Strong." The mottos are about goodness, love and resilience. We've met so many wonderful people in our work. We were perfect strangers and we were meeting perfect strangers.

When we went to Boston, while we had the Lutheran Church in common, we had never met the pastor of the downtown Boston church, Reverend Dutzmann. We headed to the church and because of the beautiful weather we were able to set up in the courtyard, with chairs for visitors and mats for the dogs. Because we have an active following on Facebook, we posted where our

ABOVE: *Boston area college students swarm around the dogs.*

BELOW: *On Wednesday evening, two days after the bombings, one of the largest running clubs in Boston came by. This was the first time many of them had seen each other since the marathon and while petting the dogs, they told their stories to each other. Pizza was ordered in and it was a wonderful evening of healing.*

Photos by Lutheran Church Charities

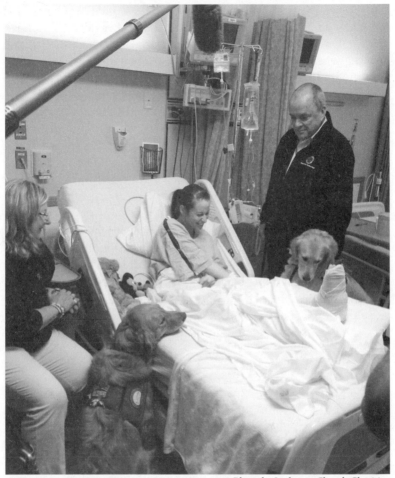

Photo by Lutheran Church Charities

Wounded spectator Lee Ann Yanni, pictured above with Ruthie, Luther and their handlers, Dona and Richard Martin, said of their visit before one of her surgeries: "It was really nice having the dogs stop by. I've always loved animals and not having been able to see my cats, it was nice to have animals as part of my recovery. Animals don't judge or talk back, they just accept you and know when you need some love."

dogs would be and it seemed like the college kids heard first and we had students from Emerson College, Northeastern University, Boston University and Suffolk University visit us; some of them waiting when we arrived. As the days went on, people came out of their homes and the community came to visit. They were able to sit down with a warm, furry dog and be comforted.

We also went to area hospitals to visit the injured victims and the hospital staff members. When we walk into a room with the dogs you can see facial expressions change. We spent a lot of time with the medical staff and they would get down on the floor with the dogs. The doctors and nurses had to perform their duties and appear strong for everyone else, but they also needed comfort. And we know the dogs did bring them some comfort. The dogs do a wonderful job with the physically impaired who are unable to reach down to pet the dog. It will put its head on the person's lap so they can be petted. "Lap" is one of the commands and the dog will put its weight on its back legs and position itself, with little, if any, pressure on the person, across the person's lap. Or they may raise their front paws on the edge of the bed.

We also provided comfort to the Boston Marathon volun-

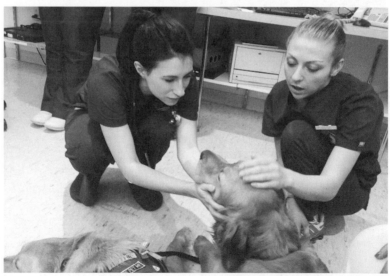

Photo by Lutheran Church Charities

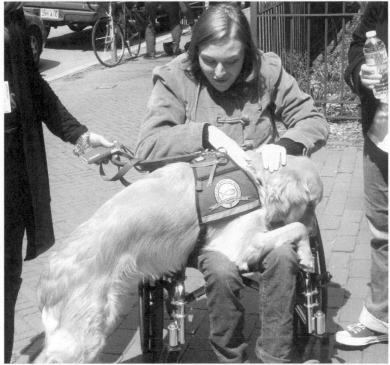

Photo by Lutheran Church Charities

teers. They were victims, too. As they passed out water and med-als, they were all of a sudden called upon to take on unbelievable responsibilities. Some of them were in the midst of the explosions. They came and told their stories and the dogs were an outlet for them to do that.

At night we went out into the community and spent time at the memorial site. That's where we found another perfect stranger story. A food cart at the memorial was fully stocked and run by New York Fire Department volunteers.

We observed in Boston a sense of community and, simultaneously, the sadness of the community and the strength of the community. On a daily basis, we were embraced by the city. We stayed at the Park Plaza Hotel along with people from all over the country and the world. When we tried to walk the dogs through the lobby in the morning, people were always crowding around us. Even going down the street was challenging in a wonderful way. The distance from the hotel to the church was only about four blocks, but it would take us about one hour to get there! We just couldn't get down the street without engaging with the most wonderful people. We've met people who've stayed in contact and have truly enriched our lives. One of them is Norine Bacigalupo, a public-relations professional who is an adjunct professor at Suffolk University, and when we returned to Boston in October, the president of Suffolk University, James McCarthy, presented our dogs with honorary Doctorate of Healing degrees.

People and businesses were so kind and generous to us. Luther had a birthday when we were in Boston and students from Emerson sang "Happy Birthday" to him. And Joe's American Bar and Grill bought Luther a birthday dinner.

We spent several long, tiring days in Boston and one night we just wanted to get the dogs back to our hotel and get a little rest. So we decided to disguise them. We took off their vests and split up, taking different routes and looking like regular people out walking their golden retrievers. One afternoon as we were walking Ruthie along Commonwealth Avenue, there happened to be a wedding going on. The mother of the bride saw Ruthie and asked, "Is that one of the comfort dogs?" We said, "Yes, she is." So Ruthie joined the wedding party and had her picture taken with the bride and groom. Ruthie was also given her own Red Sox bandana and t-shirt to celebrate the World Series win.

It has been pointed out to us countless times that "dog" spelled backwards is "God," and while we don't hide who we are — a Christian ministry — we don't proselytize. We're not there to convert anyone. We are there to offer comfort at a time when people may need it the most.

The people of Boston were so thankful that we had come from Illinois to provide comfort, and wherever we go, we're always told, "I can't believe you came all this way. It means so much that you care." We were invited back to Sandy Hook to march in their Labor Day Parade. We were so honored and happy to reconnect with these special people several months later. As we

Photo by Lutheran Church Charities

The hard working Comfort Dogs get some well-deserved pampering at a "spa day," courtesy of Fenway Bark.

marched in the parade, spectators started applauding. We looked around to see who they were clapping for. But it was for us, just thanking us for being there. It was so moving.

In Boston and other places where we are invited, the Lutheran Comfort Dogs arrive as perfect strangers but leave as perfect friends.

The Lutheran Church Charities K-9 Comfort Dog program never charges a fee to those it serves. It operates solely on donations. You can donate on line at www.lutheranchurchcharities.org. And you can follow each of the Furry Little Counselors on their own Facebook page.

Susan (Kelly) Papalia, R.N.

Finish Line Triage Nurse
Medical Sweep Team Captain
Boston Marathon 2013

W hen I learned that the L.C.C. Comfort Dogs were coming to Boston, I knew I had to see them. I had been
following the work of the dogs and their handlers for
quite some time and was especially captivated by the compassion
and love they brought to Newtown, Connecticut, immediately after the senseless murders of students and faculty at Sandy Hook
Elementary School just four months earlier. I never expected the
people of the city of Boston would soon need their comfort as
well.

The morning of April 15th was magnificent; the sunrise
was slow and deliberate, the humidity was low and the blue sky,
somehow, seemed to promise every runner a happy and memorable journey from Hopkinton to the finish line on Boylston Street.
It was a perfect day for the race.

I volunteer my time working inside the medical tents at
several races throughout the year; however, I have always chosen
to spend my time working outside during the Boston Marathon. I
am transfixed by the fever of the day, the love of family, the support for the runners and the feeling that we are all united, if only
for a single day.

It was late in the race and the crowds cheering for the
runners grew louder and then, the first explosion! Moments later,
a second one abruptly ended what was left of the 117th running
of the Boston Marathon. Despite their own fear people ran toward
the wounded, most not having any comprehension of what they
were about to witness. This wasn't a drill; it was brutal reality and
it was so much more than anyone could have prepared for.

Evening arrived and I began a long walk home all the
while trying to comprehend what had just happened. I began to

shiver as I realized that I had heard, seen and smelled pure, horrifying evil. The marathon would never be the same again and neither would I. I felt my soul growing cold.

Days passed and the constant news coverage brought immediate and even optimistic updates. I foolishly began to think that I was healing. I was angry, but wasn't that to be expected? Certainly I was sad, but wasn't that, too, understandable? I didn't eat and I couldn't sleep; nonetheless, my wounds were invisible to others so, yeah, I was okay. I never guessed I could be so wrong.

I continued to worry about my close friends, Lynn and Lucy, just two of the extraordinary nurses who were working in the medical tent at the finish line when everyone got a glimpse of hell on Earth. They tended to the severely injured until the ambulances could transport them to trauma centers.

Five days after the bombing, we decided we would meet for lunch in the Back Bay. For the three of us, it would be our first time back since that terrible day.

I knew that the Comfort Dogs would be at the First Lutheran Church of Boston on Saturday morning so I took a chance at surprising Lynn and Lucy with a visit there before lunch. I sensed that both of them had been having a difficult time in the days following the attacks and I believed that the Comfort Dogs would be a step in their healing process. I asked them to meet me in the city and bring their Boston Marathon pins with them. Along with ID badges, the pins are distributed to volunteers who proudly display them on marathon jackets worn that day. Every year I've kept mine but this year would be different; I knew that I would shortly be giving it away to someone very special.

We met and held each other but so many words remained unspoken. We walked to the church where Pastor Dutzmann had graciously agreed to retain some of the dogs until we could arrive. We entered the courtyard to find four gorgeous golden retrievers, their handlers and the pastor warmly welcoming us to join them.

In we went and sat down alongside others who had also come to find comfort with the dogs. We sat on blankets and on chairs; we lay alongside the dogs in the garden and hugged them tightly. Lynn whispered stories to the dogs with words that no one else would hear. The dogs leaned their warm bodies against us as if to help us support the weight we carried. Maggie, Addie, Isaiah and Ruthie were hard at work. Maggie placed her head in my lap and gazed at me for what seemed an eternity. I found that I couldn't stop hugging and petting her and then she did something that made me truly understand her message. She raised herself up and gently put her front paws on my shoulders near my neck, as if she was hugging me this time. I was safe.

We missed lunch by hours. We wouldn't/couldn't/didn't want to leave. We were surrounded by love and forgiveness. Lucy and Lynn laughed and cried … and I watched. I was confident that I had done something to try to help them heal by asking them to visit with the dogs that afternoon. Before we left, we took our pins, our cherished possessions, and placed them on the vests of three of the dogs. We wanted to believe that, from this day forward, Addie, Isaiah and Maggie could go out into the world carrying a part of us, and the spirit of the people of Boston, as they continue to visit with so many who need what only they can provide.

We eventually found our way to dinner and spent hours together, silently grateful that we were some of the fortunate ones to escape physical harm during the marathon. Lynn and Lucy commented that I was uncharacteristically quiet that evening but I hadn't noticed. I knew that I didn't particularly want to talk about April 15th, but I assured them I was okay. We parted ways, kissing Lucy goodbye as Lynn and I began our walk back to her car. The night was getting chilly.

We passed the Lutheran Church and, despite the hour, the courtyard was still aglow with soft light. Realizing that the Comfort Dogs may still be in there, we entered. Although the L.C.C. handlers and dogs were tired after a grueling day they stayed on solely to support us. I found myself suddenly exhausted and lowered my tired body and mind onto an empty bench.

One by one, the dogs came over to visit, some placing themselves close against my body while others simply gave me the message that they were near by should I need them. I hugged Ladel tightly and remember the beautiful scent of clean fur and warm breath. I buried myself deeper into her coat while others came to rest at my feet. Without even realizing, I began to cry. And cry. And cry. My heart, loosely pieced together with very thin strands of either courage or denial, finally broke. Here I was, in the darkness, sobbing uncontrollably into the snuggly necks of golden retrievers. I wasn't as strong and unafraid as I had convinced myself I was. I cried for so many reasons and for so many lives forever changed. I cried with gratitude for the Comfort Dogs, these angels in fur coats that encouraged me to hug them and softly confess to them my fears. Selfishly, I cried for me because at that moment I knew I would heal. How could I have ever known that the surprise that I had planned for my friends was exactly what I needed to nourish my own spirit?

It grew late. Lynn and I left the church and headed toward Boylston Street. We held hands in support and silence. As we rounded a corner, the night wind that had gathered strength blew cold in our faces. I'm not sure I noticed at the time and, if I did, I didn't mind. I had the hair, scent and unconditional love of the freshly groomed Comfort Dogs swirling around me and felt a peace I hadn't felt all week. I opened my coat. For the first time since Monday my body and my soul were warm again.

Susan Papalia urges you to consider donating to the
Lutheran Charities Comfort Dog program at
www.lutheranchurchcharities.org.

Jordan Rich

Talk Host, WBZ Radio

Boston

Heroes come in all shapes, colors, sizes and, yes, species. In a most unexpected way, I became the recipient of the compassion provided by the most perfect of strangers.

Hosting a talk show for the last eighteen years on WBZ NEWSRADIO 1030, the highest rated news/talk station in New England, has meant "being there" during many unforgettable moments. From the death of Princess Diana to the horrors of 9/11 to a slew of World Series and Super Bowl parades, it's been my honor to process and deliver news to a widespread audience, all the while offering listeners a chance to connect and share their opinions, emotions, fears and hopes.

No local event in recent memory has been as emotionally jarring as the marathon bombings. The WBZ broadcast team was devoted to covering everything from the impact of the blasts and the heroism of first responders to the struggle on the part of the victims and all Bostonians to return to some sense of normalcy.

In the fall, I was asked by listener Susan Papalia if I would host a show on the critical work done by the K-9 Comfort Dogs of the Lutheran Church Charities. They would be in Boston in October for a day of recognition for first responders.

I jumped at the chance. I'm blessed getting the chance to interview thousands of guests from all walks of life. But this assignment offered a little bonus. The women suggested they visit my home earlier that day to introduce me properly to the lovely Addie and Maggie. I rarely do pre-interviews but made an exception for personal reasons.

Allow me this explanation.

No one escapes life without their share of trauma. We Bostonians collectively felt the stinging loss of innocent life and limb on April 15th. And, like so many others, my family experienced personal trauma and sadness as well. In early August, my wife of 31 years and mother of our two children passed away after a long, grueling illness. I have dealt with grief in my own way, the best I can. I expected that spending time with the dogs would, at the very least, bring a smile to my face — did I mention how much I love animals? Little did I know how special those few hours with them would end up being for me.

The dogs and their lady companions — Susan, trainer Dina Mastropietro, and Newtown resident/volunteer Wendy Cole — stopped by on a Saturday afternoon. I learned about the dogs' intense training program, how they are matched with volunteers and some sweet stories of the dogs' impact on victims and first responders. We also discussed the ongoing mission in Newtown, where one of the dogs has been permanently stationed.

Cuddling and petting the dogs at my home for an afternoon allowed me to absorb the warmth and love these beautiful animals radiate; the palpable healing they provide for the sick, the disabled, the victimized and, as I found out, the grieving. I had a smile on my face for the rest of the day.

We met later that evening at the station to prepare for the midnight show. Addie and Maggie quickly curled up to relax by my feet. (What a terrific perk for your friendly host here!) Their human colleagues lauded their contributions, telling heartwarming, personal stories. We also saluted the amazing folks who train, house and transport comfort dogs, often on a moment's notice at their own expense.

Some heroes happen to have golden fur and selflessly offer their paws in friendship, and their hearts in unconditional love and therapeutic healing. They've helped countless people. I want to thank Addie and Maggie for helping me, too.

Jordan Rich asks you to support Boston Children's Hospital's "Until Every Child is Well" effort at www.childrenshospital.org.

Marathon Daffodils

Diane Valle, Charlestown

Marathon Daffodils is a community-based project hoping to lift the spirits of runners, volunteers, workers, residents and visitors for Boston Marathon 2014.

Hundreds of volunteers of all ages planted over 100,000 daffodils along the 26.2 mile marathon route. And, along Boylston Street and the finish line area where there is little planting space, thousands of potted daffodils will be placed, thanks to the generous and enthusiastic involvement of the Massachusetts Flower Growers Association.

The participation in this effort has been overwhelming and heartwarming, with non-profits, businesses, garden groups, schools, churches and temples, and individuals all eagerly pitching in.

With Mother Nature's help, the blooming daffodils will symbolize hope and rebirth, and provide a subliminal inspiration for all of those participating in and watching our great Boston tradition, the world's greatest marathon.

BOSTON STRONG
MARATHON DAFFODILS

The Boston Marathon will be bigger and stronger.
We will support our runners.
We will cheer them on.
We will help lift the spirits in our community and show that we have healed.

Brendan Cournane

Running Coach

85 marathons including six Bostons

Impossible, Improbable, Inevitable; a normal progression of almost every endurance runner, and a mantra I've shared with the thousands of runners I have had the privilege to coach over the years. The idea of running for 26.2 miles is daunting, maybe *Impossible* at times. But through the dedication of training, what seems impossible becomes merely *Improbable*, and by race day, the merely improbable transforms once more into *Inevitable* success.

Sometimes the sense of *Impossibility* comes from outside ourselves in the form of extreme weather, or a physical injury. Other times, the sense of *Impossibility* comes from within, when mental fatigue or self-doubt rises to the forefront of our minds. Most of these are foreseeable events and can be prepared for.

And then there are times like the afternoon of April 15, 2013. Near the finish line of the Boston Marathon, the ground shook and the throngs of spectators were rattled as the unfathomable occurred.

On the course, thousands of runners — exhausted and cramping, yet determined to finish — remained on the path from Hopkinton to Copley Square, unaware of what lay ahead. These brave souls, who had trained for months, faced a different type of *Impossible*. For them, the path to merely *Improbable* and *Inevitable* success was blocked by circumstances beyond their control.

As these dedicated athletes approached downtown Boston only to be rerouted away from their destination, confusion reigned. Some were mere city blocks from the finish line, others still miles from Copley Square. Before word of the bombing reached them runners were, understandably, confused, disoriented and angry that the prize of finishing the race was denied them.

When they learned of the attack, the initial disappointment quickly shifted to concern for those injured or killed in the explosions, as well as to the welfare of their own family and friends who had been waiting to see them cross the finish line, and to those at home who were sure to be frantic with worry.

The enduring spirit of the marathoner immediately came to the fore. Instinctively, marathoners embraced each other and sought to help those around them. As did many spectators, runners rose to the challenge to assist those in need, in many cases without immediate concern for their own safety. At Copley Square, runners, exhausted from finishing the race, summoned the adrenaline to help the wounded, forming tourniquets from their own clothing, escorting them to medical tents or simply holding their hands. Those still on the road to the finish offered comfort to the other runners around them, sharing the common bond of marathoners who had worked for months to reach a goal now unattainable, at least on that day.

In the aftermath, more than a few in the news media speculated that an event like the bombings in Boston would significantly dampen the spirit of marathoners, maybe even ending such races.

They couldn't be more mistaken.

The runners I've spoken to who were unable to complete the 2013 Boston Marathon vowed to return, to finish the race they began, for themselves and for those injured or killed by the bombings.

While it may have been *Impossible* to finish the race in 2013, the *Indomitable* spirit of the marathons makes completion of the race *Inevitable*.

Coach Brendan
™

Brendan Cournane is a running coach and motivational speaker based in Chicago. He has completed over 85 marathons, including one in each of the 50 states and all seven continents, with a marathon PR of 3:16. He has qualified for the Boston Marathon in over a dozen years and has completed Boston six times. Known for his trademark chili pepper attire and logo, Coach Brendan is certified as a coach with USATF and RRCA and can be reached through his website: www.CoachBrendan. com or, via e-mail, at Coach@CoachBrendan.com.

Why Running Still Matters

by Brian Metzler
of
www.running.competitor.com

On April 15, 2013, I walked out of the Boston Marathon post-race press conferences with the intent of hunkering down to write several stories about the elite men's and women's races. But then I looked at my watch and realized a few friends and colleagues might be finishing the race soon and decided to head back toward the homestretch on Boylston Street.

Still about a block and a half away on a side street and approaching what I hoped would be a good viewing point in front of the Lenox Hotel on the corner of Boylston and Exeter, I heard something like a loud but muffled clap of thunder. There was nothing remarkable until, moments later, a second blast sent screaming people running in all directions.

You know what happened, so there is no point in getting into the horrific details.

It struck me immediately, though, with thousands of runners still out on the course, the sport and recreational activity of marathon running suddenly didn't matter.

There wasn't any point in writing more stories about the great running in this year's race. It didn't matter if my friends and colleagues had finished, just that they were OK. Everything that happened prior to the blasts — great victories by Rita Jeptoo and Lelisa Desisa, strong efforts from Jason Hartmann and Shalane Flanagan and a new age-group world-record by 55-year-old Joan Benoit Samuelson — was completely and forever insignificant in light of the terror and bloodshed that happened at 2:49 p.m. Monday afternoon.

Nearly a year later, it's easier to put it all into perspective. And it is clear now that marathon running, and running in general, still matters. Perhaps more than ever.

For those who ran the race, those who were watching the race and everyone who worked or volunteered behind the scenes, it has to matter. For the previous 116 years of the Boston Marathon and its significance in both the international and recreational running communities, it has to matter. For the 500,000 marathoners and 50 million runners in the U.S. and millions more around the world, it has to matter. And most importantly, for those injured and the families and friends of those who were killed, running absolutely has to matter.

As runners and as a running culture, we must carry on and lead the way through this horrible situation. We can't erase it, we can't ignore it and we can't change the tumultuous state of the world. But running can still help us keep calm and help us carry on. Running doesn't restrict us, running connects us and it also lets us be free.

In fact, only running can give us the impetus to heal. Not everyone runs marathons, but running is the world's most accessible sport and, whether you run everyday or run just a few times every month, you're still a runner. And as a runner, you know it has a way of building solidarity among people, both in the common fitness goals and work ethic that running instills, but also in the shared values it fosters. That's not to say that running makes us better people than anyone else, but who would we be without it?

It began in the wake of the tragedy on April 15th. There were many runners and race volunteers among the first responders, hurrying into action to help others in ways they'd never dream of doing. Other runners, some fresh from finishing the marathon, sought out places in Boston to donate blood.

And there was an overwhelming connection among runners, their families and supporters who were stuck in hotel lobbies, restaurants and other areas as the Back Bay area of Boston turned into a surreal lockdown zone. By the end of the night, several memorial runs had been planned for the coming weeks and days, both in Boston and around the country, and the idea to wear a race shirt on Tuesday — as an act of unity and respect for the victims — went viral. Small but meaningful acts, with runners leading the way.

We owe it to ourselves, to each other and to the immediate victims of the bombings to get out there and run. Even if you weren't in Boston, have never run Boston or aren't a marathoner. Run easy. Run hard. Run short. Run long. Run alone. Run with a group. Just run. The familiar feeling of running — even the fatigue and achiness — will help each of us return to normalcy, even if it is a decidedly new normal. Focus on the good, not the bad. Spread the joy and freedom of running and indulge on endorphins.

> *Run easy. Run hard. Run short. Run long. Run alone. Run with a group. Just run.*

The Boston Marathon is back in 2014, stronger and more secure than ever. It will remain one of America's greatest sporting events, but it will forever be stained by these horrible acts and will never ever be the same as it was. This isn't the end of our innocence; that happened on 9/11. But it is a terrible reminder that nothing in these modern times will ever be as safe and secure as it used to be, not even something we cherish so dearly like running. And yet, that is a reason to be mindful, diligent and relentless in your pursuit of it every chance you get.

The best running stories from the 2013 Boston Marathon turned out to be the acts of courage, bravery and kindness that so many runners contributed. Little is remembered about the races at last year's Boston Marathon, but we'll never be able to forget this: Running will endure and we will, too, because of running.

Running still matters.

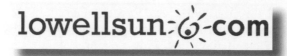

Marathon the tangible soul of Boston

By Katie Lannan, klannan@lowellsun.com

C ouldn't have been more than three hours before it happened, along the marathon route on Beacon Street.

"I love this holiday," I said to my friend. "The Boston Marathon is everything that's right with the world."

I was exaggerating, at the time, but I'm not now.

I'm not a runner. But I am a Bostonian. I was born at Brigham & Women's hospital, where SWAT teams swarmed and 26 patients were/are being treated for various injuries.

So when I got to pick my day off this week, compensating for a Sunday shift, I didn't hesitate to ask for Monday. It is not a sporting event; it is the soul of the city made tangible.

To be in Boston on Marathon Monday is to feel a buzz in the air, like it's the last day of classes before summer break, or it's 2 p.m. on Christmas Eve and your boss just sent out an email that you can all go

> "The Boston Marathon is everything that's right with the world."

home at 3. It's feeling a sense of excitement, euphoria, electricity, and to know that that sense is shared by everyone you pass. It's high-fives from strangers, it's sidewalk barbecues, it's families enjoying a day together, it's even sometimes Red Sox fans celebrating a win. It's what Disney World pretends to be.

To be on Heartbreak Hill, on Beacon Street, on Common-wealth Ave., in the home stretch on Boylston during the marathon is to feel Boston's pulse, to become a part of it. The runners are literally surging through the city's arteries.

And cheering them on are staggeringly large crowds of thousands, who spend the day screaming themselves hoarse, rallying strangers, exclaiming names Sharpied onto arms or stenciled onto t-shirts.

You root for the home team, right? Everyone's the home team. Doesn't matter if their jersey says Somerville or Greater Lowell or Mexico or Australia or even New York Athletic Club. Everyone is Boston. Everyone who runs, you want them to win, whatever that means to them.

You're not out there to catch a glimpse of the elites, to see who takes home first place. You're out there for the charity runners clad in tutus, hamburger suits and superhero capes, raising money for sick children, for the fathers pushing their sons in wheelchairs, for the cancer survivors running to prove they can, for the non-athletes honoring the memory of a loved one who died too soon. Runners like the ones who were crossing the finish line this afternoon, when Back Bay rattled.

They are out there to support a cause, a charity, a relative, their own dream ... whatever. And you're out there to support them. It's a 26.2-mile chain reaction of support, and it stretched longer than it ever has before, when a collaborative spreadsheet cropped up, full of Bostonians offering lodging to stranded strangers, when exhausted marathoners reportedly kept going until they reached Mass General and could donate blood, when the Red Cross announced they'd met their need after only a handful of hours.

When I said it, I thought it was hyperbole. But the Boston Marathon is everything that is right with the world.

Reprinted with permission. Originally published on 4/16/13.

This is Boston, a city with courage, compassion and strength that knows no bounds.

We are one Boston. No adversity, no challenge, nothing can tear down the resilience in the heart of this city and its people.

Boston Mayor Thomas Menino at an interfaith memorial service at the Cathedral of the Holy Cross in South Boston, April 18, 2013